Pedagogy and Human Movement

Across the full range of human movement studies (HMS) and their many sub-disciplines, established institutional practices and forms of pedagogy are used to (re)produce valued knowledge about human movement. *Pedagogy and Human Movement* explores this pedagogy in detail to reveal its applications and meanings within individual fields.

This unique book examines the epistemological assumptions underlying each of these pedagogical systems, and their successes and limitations as ways of (re)producing knowledge related to physical activity, the body, and health. It also considers how the pedagogical discourses and devices employed influence the ways of thinking, practice, dispositions and identities of those who work in the fields of sport, exercise and other human movement fields.

With a scope that includes physical education (PE), exercise and sports science, sports sociology and cultural studies, kinesiology, health promotion, human performance and dance, amongst other subjects, *Pedagogy and Human Movement* is the most comprehensive study of pedagogical cultures in human movement currently available. It is an invaluable resource for anybody with an interest in HMS.

Richard Tinning is Professor of Pedagogy and Physical Education in the School of Human Movement Studies at the University of Queensland, Australia, and Adjunct Professor of Physical Education in the Faculty of Education at the University of Auckland, New Zealand. As a teacher educator he has been involved in major Australian curriculum development projects for physical education, worked on large-scale professional development programs for teachers, and been a consultant to both schools and universities. His research interests are informed by a socially critical perspective and have focused on issues related to pedagogy, knowledge, identity and professional development.

International Studies in Physical Education and Youth Sport
Series Editor: Richard Bailey
Roehampton University, London, UK

Routledge's *International Studies in Physical Education and Youth Sport* series aims to stimulate discussion on the theory and practice of school physical education, youth sport, childhood physical activity and well-being. By drawing on international perspectives, both in terms of the background of the contributors and the selection of the subject matter, the series seeks to make a distinctive contribution to our understanding of issues that continue to attract attention from policy makers, academics and practitioners.

Also available in this series:

Children, Obesity and Exercise
Prevention, treatment and management of childhood and adolescent obesity
Edited by Andrew P. Hills, Neil A. King and Nuala M. Byrne

Disability and Youth Sport
Edited by Hayley Fitzgerald

Rethinking Gender and Youth Sport
Edited by Ian Wellard

Pedagogy and Human Movement
Richard Tinning

Positive Youth Development Through Sport
Edited by Nicholas Holt

Young People's Voices in PE and Youth Sport
Edited by Mary O'Sullivan and Ann Macphail

Physical Literacy
Throughout the Lifecourse
Edited by Margaret Whitehead

Pedagogy and Human Movement

Theory, practice, research

Richard Tinning

Routledge
Taylor & Francis Group

LONDON AND NEW YORK

First published 2010
by Routledge
2 Park Square, Milton Park, Abingdon, Oxon, OX14 4RN

Simultaneously published in the USA and Canada
by Routledge
270 Madison Avenue, New York, NY 10016

Routledge is an imprint of the Taylor & Francis Group, an Informa business

First issued in paperback 2011

© 2010 Richard Tinning

Typeset in Sabon by
Pindar NZ, Auckland, New Zealand

British Library Cataloguing in Publication Data
A catalogue record for this book is available from the British Library

Library of Congress Cataloging-in-Publication Data
Tinning, Richard.
The pedagogy of human movement / Richard Tinning.
    p. cm.
  1. Physical education and training—Study and teaching. 2. Human
locomotion—Study and teaching. I. Title.
  GV361.T56 2010
  613.7071—dc22   2009012480

ISBN13: 978-0-415-42844-6 (hbk)
ISBN13: 978-0-415-67734-9 (pbk)
ISBN13: 978-0-203-88549-9 (ebk)

ISBN10: 0-415-42844-0 (hbk)
ISBN10: 0-415-67734-3 (pbk)
ISBN10: 0-203-88549-X (ebk)

To my father, H.W. (Bert) Tinning, who by his example taught me about integrity, patience, caring and love, and who inspired and supported my intellectual pursuits.

Contents

Illustrations

Figures

Tables

Acknowledgments

Prof. Doune Macdonald, Head of the School of Human Movement Studies, University of Queensland, for her support at both the official level, via formal study leave to begin the book back in 2005, and at the informal level as a supportive friend and colleague who had faith that I would eventually complete the task.

Bernie Hernon-Tinning for her unflinching belief in me, and her thoughtful and critical editing of the penultimate draft of the book.

My colleagues at UQ who, over almost a decade, have challenged me to think and rethink about the nature and purpose of the field of human movement studies.

Introduction

The field of human movement studies

The field of knowledge concerned with the theoretical and practical study of human movement is variously known as human movement studies (HMS), physical education (PE) and, most recently, as exercise or sport science, kinesiology, human kinetics or human performance. Throughout this book I have chosen to use the abbreviation HMS as the descriptor for the field. HMS is an eclectic field that broadly speaking does teaching and research related to "movement culture" in general and more specifically to physical activity (including exercise and sport). There are many sub-disciplines involved in the field and these are typically represented in university courses such as motor control, exercise physiology, sociology of sport, biomechanics, history of sport, physical activity and health, sport pedagogy, sports coaching, sports management and sport philosophy. These teaching courses specifically set out to impart or (re)produce knowledge about their particular focus of human movement. Research in HMS endeavours to produce knowledge related to these sub-disciplines.

Drawing on theory, practice and research this book will provide an analysis of pedagogy and its applications in human movement. Broadly, the analysis will focus on human movement as a field of study in various educational and sporting institutions.

Each of the sub-disciplines of HMS has developed certain institutional practices and forms of pedagogy that are employed to (re)produce valued knowledge. For example, the lecture is a favoured form of pedagogy in most sub-disciplines, the laboratory class is a ubiquitous pedagogical form in science-based courses and the tutorial in sociocultural-based courses. Increasingly there is now interest in digital pedagogies that are based on the computer and Internet.

This book takes as its starting point the assumption that most sub-disciplines of HMS set out to (re)produce knowledge related to physical activity, the body and health as experienced through participation in what Crum (1986) has aptly termed "movement culture".

A professor of pedagogy?

In the year 2000 I moved from my post as professor of PE at Deakin University in the Australian state of Victoria to become professor of pedagogy in the School of Human Movement Studies at The University of Queensland (UQ). The move was more than just geographic. While I was temporarily buoyed to read that Emile Durkheim had once been professor of pedagogy in Paris and John Dewey professor of pedagogy at Chicago, Lee and Green (1997, p. 10) point out that both men "were requisitioned in the name of 'real' disciplines such as sociology and philosophy, and ... everyone has become an expert on education" (ibid.). Notwithstanding Yun Lee Too's claim that "Pedagogy is not really a discipline in its own right, and when one tries to constitute it as such, this may lead to embarrassment" (1985, p. 2, cited in Cannon, 2001), and with due cognizance to the career paths of Durkheim and Dewey, what did my new title really signify and could I really defend pedagogy as a legitimate and worthwhile sub-discipline of HMS?

At the time I arrived at UQ, the term pedagogy was used in the School of Human Movement Studies to signify the education stream of its undergraduate degree program – the pathway for students wanting to become health and PE (HPE) teachers. It still is used in that way. The other indicator of the meaning of the term at UQ was to be found in the compulsory first level course called Sociocultural Foundations of Human Movement Studies. One of my new responsibilities was to coordinate and teach this first level course. The companion first year course is called Biophysical Foundations of Human Movement Studies and together they represent two very different ways of knowing, thinking about, and researching human movement. They also have different ontological and epistemological underpinnings.

The course textbook, which bears the same title as the course (see Kirk *et al.*, 1996), includes a section that represents what, at the time, was considered to be the "pedagogical bases of human movement". This section includes chapters on "Instruction in physical activity settings"; "Learning physical activities"; "Evaluating physical activity pedagogy"; "Physical education and curriculum"; and "Beyond the formal curriculum of physical education". It was through an engagement with these issues that first year HMS students came to know about this strange new term pedagogy.

From the outset I considered that this particular representation of pedagogy did not satisfy my idea of it being a foundational sub-discipline to the field of HMS. For example, although it provides a "multidimensional view of pedagogy" (Kirk *et al.*, 1996, p. 60) and briefly refers to the pedagogical work done on the body in PE classes, and the learning of physical activity in sites such as schools, clubs and the gym, it does not provide an adequate framework for understanding how (and in what measure) HMS contributes to knowledge (re)production related to physical activity, bodies and health. Accordingly, I began to think more broadly about pedagogy. In what way(s), if any, could pedagogy be considered foundational to the field of HMS?

And what of the term "sport pedagogy"?

While sport pedagogy is now recognized as a sub-discipline in the field of HMS, this is not a book on sport pedagogy per se. It is an attempt to provide a *broader* focus on pedagogy across the field of HMS – sport pedagogy included. This is not a book about the "how to" of teaching. Rather, it sets out to explore the nature of the pedagogies employed in HMS, including their underlying epistemological assumptions and their successes and limitations as ways of (re)producing knowledge within the field. In doing so I introduce the notion of *pedagogical work* as a heuristic concept that enables us to move beyond some of the restrictive definitions and interpretations of the term pedagogy that exist within the field.

Significantly, graduates of HMS programs find employment in schools, sports clubs and institutes and in private enterprises such as health clubs and gyms, government sport and recreation departments and so on. This book will examine the forms of pedagogy used within HMS and the consequential pedagogical work on/for physical activity, the body and health. In so doing it will consider how the pedagogical discourses, practices and devices employed within the field of HMS affect and influence the ways of thinking, practice, dispositions and identities (subjectivities) of those who work in the field.

Although the initial ideas for this book began to take shape soon after I moved to UQ, it did not begin as a project in earnest until 2005 when I was on study leave at the Centre for Idreat, Aarhus University, Denmark. While much of the book is new, some of it reworks essays that I had written previously. Significantly, it has evolved from my early work, such as Pedagogies for Physical Education: Pauline's Story (Tinning, 1997) and has been informed by my recent lecturing in the course HMST1910 (Sociocultural Foundations of Human Movement Studies) and the task of trying to make sense of pedagogy to undergraduate students. Collectively I hope this book provides a useful introduction for undergraduates or postgraduate students into the ways in which pedagogy can be considered as a foundational sub-discipline in the field of HMS. I also hope that it can contribute to a new interest in pedagogy from colleagues in HMS who might not see pedagogy as central to their mission.

A word on culture and pedagogy

Most cultures expect that newcomers to that culture (whether they are born into the culture or come to live in the culture) acquire the existing behaviours, language, ways of thinking and practices such that they can participate in and contribute to the culture. There is a myriad of things that it might be necessary to know about and/or know how to do to actively participate in a given culture. This acquisition has the effect of reproducing the culture.

While not pre-empting the subject of Chapter 1, at this point suffice it to say that the acquisition of valued social practices that constitute a particular culture cannot all be left to chance. Certainly some social practices, such as cigarette smoking, are mostly acquired in informal contexts (you don't go to a class on learning how to smoke). However, enduring cultures tend to systematize the acquisition of important "things" and they do this through certain institutions (e.g. the family, the church, schooling, bureaucracies). The passing on or acquisition of cultural practices, including ways of thinking, attitudes, values and dispositions, is the "stuff" of pedagogy. Pedagogy underpins the learning of most valued cultural practices from toilet training to road rules, from religion to art, from science to commerce. Typically such practices as toilet training, eating with a knife and fork, with chopsticks, or (as in certain Eastern cultures) eating only with the left hand, are typically taught within the context of the family whereas, at least in most contemporary Westerns cultures, formal schooling is responsible for reproducing certain valued knowledge and practices such as reading, writing, mathematics, history etc. Of course, as regular debates in the media attest, the extent to which public schooling actually satisfies these expectations is hotly contested.

Culturally valued forms of human movement

In talking about pedagogy as a form of knowledge (re)production, of coming to know about human movement, then the question "What forms of human movement are valued and passed on in our culture?" is salient.

Obviously this will depend on whose culture we are talking about. Take the sport of football for example. While football markets itself as the "world game", as Franklin Froer's (2004) wonderful book *How Soccer Explains the World* explains, the meaning of football and the value placed on the game varies across different cultures. Football has a different cultural significance to Brazilians than to the English or the South Koreans. In Australia, for example, football is called soccer and, although introduced to the country back in the 1950s by immigrants from Europe, its popularity and its place in the hearts and minds of citizens remained marginal until the last decade. Football in Australia had to compete not only with the game of rugby introduced by the British colonial tradition, but also with a particular football code played nowhere else in the world – Australian rules football.

In addition to history and religion, geography and economic prosperity also play an important role in regard to valued forms of human movement within a particular culture. For example, surfing is popular in most moderate climate countries that have an ocean border and a degree of affluence sufficient to buy a surfboard; skiing is popular in developed (read "affluent") countries with a regular snow season; tennis is popular in all developed countries; hockey (ice) is big in Canada and Russia but not in Ireland, Australia or Iran; baseball is big in the USA and Japan but not in the UK or Denmark.

Also there are the sports that were geographically spread through the imperialism of the earlier major colonial powers. Cricket, for example, followed British colonialism to Australia, India, Pakistan, South Africa and the West Indies.

Sport is valued for different things in different cultures at different times. Speaking for his government in 2002, here is how the UK's Secretary of State for Culture, Media and Sport regarded sport: "The whole government knows the value of sport. Value in improving health and tackling obesity. Value in giving young people confidence and purpose, to divert them from drugs and crime. And value in the lessons of life that sport teaches us." (Jowell, in DCMS/Strategy Unit, 2002). Clearly, for some national governments, sport participation is considered as something of a magic "social pill".

In some countries that are more totalitarian than democratic, sport, and school sport, have a more specific purpose. For Hitler's Germany sports performance was used as a way to display the superiority of the Aryan race. As Susan Brownell (1995) observes in her book *Training the Body for China*, "Chinese nationalism has been very closely linked with the body, so that the act of individuals strengthening their bodies was linked to the salvation of the nation" (p. 22). Other countries (both in the West and the East) have their own reasons for including sport in the school. Nationalism, health and defence have always been significant discourses in most countries. According to Riordan and Krüger (2003):

> The various schools of physical exercises – associated with Jahn in Germany, Nachtegall in Denmark, Ling in Sweden, Lesgaft in Russia – developed as pedagogical, political and military instruments for building national identity. And that involved everybody: man and woman, squire and peasant, factory owner and worker. To learn to put one's body at the service of the nation emanated from a policy of acculturation of the common people in the same way as learning one's national language (p. 1).

But sports are a selective form of human movement. Many other forms of human movement are valued that would not be classified as sports. Think of, for instance, movement forms such as boomerang throwing, spear throwing, and horse riding that were part of daily survival for some indigenous cultures. Significantly, in many cultures the learning of the physical activity brings with it certain cultural privileges such as are attendant to demonstrating certain forms of masculinity. The early form of "bungy" jumping practiced by the men of Vanuatu is a nice example. Young men in Vanuatu participate in the ancient "art" of vine jumping because it demonstrates their developing masculinity which in turn bestows upon them the privileges of manhood. Bull riding in rodeos serves a similar function for young men in the Australian outback culture (Henry, 1996) while in Canada playing ice hockey affords young men more cultural value than being a figure skater (Gruneau and Whitson, 1993).

Think also of the place of certain forms of human movement (e.g. yoga, Tai Chi, Sumo wrestling, Wushu) that are found in Asian countries like Japan and China. These movement forms are the product of an Asian tradition that is different from the European traditions that embody the Cartesian mind/

body dualism and, accordingly, they have different cultural meaning.

Physical activity as knowledge/practice can be acquired or learned in various sites. While it is true that certain movements such as walking are "wired-in" genetically, they still require a period of learning. What is wired in (in the genes) is a potentiality, and given the right environmental or nurturing conditions most humans can learn to walk after a period of trial and error. No formal instruction is required. Learning a tennis overhead serve is, however, somewhat different. A tennis serve, like most other movements that constitute physical activities common to our sports and recreations pursuits, is not a "natural", pre-wired, movement pattern. It must be purposefully learned. A pedagogical question that fills the pages of many textbooks in our field is how that learning can be best facilitated by the teacher/instructor.

No matter which way we look at it, special forms of human movement have been, and continue to be, very important dimensions of most cultures – for survival purposes, national identity, individual identity, health or merely entertainment. Being able to do certain physical activities gives access to certain cultural capital (Bourdieu, 1977) and is thus a significant factor in the lives of millions of people. Access to, participation in, and understanding of "movement culture" is a significant right in many countries and the field of human movement studies is a central "player" in this educative process. Understanding something of the pedagogies used specifically to facilitate the reproduction of such movement and the possible pedagogical work done by particular pedagogies is a focus of this book.

Physical activity, the body, and health as the focus of HMS

Physical activity, in all its forms, is the focus of much of the work of those in the human movement profession. In universities, sport sociologists study the structural and agentic dimensions of participation in physical activity. Exercise scientists study the biophysical responses to, and mechanisms facilitating, performance in physical activity. Physical activity and health specialists study the epidemiological evidence related to activity, morbidity and mortality of populations and conduct intervention studies to measure the effect of physical activity on certain health parameters. Sport psychologists study individual motivation for/in participation in physical activity. Sport historians study the historical origins and significance of physical activity in various cultures. And sport pedagogy specialists study the pedagogical processes used in teaching physical activity.

In schools, sports clubs, health clubs and dance studios, teachers, coaches and instructors assist their charges in how to perform physical activities. Sometimes, but by no means universally, they will use some of the findings of their university colleagues to inform their pedagogical practices. Often, however, their pedagogies will be informed by tradition rather than research.

In approaching the task of discussing pedagogy and human movement I begin with the assumption that when one participates in movement one must engage or use one's body. Accordingly, there can be no pedagogy for physical activity that does not also embody a pedagogy for the body. Moreover, this bodily engagement will often have certain consequences for one's health. For example, when a person takes dance lessons they will learn not only about the dance as a physical activity (how to do it), they will also learn also about the(ir) body and about health.

For my purposes I will focus attention on how, and by what means, knowledge (both practical and theoretical) about physical activity, the body and health is (re)produced within the field of HMS. Although I discuss pedagogies for physical activity, the body and health in separate sections of this book, this is only a textual convenience and, in "real life", pedagogical work often occurs simultaneously across these categories. In many cases throughout the book there is considerable blurring of the categories, especially when talking about the body and health.

Since I live and work in Australia I have used many examples from the Australian context. Often I will use an Australian example of a broader trend that, while not generalizable in its specifics, in nonetheless indicative. I trust this will not be a frustration for European or North American readers – in reply I can add that in company with my Antipodean colleagues I have "grown up" with the northern hemisphere as the example for all valued cultural practices even when the transfer is patently absurd (e.g. a white Christmas). Reading this book will involve you in a pedagogical encounter and, as with all pedagogical encounters, you, the reader, the learner, will be the judge of the relevance of these pages to your professional world.

Part I

Introducing pedagogy

1 Languaging pedagogy[1]

The term pedagogy (pronounced with a hard "g", and then a soft "g") has become ubiquitous in the field of kinesiology and sport pedagogy is now firmly established as a credible academic sub-discipline. Notwithstanding the fact that our European colleagues had been employing the concepts of pedagogy and sport pedagogy for many years (see Crum, 1986; Haag, 2005), the English speaking world of PE has only relatively recently embraced the terms. However, increased usage does not necessarily equate with coherent or shared understandings of what the terms mean. Accordingly, the purpose of this chapter is to do some "languaging" (Postman, 1989; Kirk, 1991) in order to shed some light on the meanings of pedagogy and sport pedagogy and in so doing perhaps stimulate further consideration of their use in HMS. I will argue for a notion of pedagogy that is generative in enabling us to think about the process of knowledge (re)production across the many sub-disciplines of the field of HMS, including but not limited to sport pedagogy. Finally I will consider the notion of pedagogical work as providing a useful concept for analyzing the contribution of sport pedagogy to understandings related to how we come to know about physical activity, the body, and health.

Languaging pedagogy: One version

While Kirk (1991) has previously done some languaging of the meaning(s) of PE teaching, this chapter focuses on the terms pedagogy and sport pedagogy. There are multiple ways in which the term pedagogy is used within HMS. Silverman (2007), for example, essentially equates pedagogy with PE while Rink (2007), writing in the same issue of *Quest*, suggested that the field PE morphed into Kinesiology and now PE is seen as a sub-discipline of kinesiology and as synonymous with pedagogy. In what follows I begin with a brief account of how the term pedagogy is understood generally and then will consider the use of the term specifically within sport pedagogy, a term unique to our field.

Twenty years ago David Lusted (1986, p. 2) claimed that "pedagogy is under-defined, often referring to no more than a teaching style, a matter of personality and temperament, the mechanics of securing classroom control to encourage learning, a cosmetic bandage on the hard body of classroom contact". Lusted also considered pedagogy to be an ugly term and rarely used by teachers. Buckingham (1998) adds that pedagogy "derives from an academic discourse about education which is largely sustained within the walls of the elite universities and in the pages of obscure academic journals" (p. 3).

Edgar Stones (2000) suggests that pedagogy is ubiquitous and resembles an amoeba (shapeless and perpetually changing). Grossberg (1997) argues that "the very concept of pedagogy has been exploded and multiplied" (p. 12) and we get some sense of this explosion when we see the range of references to pedagogy in the fields of education, cultural studies and feminist studies. We read of:

- Pedagogy of the oppressed (Friere, 1972)
- Pedagogical pleasures (McWilliam, 1999)
- Cultural pedagogy (Trend, 1992)
- Critical pedagogy (Giroux, 1989)
- Visual pedagogy (Goldfarb, 2002)
- Border pedagogy (Giroux, 1992)
- Phenomenological pedagogy (van Manen, 1982)
- Feminist pedagogies (Luke and Gore, 1992; Lather, 1991; Ellsworth, 1989)

In the field of HMS we read of:

- Pedagogical kinesiology (Hoffman, 1983 and many university courses in the USA)
- Sport pedagogy (Haag, 1989; Crum, 1986)
- PE pedagogy (Lee and Solmon, 2005)
- Critical pedagogy (Kirk, 1986)
- Feminist pedagogies (Bain, 1988; Dewar, 1991; Scraton, 1990; Wright, 1990)
- Critical postmodern pedagogy (Fernandez-Balboa, 1997)
- Pedagogy as text in PE (Gore, 1990)
- Performance pedagogy and modest pedagogy (Tinning, 1991c and 2002)

Clearly multiple meanings can be a problem when trying to work with the term. So what are the ways in which pedagogy is understood? What theoretical perspectives underpin the meanings ascribed to pedagogy in different educational "camps"? And why do some resist the term with a passion (see Cannon, 2001)? To my continuing frustration, the word pedagogy is often resisted by HMS or kinesiology students who ironically offer no resistance to learning difficult specialist Latin derived anatomical terms such as coricobrachialis or semimembranosis.

The roots of the term are to be found in the ancient Greek word *Pedagogue* which referred to "a man having the oversight of a child or youth, an attend-ant who led the boy from home to school, a man whose occupation is the instruction of children or youths, a schoolmaster, teacher, preceptor" (OED, 1989, p. 417). However, as in all languages, the meaning of words seldom remains fixed in perpetuity. How the Greeks used pedagogy is not how the word is typically used today. Moreover, how the term is often understood in Anglophone countries is different to how it is understood in Continental Europe or Scandinavia. For example, to some in the Czech Republic peda-gogy is considered a pejorative term connected to the ideological state apparatus of the previous communist state. In Sweden it is common to hear pedagogy in connection with family and child rearing practices. As a Swedish academic outlines, "Pedagogy as a discipline extends to the consideration of the development of health and bodily fitness, social and moral welfare, eth-ics and aesthetics, as well as to the institutional forms that serve to facilitate society's and the individual's pedagogic aims" (cited in Marton and Booth, 1997, p. 178).

Carmen Luke (1996) found that her colleagues in Slovenia also had prob-lems with the word pedagogy since "generations of Slovenians have been subject to *pedagoski* – a centralised national curriculum and pedagogy of indoctrination, via nineteenth-century Prussian and twentieth-century com-munist models" (p. 2).

Importantly, the OED (1989) adds that the word pedagogue is "Now usu-ally used in a more or less contemptuous or hostile sense, with implications of pedantry, dogmatism, or severity" (p. 417). So when one of my colleagues (a neuroscientist) loudly greets those of us in my department who self-define as teacher educators with "morning pedagogues" in what sense is he using this term? Is he using the term as one of affection, respect, or of ridicule?

In considering the meaning(s) given to pedagogy in kinesiology it is first necessary to engage some of the literature from the field of education in which the term pedagogy has traditionally had most currency. Although pedagogy as a concept has a long history within European educational discourse up until the early 1960s there was "no obvious English language pedagogic mainstream ... with which educationalists could identify" (Gage, 1963, p. 18). In languaging the term I will draw heavily on the American aca-demic literature but will reference the European context where appropriate. I begin by briefly considering the popular synonyms for pedagogy and then will outline three orienting theoretical perspectives that have been prominent in the research and scholarship related to pedagogy. Although I will draw significantly on mainstream education literature, I will also connect with specific PE and kinesiology literature where appropriate.

Pedagogy synonyms

Reading about pedagogy in both the fields of education and kinesiology one often sees pedagogy equated with teaching and instruction equated with didactics. This slippage or lack of conceptual clarity is at times confusing and making definitive distinctions between these terms is difficult.

If we go to a dictionary for a clear and useful definition of pedagogy the *Oxford English Dictionary* (OED, 1989) offers "the art or science of teaching" (p. 418) and the Encarta® *World English Dictionary* (1999) provides overlapping meanings:

ped·a·go·gy n the science or profession of teaching Also called pedagogics	*di·dac·tics* n the science or profession of teaching (formal) (takes a singular verb)

teach·ing n
1 the profession or practice of
   being a teacher
 	
2 something that is taught, for
   example, a point of doctrine
   (often used in the plural)
	in·struc·tion n
	1 teaching in a particular subject
	   or skill, or the facts or skills
	   taught
	2 the profession of teaching or
	   the teaching process

Considering the use of the term pedagogy within educational research literature in the USA, it is interesting to note that in the first *Handbook of Research on Teaching* (Gage, 1963), the *Second Handbook of Research on Teaching* (Travers, 1973), and the third edition of the *Handbook of Research on Teaching* (Wittrock, 1986) there was no reference to the term pedagogy. It was all about teaching.

In the widely cited edited book *Research on Teaching* (Peterson and Walberg 1979) which synthesized much of the then current educational research thinking and evidence on the nature of teaching effectiveness, we find only one oblique mention of the term pedagogy. It seemed that for the leading educational researchers in the USA during the late 1970s the term pedagogy was not part of their lexicon when talking about teaching or research on teaching. This omission of the term pedagogy was not an oversight. Until very recently, within the educational literature of the USA, the word pedagogy was rarely used.

It was not until the publication of the fourth edition of the *Handbook of Research on Teaching* (Richardson, 2001) that we can find the term pedagogy included in the subject index, although most contributors still avoided the term. In this edition we also see the inclusion of a chapter on research on teaching PE by Kim Graber (2001) in which, with the exception of a brief discussion of Shulman's (1986) notion of pedagogical content knowledge, there is no reference to the term pedagogy.

Another term that is often used in conjunction with pedagogy is *curriculum*. It is instructive to note that in the USA in particular there has been a long tradition in distinguishing curriculum *from* instruction. Indeed, in many

American universities this distinction is formally institutionalized in the official naming of the Departments of Curriculum and Instruction. Writing in the *Handbook of Research on Curriculum*, Walter Doyle (1990), however, suggested that "The meeting point between these two domains [curriculum and instruction] has always been somewhat fuzzy, in part because these terms denote separate but interrelated phenomena" (p. 486). We now often see reference to the terms curriculum and pedagogy as separate but interrelated concepts.

In the introduction to *The Handbook of Physical Education* (2006), which should have been titled more accurately *The Handbook of Research in Physical Education*, editors Kirk, Macdonald and O'Sullivan explain that they "have located the term pedagogy at the centre of [the] handbook, as a means of providing an organizing principle for the text. The notion of pedagogy we are working with here can be defined by its three key elements of learning, teaching and curriculum" (p. xi). They explain that they recognize the three "elements" to be interdependent but nonetheless separate them for organizational purposes. Having so defined the focus of the handbook it is interesting that only one of the 65 chapters actually includes the term pedagogy in the title.

As we will see later, the notion of pedagogy which I am advocating tries to avoid artificial distinctions between pedagogy and curriculum and the more reductionist and instrumental logic that underpins frequently held ideas of pedagogy within kinesiology. Moreover, and importantly, I will argue for a broader view of pedagogy than one restricted to the practice of teaching PE or of PETE.

Conceptual orientations in/on pedagogy

The ways in which people think about pedagogy are underpinned or informed by particular knowledge paradigms and ways of seeing the world. While there are various ways to categorize these different paradigms (see for example Section 1 of *The Handbook of Physical Education*, Kirk *et al.*, 2006), I will briefly discuss three perspectives that influence very different conceptions of pedagogy.

Pedagogy as the science of teaching

One popular conception of pedagogy is as a science of teaching (see the dictionary definitions above). Although teachers might not think of their work as a science, educational researchers from the behavioural psychology tradition considered that pedagogical practice was underpinned by behavioural principles that were amenable to scientific study. Mainstream educational research had, during the 1960s and early 1970s, begun to establish a tradition of research that can be characterized as scientific in nature (see for example Gage, 1963; Petersen and Walberg, 1979; Travers, 1973) because it employed scientific methods, and also because it sought to identify, analyze and understand what Gage (1977) called "the scientific basis of the art of teaching". This research tradition was predicated on the perspective that teaching can be reduced to a set of variables that can be observed and measured (see Dunkin and Biddle's [1974] presage, process, product model).

In a commentary on research in PE pedagogy Larry Locke (1977) suggested that there was "new hope for a dismal science" (p. 2). In essence he was referring to the developing state of scientific-like research in PE pedagogy and comparing it with the growth of research into the science of teaching within mainstream educational research at that time.

Throughout the 1970s and 1980s, within the field of kinesiology, research in PE pedagogy was dominated by an attempt to develop a scientific basis to inform pedagogy within formalized institutional teaching (particularly in school PE classes and PETE programs). The instrumental focus on technical issues related to improving the practice of teaching was characteristic of much of the early work of researchers like Piéron (1983); Siedentop (1983a); and van Der Mars (1987).

Part of the agenda of this chapter is to move beyond the early critiques of instrumental and technocratic conceptions of pedagogy as a science (see Kirk, 1986; Tinning, 1987) and to offer a broader notion of pedagogy that has greater potential for the pedagogical agendas of HMS.

Pedagogy and didactics

In the English speaking world the term didactic is mostly used as a pejorative for a doctrinal, moralising form of instruction. For example in the Encarta® World English Dictionary © 1999 we find the following definition:

> di·dac·tic adj
> 1   containing a political or moral message
> 2   tending to give instruction or advice, even when it is not welcome or not needed

According to Hamilton and McWilliam (2001) the term didactics was originally associated with the art of teaching and "embraced procedures for the efficient transmission – or inculcation – of received knowledge" (p. 17). Later, with the rise of behavioural science it became associated with a science of teaching. But "Modern pedagogy ... broke away from didactics" with pedagogy becoming seen as a process rather than a technique (ibid.).

Up until the early 1960s educational research in the USA, as represented in the first *Handbook of Research on Teaching* (Gage, 1963), was primarily concerned with didactics. Indeed in the early 1960s there was still "no obvious English language pedagogic mainstream ... with which educationalists could identify" (p. 18). Research into teaching PE was, however, still in its infancy in the 1970s and it focused initially, like in mainstream education, on didactics rather than pedagogy. Research into *pedagogy as a process* in the context of PE lagged at least 10 years behind mainstream education. Accordingly, when much of the educational research community had began to move beyond attempts to find the best teaching method or the laws that underpin teaching (see Tousignant, 2005), PE researchers were still seeking answers to those very questions through quasi-experimental research (e.g. van Der Mars, 1996).

However, the use of the term didactics has considerable currency in Continental Europe, particularly in France and to a lesser extent in Germany. The German Herbert Haag (2005), for example, argues that sport didactics is essentially a synonym for sport instruction and relates to "all the factors which are important for an optimal realization of teaching-learning processes" (p. 47). As Chantal Amade-Escot (2006) explains, "In German educational language and in most European languages, didactics concerns the practice of teaching and its methods in general and/or related to specific subject matter" (p. 347). Amade-Escot, one of the leading didactics scholar/researchers in French PE makes a point of distinguishing the French *didactique* tradition from the English understanding of the term didactics. She argues that "In the French speaking world of educational research, the noun 'didactics' and the adjective 'didactic, didactical' are to be understood in terms of research that studies teaching and learning processes with a special focus on the content knowledge taught" (p. 348). Moreover, "Research into *didactique* studies the functioning of the 'didactic system' which is defined as the irreducible three way relationship linking teacher, students and a piece of knowledge to be taught and learned" (p. 349). To me this seems to locate the French *didactique* more in line with current conceptions of pedagogy (e.g. see the introductory chapter to *The Handbook of Physical Education*, Kirk *et al.*, 2006) and certainly different from the pejorative notion of didactic in English speaking contexts.

In his etymology of pedagogy, Brent Davis (2004) explains the link between pedagogy and didactics as follows:

> In some European languages other than English, pedagogy is paired up with didactics to describe the role of the teacher. Neither word has direct English translation. Didactics is roughly synonymous with instructional techniques or methods, but is also used to refer to the teacher's command of the subject matter knowledge, ability to interpret student responses, and other personal competencies. In complement, pedagogy is more a reference to the teacher's interpersonal competencies, and is thus used to refer to the moral and ethical – as opposed to the technical – aspects of the teacher's work with learners. It is in this sense of responsibility to learners that prompted many critical education theorists to adopt the noun pedagogy (pp. 143–144).

I return to the work of the critical education theorists later but first it is necessary to consider some other frameworks that have been used in thinking about pedagogy.

Phenomenological pedagogy

There is a stream of work in pedagogy that connects directly to the particular relationship between the teacher and the child (learner). According to Max van Manen (1980), "Pedagogy is the most profound relationship that an adult can have with a child" (p. 290). The pedagogue is the adult who shows the child the way in the world. This is an important point for the pedagogue, in showing the way in the word, is introducing the child to much more than subject matter knowledge, he is also teaching about the moral-ethical and political life. This is likened to a process of initiation (R.S. Peters, 1981) or guidance (Rogers, 1967). Van Manen suggests that being a pedagogue is a "calling" (p. 285) and we can see a direct link back to the notion of pedagogy as a moral and political enterprise as discussed above by Davis (2004). For van Manen (1979),

> Pedagogic thought and practice rely on phenomenological analysis of what it is like to live as a young person in present-day society, in the modern family ... Educators need to focus on the child as a way of being in the world; how the young person actually and concretely experiences being at home, in the neighbourhood with friends, among peers, on the way to school, in the classroom, and so forth (p. 5).

Like van Manen (1980) and Spiecker (1984), Nel argues for a phenomenological analysis of pedagogy that revolves around a special relationship between child and adult (pedagogue). According to Nel (1973), "On the continent of Europe the tendency is to use the term *pedagogy* for the science or theory of upbringing and schooling of the child, and the term *education* for the practical activities in the school as teaching, school and class organization etc." (p. 201). Physical educator Stephen Smith also advocates a phenomenological perspective in his book *Risk and Our Pedagogical Relation to Children: On the Playground and Beyond* (Smith, 1998) and argues that "Pedagogy connects us with the practice of being with children where there is the intention of guiding them towards 'mature adulthood'" (p. 27).

Importantly this guiding is not merely a technical process. This view of pedagogy implies the need for critical self-reflection about what it means to achieve "mature adulthood". It requires having a clear sense of the ethical and political principles that ought to underpin the guidance of the child toward a particular social life. Without such a reflection, without a clear sense of principles and purposes, the "pedagogue" may become a mere instructor in the sense of enacting prescriptions for practice, or more problematically, may be guided more by their own conditioning developed during their own childhood home and schooling experiences (see for example Miller, 1990; Fernandez-Balboa, 1999).

With the exception of the work of Smith (1991, 1998), Connolly (1995), and Nilges (2004), we have not seen much of the phenomenological focus on pedagogy within HMS.

Pedagogy and knowledge (re)production

Influenced variously by the early neo-Marxist work of such scholars as Bowles and Gintis (1976) and Willis (1975), the critiques of education as social reproduction by Freire (1971), Bourdieu and Passeron (1977) and Bernstein (1975), the sociology of knowledge (e.g. Young, 1971; Bates, 1986) and Habermas' (1972) knowledge and constitutive human interests, scholars such as Michael Apple (1982), Aronowitz and Giroux (1985), Carr and Kemmis (1986), Smyth (1987) and Luke and Gore (1992) began to consider pedagogy with the broad frame of knowledge (re)production. They asked questions relating to whose interests are served by particular curriculum choices and pedagogical practices. In other words, these critical pedagogies gave attention to both the intentions and the consequences of pedagogy. In the field of HMS, advocates of critical pedagogies such as Kirk (1986), Bain (1989), Tinning (1988) and Fernandez-Balboa (1995) began to argue for a similar perspective on pedagogy.

According to Goldfarb (2002), Paulo Freire's *Pedagogy of the Oppressed* (1970) inspired three decades of scholarship in education based on the premise that pedagogy is a form of cultural politics, not a science of knowledge transmission. In the 1980s numerous feminist scholars began using the idea that pedagogy is a form of cultural politics and were applying their increasingly sophisticated theorizing to critique the patriarchal underpinnings of education (see for example Ellsworth, 1989; Friedman, 1985; Lather, 1991; Luke and Gore, 1992; Maher, 1985). In kinesiology some feminist scholars such as Alison Dewar (1990), Jennifer Gore (1990) and Linda Bain (1989) were also using a notion of pedagogy that was informed by the discourses of the emerging field of cultural politics.

In HMS, it was Gore (1990) who was the first to problematize the concept of pedagogy in HMS (in the English speaking world at least) and to begin to use it to refer to a discourse on knowledge production and reproduction. She introduced the idea of pedagogy as text, and using Lungren's (1983) concepts distinguished between texts *for* pedagogy (texts from which teachers could teach, or the formal curriculum) and texts *about* pedagogy (texts that theorize or describe pedagogy). Most of the PE texts at the time were texts for pedagogy. Gore's work followed how the term was increasingly being used in the then emerging field of Cultural Studies, particularly by those in the Birmingham tradition (e.g. Hytten, 1999) and how it was being used in the work of Lusted (1986) as one of the conceptual springboards for her work *The Struggle for Pedagogies: Critical and Feminist Discourses as Regimes of Truth* (1993).

Lusted's (1986) interpretation of pedagogy specifically relates to knowledge (re)production. According to Lusted (1986), pedagogy is an important concept because "it draws attention to the *process* through which knowledge is produced" (p. 2; emphasis in original). It enables us to ask questions concerning "under what conditions and through what means we "come to know" (p. 3). It is Lusted's conception of pedagogy that I will argue is most useful to HMS.

Another conceptual framework used for understanding pedagogy as knowledge (re)production is that provided by Basil Bernstein (1975, 1996). Bernstein's concept of pedagogical practice is "somewhat wider than the relationship that goes on in schools." (1996, p. 17). His notion of pedagogical practice is as a "fundamental social context through which cultural reproduction – production takes place" (ibid.). In this sense it is somewhat similar to Lusted's notion of pedagogy. Bernstein's work offers an explanation of "the inner logic of pedagogical discourse and its practice" (p. 18). He claims that in order to understand how "pedagogic processes shape consciousness differentially [we need some] means of analysing the form of communication which bring this about" (ibid.). In this sense his work on pedagogical discourse is concerned with the rules of construction, distribution, reproduction and change of a pedagogic text (Glasby, 2000).

In the view of PE researchers Evans *et al.* (1999), "Bernstein (1996) has articulated more eloquently than most how this complex relationship between education and socialization is simultaneously embedded in the act of teaching" (p. 10). However, notwithstanding this observation, although popular in educational research literature, relatively few scholars in kinesiology have used Bernstein's framework to analyze pedagogy from a perspective of knowledge, power and control (exceptions include the work of Evans *et al.*, 2003; Glasby, 2000; Hay, 2007; Johns, 2005; Macdonald, 2003; Macdonald *et al.*, 1999; Chan, 2008).

The important thing about these examples of conceptual orientations is that each has its own particular (even if broad) notion of pedagogy. They each exist, and make sense, in different discourse communities (Ovens, 2002). There is little common ground and accordingly communication across advocates of these perspectives is often difficult.

Languaging sport pedagogy: one version

In order to "language" sport pedagogy it is necessary for me to trace how the terms pedagogy and sport pedagogy have been used within some of the major conferences and texts of kinesiology. But first we need a little languaging of the term sport. It is important to recognize that there is frequently a blurring of the categories of sport and PE in the context of formal schooling and society in general. Sometimes the terms are used as synonyms. As we can see in the pages of *Education though Sport: An Overview of Good Practices in Europe* (Janssens *et al.*, 2004) in the European context (from where sport pedagogy originated) the term sport is a much broader and inclusive term than is commonly understood in Anglophone countries like the UK or USA.

Sport pedagogy, like pedagogy, is amorphous (Erdmann, 1996). Notwithstanding this, it is now generally accepted that *sport pedagogy* is a sub-discipline of the field of kinesiology. It is now commonplace to see advertisements for academic positions in sport pedagogy within universities in the USA and the UK. Back in the 1980s such positions would most likely have been advertised as PE ones.

The 1996 publication of the UK based journal *Physical Education and Sport Pedagogy* signified the contemporary acceptance of the term sport pedagogy in the Anglophone world of kinesiology. However, as *sport* pedagogy is often seen as synonymous with *PE* pedagogy perhaps the new journal is seeking to cover all bases. In the UK, Europe and the USA different meanings are attached to the terms pedagogy and sport (see Crum, 1986; Haag, 1989). In general, the European meaning of both pedagogy and sport is much broader than their meaning in the USA and in Asian countries (such as Taiwan, Korea and Japan) that look to US scholarship and research for their leadership.

The term sport pedagogy was first used in Germany in the early 1970s (Grupe and Krüger, 1996) and has been in use in work on kinesiology in English since the late 1970s (see Crum, 1986; Haag, 1989). In 1978 Herbert Haag wrote that "Sport pedagogy as one major theoretical field of sport science is in urgent need of clarification of its nature" (p. x). Later (1996) he argued that sport pedagogy is a theory field (like sport biomechanics or sport psychology) and not like (not synonymous with) PE, which he regards as a "total academic field". In Europe, the "total academic field" of PE is now mostly referred to as sport science (*Sportwissenschaft* in German). Importantly, as Haag points out, *Sportwissenschaft* "includes aspects of natural science as well as behavioural science, arts, humanities in relation to movement, play and sport" (p. 1).

Haag (1989) asserts that sport pedagogy is "the description of the field of theoretical research or sub-discipline of sport science which deals with the educational aspects of physical activity: sport, play, games, dance etc." (p. 6). Moreover, "It becomes evident that sport pedagogy has a central position within sport science, in every teaching and learning process in physical activity" (p. 9). Significantly, Haag positions sport pedagogy as "residing" between sport science and the science of education. Bart Crum (1986), also providing a European interpretation, argued that sport pedagogy is a "field of scholarly work on and disciplined inquiry [into] all educational interventions in the domain of human movement" (p. 212). He forcefully claims that

> There should be no doubt that the subject matter of sport pedagogy (as a field of research) is a *pedagogical practice*, in particular a sport pedagogical practice, and that the subject matter of research on teaching physical education [sport pedagogy research] is not sport but teaching, in particular the teaching of movement and sport (p. 212).

Larry Locke (1979) was one of the first US scholars to use the term sport pedagogy in an address to an ICHPER (International Council for Health, Physical Education and Recreation) conference in Kiel, Germany. Perhaps the location of the conference motivated Locke to use the term that already had currency in Europe. In his paper titled "Teaching and learning processes in physical activity: The central problem of sport pedagogy", Locke argued strongly that "Teaching and learning are the processes at the heart of Sport Pedagogy, and research which probes the problem of their nature forms the content of that discipline" (p. 1). This is very similar to how Haag (2005) described the essence of the European usage of sport didactics.

Significantly, when sport pedagogy was imported from Germany into North America the German word for science (*Geistes*) was interpreted in a narrow technical sense and, in the US in particular, sport pedagogy came to be interpreted as a scientific (read technical, empirical) approach to pedagogy in human movement (Crum, 1986). The German term *Sportpädagogik* (sport pedagogy) refers to both educative practice (e.g. school PE) and to scholarly work about/for such practice. Unfortunately for those of us who speak only English, there are numerous resources on sport pedagogy that are only available in German (see for example, Haag and Hummel's (2001) edited collection of writings *Handbuch Sportpädagogik* [Handbook of sport pedagogy] cited in Haag, 2005).

In 1982 Purdue University in Indiana hosted a conference under the auspices of the Committee for Institutional Cooperation (CIC) among the "Big Ten" universities of the USA. The conference was significant because it was the first time that the Body of Knowledge Symposium Committee of the CIC held a symposium on research on teaching in PE. Previous symposia between 1968–81 had addressed all other sub-disciplines of the field of kinesiology that had status as an academic research area of study. Ironically, the "parent" that conceived them all, namely PE (Haag's (1996) "total academic field"), was not deemed to have a coherent or emerging research culture until the Purdue conference. This prompted Daryl Siedentop (1993a) to comment that this state of affairs was rather like being part of the family (of PE) yet being considered more like the bastard child. The conference proceedings (Templin and Olson, 1983) make for interesting reading. Although the editors claim that the proceedings reflect information that was "currently at the forefront of pedagogical research in physical education" (p. xii), the word pedagogy was used by only one presenter (Hoffman, 1983) and the term "sport pedagogy" was not mentioned at all.

Sport pedagogy as a term has long been used in the professional association known as the Association Internationale des Ecoles Supérieures d'Education Physique (AIESEP) and some tracing of the conferences of this association is informative. One of the significant presentations at each annual AIESEP World Congress meeting is the memorial Cagigal lecture. In 1990 American scholar Linda Bain titled her Cagigal lecture "Research in sport pedagogy: Past, present and future". Bain began her address with an examination of the differences within sport pedagogy and the continuing struggle over meaning within the field. She identified the three dominant research traditions that have been used in North American sport pedagogy as: behaviourist research; socialization research; and critical theory research. In highlighting the gendered nature of the development of sport pedagogy, Bain pointed out that although there were many early women leaders in PE who had an interest in pedagogy, "most of those who led the effort to transform sport pedagogy into a scientific area of study were men" (p. 32). Perhaps as a consequence it is the curriculum dimension of sport pedagogy that has become so popular for women.

The following year in Atlanta, Georgia, German scholar Wolf Brettschneider (1991) titled his Cagigal address "The many faces of sport as a challenge for sport pedagogy and physical education". Brettschneider (1991) suggested that sport pedagogy in the early 1990s was in a crisis. He claimed that "Sport pedagogy is at present a discipline without a recognisable core … It is neither sure of its subject matter and its objectives, nor of the direction to take" (p. 60). Two significant issues of the crisis related to the nature of sport (as a narrow or broad conception) and the pedagogical nature of sport (was it purposeful for developing certain human attributes).

American Paul Schempp delivered the Cagigal lecture in 1993 titled "The nature of knowledge in sport pedagogy". Schempp (1993) turned to the International Council for Sport Pedagogy and their specific publication *An Introduction to the Terminology of Sport Pedagogy* for clarity on a definition of sport pedagogy. He claimed to have found "no less than six distinct definitions" (p. 123). What was common to all definitions was that "sport pedagogy is constituted in the actors and actions of teaching and learning purposeful human movement" (p. 107). Significantly Haag, Crum, Siedentop, and Schempp all focus on pedagogy as related to purposeful knowledge. Schempp (2000) used Habermas' (1972) notion of knowledge-constitutive interests in his exploration of the nature of knowledge in sport pedagogy. He described three types of disciplined inquiry that have been used in educational research and sport pedagogy research: empirical analytic (positivist) science, historical-hermeneutic (interpretive) science; and critical science (see Carr and Kemmis, 1986; Tinning, 1992).

The conference proceedings of the AIESEP World Sport Science Congress held at Adelphi University, New York in 1998 reveal a collection of different terminologies. Sections included Pedagogy – Teacher Education; Pedagogy – Foundations; Pedagogy – Culture; and Sport Pedagogy and Social Issues. Implicit here is a distinction between pedagogy and sport pedagogy but there is no hint as to what it might be. Moreover, none of the speakers actually used the term sport pedagogy in their presentation titles.

In October 2007 Lynn Housner from the University of Pittsburgh organized a major "pedagogy" conference titled "Historic Traditions and Future Directions in Research on Teaching and Teacher Education in Physical Education". Arguably this was the largest conference held in the US with a focus on research in PE and PETE and although overseas presenters attended, the majority of presenters were American. Of all the presentations there were only six that used the terms pedagogy or sport pedagogy in their abstract title. Of these, only one was from the USA, the other five were from the UK, Norway, Spain, Canada, and New Zealand. Clearly, in the USA at least, the terms pedagogy and sport pedagogy are not preferred when reporting on research in PE and PETE.

The use of the term within some of the influential textbooks is also informative. Notwithstanding the increased use of the term sport pedagogy as a sub-discipline of kinesiology there are many textbooks written for the Anglophone audience that avoid the term sport pedagogy and instead continue to use terms like PE curriculum and instruction, teaching and learning in PE or PE pedagogy.

In the first edition of Siedentop's (1990) influential American text *Introduction to Physical Education, Fitness and Sport*, there is a section on the (then) new sub-discipline of sport pedagogy. Actually Siedentop, like Haag (1989), called it the field of sport pedagogy but since "field" has many broader meanings (for examples see Bernstein, 1975; Bourdieu and Passeron, 1977) calling it a sub-discipline of the field of kinesiology is more appropriate. According to Siedentop, "Sport pedagogy is the study of the processes of teaching and coaching, of the outcomes of such endeavours, and of the content of fitness, physical education, and sport-education programs" (p. 316). At that time Siedentop claimed that in the USA at least, the field of sport pedagogy was typically called teacher education or curriculum and instruction. It is interesting to speculate, however, as to why, if sport pedagogy is "a term used widely in international and physical education and sport science" (Siedentop, 1990) we find no reference at all to the term in the fourth edition of his famous *Developing Teaching Skills in Physical Education* (Siedentop and Tannehill, 2000). Perhaps, in writing for an American audience, Siedentop considered that the term had little currency given the restricted meanings ascribed to both sport and pedagogy in the USA.

Silverman and Ennis (1996) use the term PE pedagogy rather than sport pedagogy in their *Student Learning in Physical Education*. They claim that "The field of research in physical education pedagogy, sometimes called *sport pedagogy* in the international community" (p. 3; emphasis in original) is comprised of three sub-areas: curriculum; teaching; and teacher education. Presumably their choice to avoid the term sport pedagogy was a conscious one and was perhaps influenced by the fact that the text was predominantly targeted at the American market.

In the UK the edited volume by Laker (2003) titled *The Future of Physical Education: Building a New Pedagogy* makes no specific reference to sport pedagogy (with the exception of the chapter by Silverman who self-identifies as a sport pedagogue). Even more interesting is that the Dutch publication *Education through Sport: An Overview of Good Practice in Europe* (Janssens *et al.*, 2004) also avoids using the term sport pedagogy. While they use the terms pedagogical perspective and pedagogical action (p. 29), the term sport pedagogy is absent. Perhaps this is because the book is written in English and is not intended for a continental European audience.

So it appears that in regard to the systematic use of the term sport pedagogy, all we can say is that some researchers and scholars do (sometimes) and some don't (sometimes). Since there is no international agreement on the preferred terms (sport pedagogy or PE pedagogy) it seems that personal preference and local traditions (including national language differences) will continue to largely influence the choice of term. Personal investment in self-defining (e.g. as a sport pedagogist) is also important. Those who have created their careers as PE pedagogy scholars may be reluctant to re-label their work as sport pedagogy. Whatever the reasons, it seems likely that, at least in the immediate future, sport pedagogy will not become a universal signifier for research and practice in all matters relating to pedagogy and human movement.

The idea of pedagogical work

As Ellsworth (1997) informs us "all curricula and pedagogies invite their users to take up particular positions within relation of knowledge, power and desire" (p. 2). Moreover, "pedagogy is a much messier and more inconclusive affair than the vast majority of our educational theories and practices make it out to be" (p. 8). I take these two statements as a basis for the way I am using pedagogy in this book. I assume that pedagogy is concerned with processes of knowledge (re)production and also the (re)production of values, attitudes, dispositions, subjectivities and identities. In order to argue this case and carry this notion throughout the book let me first define what I am taking as the meaning of these particular terms. The following definitions are taken from the Encarta® *World English Dictionary* and provide a commonplace starting point:

> *knowl·edge n*
> 1 general awareness or possession of information, facts, ideas, truths, or principles
> 2 clear awareness or explicit information, for example, of a situation or fact
> 3 all the information, facts, truths, and principles learned throughout time
> 4 familiarity or understanding gained through experience or study
>
> *val·ues npl*
> 1 the accepted principles or standards of an individual or a group
>
> *at·ti·tude n*
> 1 an opinion or general feeling about something

2 a physical posture, either conscious or unconscious, especially while
   interacting with others

dis·po·si·tion n
1 somebody's usual mood or temperament
2 an inclination or tendency to act in a particular way

Although these four terms are relatively straightforward to define, the distinction between subjectivity and identity is more difficult. I think the following from Michael Gard (2006) is the most understandable I have read:

> I define 'subjectivity' to mean a sense of one's separateness from all other things in the world, the sense that 'I' am an individual self in a world of other selves. I take 'identity' to indicate the specific content or shape of a particular person's sense of themselves. That is, identity is the answer to the question 'who are you?' As such it is a dimension of subjectivity (pp. 11–12).

Pedagogical work as a concept is not new. David Kirk and I may have been the first to use the term in the HMS/PE context (at least in a title) in a paper delivered to the American Research Association in San Francisco back in 1992 (Kirk and Tinning, 1992a). At that time we used the notion of pedagogical work to "conflate tasks centred around curriculum and instruction" (p. 2). In so doing, we proposed that "all work which is of direct relevance or significance for teaching and learning in physical education is pedagogical work" (ibid.). Ours was an attempt to show that curriculum work and instructional work were an interdependent dynamic dialectic rather than, as often depicted, separate unrelated processes.

While this notion of pedagogical work was useful at the time, more recently the term has become increasingly widely used yet never defined or explained. Accordingly I am articulating a particular conception of the term found in the Encarta® *World English Dictionary*, one that takes "work" to mean:

work n
6 that which has been made or done as part of a job or as a result of
   effort or activity requiring skill (often used in combination)

Pedagogical work, as I am using the term, is a consequence of the intentions of pedagogy. It is a result of pedagogy. While pedagogy refers to a practice or set of practices, the purpose of which is to pass on or produce knowledge, the idea of purpose or intention is important. Someone may learn something from an experience or an encounter with a device or piece of equipment (e.g. a young child finds a football in the backyard and through trial and error learns to kick the ball), but if there was no explicit intention to pass on knowledge by someone (teacher, coach, parent, or other pedagogic device) then there has been no pedagogy and no pedagogical work done.

Pedagogical work, therefore, foregrounds the *consequences* of pedagogy. It is not concerned with what particular pedagogical practices are said to do, but rather is concerned with what knowledge(s), ways of thinking, dispositions and subjectivities are actually (re)produced in/through particular pedagogical encounters. The reason I have chosen to so limit what stands for pedagogy is that without this restriction pedagogical work would be everywhere yet nowhere in a similar way that discourse and text sometimes are seen to be all pervasive. It simply makes no practical or theoretical sense to consider all acts of learning as the result of pedagogy.

This understanding of pedagogy is different from Siedentop's (1993b) claim that "For pedagogy to have occurred, certain student outcomes must be attained. No outcomes, no pedagogy!" (p. 7). In my view, for pedagogy to have occurred there must be a purposeful encounter between teacher, learner and subject matter and the purpose is to (re)produce knowledge. There will always be outcomes (consequences or learning) but they are often unpredictable and always dependent on meaning making processes which are beyond the control of the teacher. This view connects my notion of pedagogy with Giroux and Simon's (1989) view that "any practice which intentionally tries to influence the production of meaning is a pedagogical practice" (p. 230).

Importantly, the pedagogical work done may not be that which was intended. There are, as I shall argue, possibilities for learning certain ethical and political values, attitudes and dispositions that might not be part of the initial intention of the pedagogy. For example, an exercise science lecturer might have the pedagogical intention to develop in students an understanding of the principle of progressive overload as it applies to exercising. However, the students learn not only how progressive overload works, but also that such exercise regimes are aversive and to be avoided at all costs. The pedagogical work done as a consequence of the pedagogy was therefore both intended and unintended. In another example, a PE lesson intended to teach students gymnastics might have unintended consequences whereby some of the students learn that their body shape and strength limit their ability to perform that activity. Again, pedagogical work is done, but it is not what the teacher intended.

In the case of HMS as formal institutional practice in universities, *pedagogical work* is that effect or influence on ways of thinking, beliefs, practices, dispositions and identities regarding physical activity performance and participation, bodily practices, and understandings and self-awareness related to health and well-being that is produced by an individual's encounter with certain prescribed pedagogical practices and devices. When I use the notion of knowledge (re)production I am including as knowledge not only a taxonomic range of cognitions (e.g. Bloom, 1956) and motoric skills (e.g. fundamental movement skills, see Walkley *et al.*, 1993) but also knowledge as represented in particular ways of thinking, attitudes, beliefs and dispositions. Importantly, pedagogical work can also apply to the "transformation of consciousness that takes place in the intersection of three agencies – the teacher, the learner and the knowledge they produce together" (Lusted, 1986, p. 3).

Sites of pedagogy

All cultures attempt to reproduce themselves. They pass on valued knowledge by means of modelling, stories and metaphor, dance, art, books, speeches, billboards, TV, radio, the Internet and so on. The passing on of knowledge sometimes occurs in "formal" institutional sites such as churches, hospitals, universities, schools or factories, sports clubs, theatres, and ski resorts. In all these places there is an explicit attempt to "pass on" valued knowledge. But we also find pedagogical work done in non-formal sites such as families (e.g. manners training, toilet training and other forms of behaviour shaping), local parks (e.g. in "fitness stations"), playgrounds, and even T-shirts. As in the formal institutional sites, in these non-formal sites the pedagogical practices or devices are intended to (re)produce certain valued knowledge. There is an intention to do certain pedagogical work.

Simon (1997) gives a useful example of how a T-shirt can do pedagogical work. He describes a T-shirt with a picture of a sailing ship and an inscription "How could Columbus have discovered America when Native Americans were already there?" (p. 130). The question is intended to offer a statement of "counter-commemoration" that refers to the struggle to resist the 500th anniversary of the Columbus landfall as the "discovery" of America. In other words the T-shirt offers an alternative reading of history and in doing so affords the possibility of doing pedagogical work regarding knowledge (re) production regarding history. This example reveals something of the ways in which cultural studies as a field considers pedagogy as a very broad dimension of cultural politics.

Importantly, as the T-shirt example shows, the "teacher" in a pedagogical encounter need not be a flesh and blood human or even a computer instructional program. Pedagogical work is done if an individual gains some knowledge (comes to know), either consciously or sub-consciously, as a consequence of engaging in a pedagogical encounter which has as its purpose the passing on of certain knowledge/understanding. In the case of the T-shirt example the intention of the text was to inform/educate about the problematics regarding the "discovery" of America.

Also importantly, what is learned in a pedagogical encounter might not be what is intended by those who created the particular pedagogical device or encounter. Pedagogical intentions are often unfulfilled. Administrators and teachers (in both schools and universities) are only too familiar with the differences between intentions (curriculum goals) and actual learning outcomes. Considering that knowledge is what is understood rather than what is intended, I consider that thinking about *pedagogical work* helps take our focus off specific pedagogical practices and helps us focus instead on what is *understood* by the learner as a result of some pedagogical encounter.

There is a resonance here with the notion of the hidden curriculum (Dodds, 1993) and with what Billett (1999) called unintended learning. However, I have chosen to use pedagogical work because it relates more specifically to the outcomes of a pedagogical encounter; that is an encounter between student, subject matter and teacher in which there was specific pedagogical intent.

Pedagogical work in HMS

HMS, as a field of knowledge, is part of the formalized institutional context. Teaching in HMS sets out to reproduce knowledge (in the broad sense described earlier) related to the sub-disciplines of the field (e.g. biomechanics, motor control, sociology of sport, exercise physiology, exercise and sport psychology, history of PE and sport). Research in HMS endeavours to produce knowledge related to the sub-disciplines.

In HMS pedagogical work is done relating to three interrelated dimensions: Physical activity, bodies and health. In a dialectical manner, the pedagogical practices and devices used to bring about the intended pedagogical work also affects and influences the ways of thinking, practice, dispositions and identities (subjectivities) of those who work in the field of HMS. Importantly, however, pedagogical work on/for bodies, physical activity and health is not the sole preserve of our field. Other cultural players have vested interests in (re)producing certain knowledge about bodies, physical activity and health and such knowledge will, in various ways, impact on the pedagogical work done in kinesiology (Tinning and Glasby, 2002).

If we are to consider sport pedagogy to be a foundational sub-discipline of the field of HMS and not just applicable to PE teaching and sport coaching, then it should be informed by a notion of pedagogy that allows us (professionals of the field) to interrogate and analyze not just the pedagogical practices and devices of formal institutions like schools, universities and sports clubs, but also those of non-formal sites such as families, TV, video games and T-shirts. It should enable us to gain an understanding of the pedagogical work that is consequential to all pedagogical encounters wherever they take place. It should enable us to better understand how and what knowledge is (re)produced related to physical activity, bodies and health by both the field of HMS and other cultural players across all possible sites.

Unfortunately there has been virtually no systematic study of pedagogy as a process of coming to know used within the sub-disciplines of HMS such as biomechanics, exercise physiology, sport history, sport sociology, and accordingly we actually know very little about the pedagogical work done in those contexts.

If we are to gain a better understanding of the actual impact of our institutional pedagogical work we also need to understand the pedagogical work done by other cultural players that has the potential to reinforce or undermine the intentional pedagogical work done by HMS specialists. Consider the issue of obesity. Our field does intentional pedagogical work to educate and provide advice on exercise, nutrition and lifestyle factors effecting obesity (e.g. Sallis and McKenzie, 1991) while at the same time there are other cultural players, such as certain drug companies and media advertising agents, who have vested interests in obesity as a profit making opportunity to do pedagogical work that might be counter-productive to that of the HMS field.

At this point it is worthwhile asking if sport pedagogy as a sub-discipline of HMS currently allows for an analysis and understanding of such broadly conceived pedagogical work. For example, would the chapter by Saltman (2002) titled "Embodied promise: The pedagogy of market faith in body-building" be considered a project of sport pedagogy? Perhaps Haag's (2005) definitions are broad enough to capture it, but certainly restrictive definitions that confine the focus of pedagogy to an instrumental analysis of instructional processes are not.

Over a decade ago Zakus and Cruise Malloy (1996) made a thoughtful evaluation of pedagogical approaches in kinesiology and offered praxis oriented critical pedagogy as a way forward. More recently I have argued for what I called a modest critical pedagogy (see Tinning, 2002) that enables a more sophisticated analysis of pedagogical work done within HMS and beyond. Both of these examples represent a challenge to orthodoxy in pedagogy but more importantly they offer the possibility for sport pedagogy to move beyond a narrow, yet important, focus on school PE and PETE, and towards a contribution to HMS that is foundational.

While I agree with Silverman's (2007) argument that pedagogical knowledge can be useful for kinesiology, I am not talking about the use of teaching skills or pedagogical practices in the various sub-disciplines of the field. As a foundational sub-discipline of kinesiology, sport pedagogy would need to extend "to the consideration of the development of health and bodily fitness, social and moral welfare, ethics and aesthetics, as well as to the institutional forms that serve to facilitate society's and the individual's pedagogic aims" (as cited in Marton and Booth, 1997, p. 178).

Accordingly, sport pedagogy should embrace a conception of pedagogy that allows us to seek the "multiple connections between things that have [apparently] nothing to do with each other" (Mercer, 1992, p. 39). It should enable us to "connect the dots" (Klein, 2000) between all pedagogical work that is done relating to the various orientations of our field – between physical activity, the body, and health. A sport pedagogy conceived in this way has the potential to be genuinely foundational to HMS and not of relevance merely to PE teaching and sports coaching.

Note

1   An earlier version of this chapter was originally published as Tinning, R. (2008). Pedagogy, sport pedagogy, and the field of kinesiology. *Quest*, 60, 405–424.

Part II

Pedagogy for physical activity

2 Sites of pedagogy for physical activity

Physical activity in all its forms is the subject of serious pedagogy. A useful beginning question to ask is "Who is involved with pedagogy for physical activity?" Casting our search widely we can see that the range of interests is diverse indeed. Schools have long used pedagogies for physical activity in formal PE lessons and sport sessions. Some universities (particularly in the USA) require all students to attend courses in PE in which they learn certain physical activities (e.g. swimming, tennis, softball). Coaches in sports clubs for juniors and seniors are involved with pedagogies focused on their particular sport. Elite sports institutes focus on the achievement of high performance in certain sports. Local gyms employ instructors who use certain pedagogies to assist their clients to learn the physical activities. Individual instructors teach yoga or Tai Chi in local halls and parks. Ski schools (in most alpine regions), scuba diving and surfing schools are run as commercial businesses that focus on pedagogies that are meant to maximize success in helping their clients acquire the skills of the specific activity. Instructors in dance studios use pedagogies of physical activity to teach various forms of dance from ballet to salsa. And various forms of the media also engage in pedagogies for physical activity.

In this chapter I will consider the pedagogies utilized in/for the learning of physical activity and the pedagogical work they might produce. I will consider how pedagogy for physical activity is theorized and practised in various sites (e.g. universities, schools, sport clubs) and will discuss the implications of various pedagogical choices used in both PE and sports coaching contexts (including sports clubs, and elite sport institutes). I will also discuss various popular models of pedagogy that are found in PE and sport contexts and why one particular model is dominant. These are examples only and are not meant to be an exhaustive range of all the possible sites of pedagogy for physical activity.

In schools

In 1978 the United Nations Educational Scientific and Cultural Organization (UNESCO) issued its *International Charter of Physical Education and Sport*.

The first of 11 articles reads as follows:

Article 1. The practice of physical education and sport is a fundamental right for all

1.1. Every human being has a fundamental right of access to physical education and sport, which are essential for the full development of his personality. The freedom to develop physical, intellectual and moral powers through physical education and sport must be guaranteed both within the educational system and in other aspects of social life.

1.2. Everyone must have full opportunities, in accordance with his national tradition of sport, for practising physical education and sport, developing his physical fitness and attaining a level of achievement in sport which corresponds to his gifts.

1.3. Special opportunities must be made available for young people, including children of pre-school age, for the aged and for the handicapped to develop their personalities to the full through physical education and sport programmes suited to their requirements.

(Adopted by the General Conference at its twentieth session, Paris, 21 November 1978; available online at http://portal.unesco.org/shs/en/ev.php)

This article is the official imprimatur of the place of PE and sport within school. Although written in a gendered language that would be unacceptable today, it is testimony to the longstanding commitment at the level of rhetoric to PE and sport as valued cultural practices. There is often, however, considerable slippage between rhetoric and reality. This has meant that the translation of this principled rhetoric into policy and actual practice has been highly variable across countries and even within countries. Notwithstanding this variability, the PE lesson and the sport class are ubiquitous sites of pedagogy for physical activity.

The PE lesson

You either loved it or hated it, looked forward to it or dreaded it, but we've all been forced to do it. Sometimes a note could get you out of it, but the following week there you'd be again, writhing on a cold and dusty gym floor in your underwear. We've all forgotten our kit, endured the sweaty changing rooms, the freezing cross-country runs, the pubescent torture of communal showers supervised by a (fully clothed) teacher. PE is one of life's great levellers, a uniquely ruthless aspect of school experience which shapes us all and leaves its traces in unexpected and lingering ways.

(Publisher's note, Dust cover, Myerson, 2005)

Certainly we might like to think that PE classes are no longer a "ruthless aspect of school experience", and most advocates would like to think that one of the traces it leaves is an enduring love for, and involvement in, physical activity. However, as Evans and Davies (1993) argued some time ago, PE continues to make friends and enemies of young people.

Notwithstanding its problematic pedagogical work, the PE lesson is the most ubiquitous formal encounter with learning physical activities that most young people experience. In schools in Britain and Ireland, Continental Europe, Scandinavia, Australasia, North America, South America, Africa, China, Japan, Korea etc. young people have PE classes. To be sure there will be considerable variation between contexts with regard to such things as frequency and duration of lessons; the physical resources available at the school (playing fields, gymnasia, balls and other small equipment); the climatic favourableness to outside physical activity; and the training and expertise of the teachers. These factors will obviously affect the experience that pupils will have in PE class but the fact remains that PE classes tend to be a universal experience across most education systems.

Internationally, the development of PE has been a battleground for ideas regarding the most appropriate pedagogical strategies to achieve specific objectives. The PE lesson has variously been conceived as an education *in*, *through* and *about* movement (Arnold, 1988) and at different times in its history there has been differential emphasis on each of these possibilities. In the Australian context, since the beginning of the twentieth century we have seen school PE characterized by drills (Swedish gymnastics), physical skills (Gray, 1985a), movement education (Gray, 1985b), sports science (Gray, 1985c), health related fitness (Tinning, 1990), and intelligent performance (Kirk, 1983). I will discuss some of these later in this chapter.

While individual PE lessons might focus on skill practice, games playing, fitness activities, or the study of the theoretical aspects of human movement (e.g. biomechanics and exercise physiology) there has been a trend, in Australia at least, for there to be less teacher focus on pedagogies for physical activity per se, and more emphasis on pedagogies for the instrumental or secondary outcomes (Tinning, 2000) that are considered to result from engagement in physical activity (for example health). As to whether that is OK or not will depend on your view regarding the purposes of PE. However, this shift has, along with other changes in the educational context, meant that many graduating PE teachers now know less about the appropriate pedagogical strategies for teaching particular forms of physical activity. In contemporary parlance, neophyte PE teachers of today probably know less about pedagogical context knowledge for physical activity than their equivalents of two generations ago.

I think it is useful to think about pedagogies for physical activity in PE as concerned, in part, with the development of *physical literacy*. Margaret Whitehead's (2001) notion of physical literacy includes dimensions of:

- Physical competence (to do certain movement tasks or skills).
- Spatial awareness (which some call spatial literacy), which allows for reading physical space as in knowing where one's body is in space (useful for example for a gymnast or a diver), and/or in relation to others (useful for example in soccer or hockey).
- Sport/movement literacy, which enables a person to understand games and sports with respect to strategies, tactics, rules, values, traditions etc.

Although validly criticized as lacking reference to "the social and cultural contexts in which we learn and use movement" (Wright and Burrows, 2006), Whitehead's physical literacy has some similarities, and some important differences from, Rossi and Ryan's (2006) notion of movement literacy. Whether movement literacy or physical literacy is the preferred term, they both focus our attention on the physical activity aspects necessary to participate in the movement culture (Crum, 1993) and therefore allow us to appreciate the contribution that school PE lessons can make through specific pedagogies for physical activity. Of course the pedagogical work that is done as a consequence of pedagogies for physical activity in PE classes is, as the above extract from Julie Myerson's (2005) book attests, too often problematic.

Although it is not possible to give a description of a typical PE lesson, in many countries there is often considerable overlap between a PE class and a sports class. Indeed this overlap has long been a major concern for many physical educators (e.g. Evans, 1990) and the place of sport within the PE curriculum is still a contested issue in our field.

The sports class

What stands for the "sports class" will also vary considerably across contexts. Some will be well organized and probably contain skill development activities and some form of organized competition between selected sides. Others will be an opportunity for truancy for those who are "not games people" (Myerson, 2005) or participation in forms of "motley" competition between those left behind (i.e. those not selected in the real teams). Of the teachers who are given the responsibility of overseeing the sports class some are interested in sport, knowledgeable and enthusiastic, some are enthusiastic but not knowledgeable, some will be ambivalent and still others resistant and resentful at having to spend their time overseeing sport.

While some physical educators lament the fact that too many PE classes look no different from a sports class, to the extent that there is a recognizable difference, it would be more unusual for a sports class to look like a PE class. One reason is that most sports classes do not spend much time on instruction in sports skills. Typically they move quickly into the game-playing situation. The sports class is not primarily about doing pedagogical work on/for sports skills per se – it is usually assumed that pedagogical work will accrue or follow from participation in competitive sports.

Sport in the school curriculum (or as extra-curricula) is intended to do important pedagogical work well beyond the learning of some physical skills and games play. The following quotes give some idea of the huge expectations for sport in school. In 1994 the British Prime Minister John Major exhorted that:

> I don't regard sport, especially team sport, as a trivial 'add-on' to education. It is part of the British instinct; it is part of our character. Sport is fun, but it deserves a proper place in the life of all our children. ... We are therefore changing the National Curriculum to put competitive games back at the heart of school life. Sport will be played by children in every school from five to 16 and more time must be devoted to team games.
>
> ("Sport in Schools" – Conservative Party
> Conference, 14 October 1994).

Major's words say what sport advocates in many other countries also believe to be true about the value and place of school sport. His comments embody the British conceived "Muscular Christianity" that was "part of a complex ideology which also embraced imperial duty, nationalistic pride, and moral character" (Vamplew *et al.*, 1997, p. 297). These beliefs underpin support for sport in schools. Of course sport might not live up to (deliver) on these expectations but the point is that this is the *intended* purpose of including sport in the curriculum of British schools. However, the pedagogical work that school sport actually does might well be (and is) somewhat different.

School sport not only does pedagogical work related to knowledge about how to play sport (including rules and traditions), it also does pedagogical work related to values, attitudes, dispositions, subjectivities and identities. For example, there is considerable research evidence that school sport privileges certain masculinities (heterosexual, physical) and, in so doing, reinforces and facilitates the reproduction of particular values, attitudes, dispositions, subjectivities and identities that are associated with this form of masculinity (see for example Hickey and Fitzclarence, 1999; Burgess *et al.*, 2003; Hickey, 2008).

Canadian scholar Brian Pronger (2002) suggests that "learning a sport is never purely a technical matter" and "When one is learning the technical skills of sport one can at the same time and in the same setting – depending on how the sport culture is structured – learn, internalize, and operationalize oppressive cultural discourses, such as classism, racism, sexism, heterosexism and homophobia" (p.13). This is a clear statement of what Pronger considers to be some of the possible *pedagogical work* that might result from pedagogical encounters within sports participation. Certainly many other critical sports sociologists (see for example Hoberman, 1984; McKay, 1991; Eitzen and Sage, 2003) have informed us that the effects (pedagogical work) that are produced through pedagogical encounters within sport are often problematic.

The actual nature or form of the typical school sports session is worth considering. Although "typical" is a rather contentious term since there are many variants on the theme, I suggest that the pedagogy of the sports session is more often than not a pedagogy of sports coaching. By this I mean that sports sessions rarely involve pedagogical forms which have as their basis rationales like those of TGfU (Teaching Games for Understanding) or game sense (see Chapter 3). Although there might be some use of modified rules and equipment, most school sports sessions take their pedagogical form from the ways in which particular sports are coached and organized. For example, they might include versions of mini-games and drills (e.g. 3 against 2 Soccer) and they might also try to emphasize the tactics and strategies of the game in focus.

In these contexts, for many students the pedagogical work might be that which the teacher or coach anticipates (i.e. the improvement in game skill and play). But there might be other pedagogical work done for those students who, when placed prematurely in competitive game situations, learn to become competent bystanders and avoid the action for fear of failure or injury.

There is ample evidence that enjoyment in school sport (and PE) is closely related to ability. For example, as Wellard (2006) argues, "Claims that all children benefit from sport fail to recognise the differing experiences faced by boys and girls, particularly in organised sports and physical education" (p. 117). For many young boys the differing experiences can be related to the favouring of hegemonic masculinity and specific skill-based perform-ances (e.g. Hickey, 2008). Wellard also refers to Fernandez-Balboa's (2003) use of Miller's (1990) concept of "poisonous pedagogy" as it applies to the PE and sport experiences of some young people. According to Fernandez-Balboa, the pedagogical form of much PE and sport maintains "vicious cycles in which certain pedagogical principles are automatically applied as if they were beneficial to all students while, in reality, their effects are socially and psychologically pernicious" (p. 148). This is what I am referring to as the pedagogical work done by certain pedagogical practices that dominate school sport sessions.

Interestingly, in the literature of our field, there is relatively little attention given to the pedagogical forms of the school sports class. I return to this issue in Chapter 3 where I discuss the recent interest in situated learning and sport contexts.

The dance lesson

There is no doubt that dance is physical activity and as such has a history of being included as part of school PE curriculum. However, as Michael Gard (2004) argues, the nature and place of dance as physical activity in the school curriculum is often problematic. Certainly dance is far more than physical activity and accordingly its inclusion in PE is highly contested. In Gard's words:

> dance is qualitatively different from activities such as competitive and recreational sports, and the things which make it distinctive can also be the things which make it unattractive to physical educators (p. 93).

Accordingly, there are many (including some PE teachers) who consider that dance is fundamentally a performing art and should not be seen as part of PE. Notwithstanding this important recognition, dance is a site for pedagogy of physical activity and accordingly it finds a place in this chapter. With a small number of exceptions (e.g. Bibik, 1996; Vertinsky *et al.*, 2007) pedagogy for dance lessons in schools has been largely ignored in PE research.

Here are some notes I made after watching a school dance lesson *circa* 2007:

There is a crowd of kids at the edge of the dance studio. As each student enters the studio they place (drop) their bag near the piano and proceed to pull-on their tights, socks, slippers and other clothing that, while functional for dance, also helps mark their particular identity making process. Dressed to dance, one by one they move to a space on the floor and begin to warm up. Their stretches are slow and purposeful and as they move they chat to one another. By the time that Maree calls for their attention they are all warming up on the floor. Maree seamlessly begins to structure the collective warm up exercises of the class by leading from the front. Since dance is an elective subject for students she tends to only get students who are motivated and enjoy dancing.

After about 5 minutes of this mass warm up activity Maree stops the class and begins to briefly outline what they got up to last session. They are working on a class dance that Maree has lead choreographed to one of the contemporary songs popular with the class.

Maree demonstrates the moves they practised last session and then, with her back to the class, leads the whole class in revision of the moves. This is done first without music and then later with music added. After about 5–6 minutes of this practice Maree stops the class, gets them to sit down and proceeds to explain and demonstrate the next sequence of moves in the dance. This is followed by more class practice led by Maree without music and then later with the addition of music. In this pedagogical format of demonstration, explanation and practice the class progressively learns all the moves of the entire dance in sequence and to music.

Maree has probably never thought too much about the pedagogy she uses. She just replicates the way she was taught. She reproduces a dominant pedagogical form found in PE classes everywhere.

Interestingly, while dance may be "qualitatively different from activities such as competitive and recreational sports", the pedagogical form of the lesson described above was identical to that seen in most PE and sport lessons

– namely demonstration, explanation and practice. The lesson I observed was, from what I could ascertain, a highly enjoyable lesson and connected strongly with some dimensions of what makes dancing a reinforcing activity for some people. Notice that this was an elective class and so students had self-selected according to whether or not they liked dance. The same movement experience might not be seen as enjoyable to some other young people.

Also interestingly, this lesson, while enjoyable and useful in developing certain dance competence, was not creative in the sense that the students were not required to problem solve in movement. It didn't tap their "creative juices". For some boys (and I presume some girls) the pleasure of dance itself is enough reason to justify dance in the school curriculum (Gard, 2008). But it can offer considerably more educational value since, as Gard (2004) suggests:

> Dance, as a primarily social (as opposed to competitive) and aesthetic (as opposed to instrumental) form of physical activity, has the potential to greatly extend the pedagogical possibilities of physical education. As yet, this potential remains largely untapped (p. 103).

In Blume's (2003) opinion, "Physical education programs that include instruction in both dance technique and critical self reflection can help to erase the subjugated knowledge of the body in the school curriculum" (p. 201). But dance can also be an extreme form of body disciplinary practice. As Bresler (2004) points out, ballet lessons discipline the body in particular well-established and codified traditions and "this orientation with its elitist connotations and goals does not fit well with the general school missions and priorities" (p. 128). For this reason dance as ballet is usually pursued in ballet "schools" and other commercial dance sites.

The swimming lesson

Swimming has long been part of PE in many countries. However, although swimming is essentially just another form of physical activity, the fact that it is conducted in the water means that it is a challenge to teach. The aquatic "classroom" is different to a regular classroom and presents some special problems and challenges for the teacher. Not the least of these is that inappropriate pedagogies might result in serious injury or even death. Accordingly, the swimming lesson is usually heavily controlled in terms of regulation.

In the Australian state of Queensland the following requirements must be adhered to for the swimming lesson:

> *At least two adults should be present, except in the situation outlined below.*
> One of the adults should have the ability to:
> • implement safety procedures
> • effect a recovery of a student from the water at the teaching venue

- perform first aid
- perform cardiopulmonary resuscitation

At least one adult should be ready at all times to enter the water to assist a student. At no time should an adult leader rely solely on students to effect a recovery of a swimmer in difficulty.

Provided that students have been trained to respond correctly in an emergency in Years 8–12, one teacher may be sufficient to fulfil both recovery and supervision roles required by the emergency plan for a water venue. Their correct response should include clearing the water and providing adequate assistance, such as going for adult help, summoning an ambulance and/or acting in a support role in resuscitation, if necessary.

The qualifications listed in this section are minimums for each type of situation.

The leader should be:
- a registered teacher with:
  — experience (previous involvement) in the teaching of swimming
  — experience (previous involvement) in the implementation of safety procedures
- where no teacher with these qualifications is available, an adult who has either:
  — Level 1 Swimming Certificate of the National Coaching Accreditation Scheme OR
  — Certificate of the Australian Council for the Teaching of Swimming and Water Safety (Austswim) OR
  — equivalent qualifications, as determined by the Department of Education

(http://education.qld.gov.au/strategic/eppr/
health/hlspr012/swimming.html)

As Terret (2004) reveals with his example from France, the sites of pedagogy for swimming have, over the years changed significantly. Conducting swimming lessons in rivers, dams, watercourses, lakes or the ocean are particularly problematic since there was little control over the depth of the water, the evenness of the bottom, the entry and access points, and the visual clarity of the water. Accordingly, countries have tried various ways to bring a measure of standardization to swimming. The French, for example, introduced portable, transportable above ground pools in the 1950s. Many primary schools in the warmer states of Australia built their own small in-ground pools. Nowadays, in many countries swimming is taught in a local community pool that not only functions as a learn-to-swim venue but has other commercial and recreative functions as well.

Originally, swimming lessons were conducted in sites that were not standardized and therefore problematic in the context of schooling. In this respect, Thierry Terret (2004) asks the question:

> How, then, could the needs of the school be adapted to the particular constraints of water spaces? Historically, how did the school succeed in managing the contradictions between the role of the class or gymnasium as a privileged space for rationality, and the medium of water, whose characteristics were, on the surface, unfavourable to teaching and disciplinary work? (p. 40).

As we will see in Chapter 6 (Pedagogies for the body) historically there have been some novel approaches to the pedagogical dilemma of swimming. Many of the pedagogical devices, such as the Beulque apparatus (see Chapter 6) in France were unsuccessful and abandoned in favour of "simple" poolside controlled pedagogies.

Swimming lessons can be traumatic for some kids who are unfamiliar with, or have strong fear of, water. Typically there are introductory water familiarization activities that can be employed to develop the confidence necessary to move to learning specific strokes. I remember when I taught swimming as a young teacher we had an activity called the "Dead Man's Float". The activity was intended to facilitate confidence in the water but the irony of the term "dead man" was not lost on most kids, and accordingly the pedagogical work of the activity was something different than intended.

With a few notable exceptions (Moran, 2001, 2002, 2008; Light, 2008), there has been little research into the pedagogy of teaching swimming.

In universities

Although explicitly focused on the development of the intellect, universities have long given varied status to the notion of a healthy mind in a healthy body and accordingly some have had a long tradition of PE for the general population of students. This has been particularly the case within universities in the USA that require undergraduates to complete a number of PE courses as part of their graduation requirements. Even elite private universities such as Harvard and Berkeley complied with this tradition. It was a manifestation of a notion of what it meant to have a liberal education that embodied the value of "healthy mind in a healthy body". The PE classes were in fact instructional classes in physical activity (e.g. tennis, swimming, weight-training, racquet ball etc.). Indeed, countless HMS postgraduate students earned their way through graduate school by teaching these physical activity courses to the general student body.

This tradition seems not to have been part of university culture in the UK or Europe but there were examples of specific mandatory requirements for PE classes in medical schools within Australian universities at least until the early 1970s (e.g. the University of Queensland).

PETE students

For university students training to become PE teachers, learning about pedagogies for physical activity is, or at least was, a major part of their curriculum. Not only are there classes that focus on developing PETE students' subject matter content knowledge (Shulman, 1986) related to physical activity (e.g. knowledge about how to play soccer, "do" gymnastics, swim the crawl stroke etc.), there are also classes that focus on the development of pedagogical content knowledge related to physical activity (e.g. how to teach soccer, swimming etc.). In some contexts these two foci are subsumed into one class such that, in the process of learning to swim, for example, PETE students also learn how to teach swimming.

As I mentioned earlier, however, the rise of the importance of the sub-disciplines of HMS, together with contemporary teacher registration demands in many countries, has resulted in many new PE teacher graduates being less knowledgeable regarding pedagogies for physical activity.

In sports clubs and sports institutes

The sports club

Sports clubs are a common feature of the movement culture landscape in many countries. The clubs are usually sport-specific (e.g. hockey, handball, football, gymnastics, swimming, tennis etc.) and young people and adults join the clubs voluntarily. Such clubs usually offer varying levels of sports coaching and participation in organized competitions with other clubs. A fundamental part of much of the sports coaching offered by sports clubs focuses on the pedagogy for physical activity.

For many young people who attend schools that do not provide a comprehensive or adequate PE curriculum, access to the knowledge and skills necessary to participate in aspects of the movement culture is available through local sports clubs.

Resources and facilities vary considerably across clubs. Some are affluent, some are poor but most participate in local or district/county-wide competitions on a regular basis. Community sports clubs are more significant in European countries, the UK, Australia and New Zealand, where progression to elite and professional sport is via participation in community clubs. Another pathway is provided through sports schools and sports institutes. In the USA progression to elite and professional sport is usually via college/university sport, and hence community based clubs are less significant.

At the sports club there will usually be junior sport and senior level sport and often young players progress from junior to senior grades as they mature. At the junior sport level there will be instructional coaching sessions that are designed to enable young players to learn the game and to take their place in the teams of the club. The instructional competence of the coaches/instructors is often variable but increasingly in countries such as the UK, Canada, Australia and New Zealand amateur coaches/instructors are required to have completed a certificate of coaching (offered at various levels and increasingly nationally accredited) to demonstrate their level of competence. HMS trained professionals are often employed to teach these accreditation courses for junior coaches.

The sports institute

In many countries elite athletes are often attached to a national or regional institute of sport. The institute is a focus for high performance and will usually employ coaches/managers, skills coaches, fitness coaches, biomechanists, sports psychologists, exercise physiologists, massage therapists and physiotherapists as part of a "team" approach to developing champions in a given sport. Many/most of these professionals will be trained in the disciplines of sport/exercise science. These professionals provide advice to athletes (instructing them on how to do a particular exercise or whatever) and in this sense, whether they recognize it or not, they will be working with pedagogy. But it is the coach who in particular needs special understandings of pedagogy.

The skills coach will often have the task of working with athletes on particular skills or movement patterns. Their task is diagnosis of errors, communication to the athlete, and the devising of appropriate remediation or corrective practices. This requires the coach to have sophisticated subject matter knowledge (the specifics of, for example, how to trap a ball at waist high) and pedagogical content knowledge regarding how best to teach this skill.

As we will see in Chapter 4, there are considerable similarities in the pedagogical methods employed across sport coaching sites and other sites that operate pedagogies for physical activity. There are also some important distinctions across some sites that have much to do with the nature of the learner and the objective of the pedagogy.

Commercial sites for physical activity instruction

There is huge investment in the industry of physical activity. Outside the institutions of schools and sports clubs are numerous sites devoted to the pedagogy of particular physical activities. Think of, for example, the ski school, the ballet school, the aerobics class, the yoga class, the gym, the personal trainer. These are just some of the organizations and people that earn their living from the provision of instruction in physical activity. One way or another all these providers have their chosen, preferred forms of pedagogy. The following are but a few examples of the multitude of sites where pedagogies of physical activity are presented or used.

The ski school

If you have ever been snow skiing perhaps you have had a lesson or at least seen people having lessons in one of the many ski schools that operate on most commercial mountains. The ski lesson is a site of pedagogy. The instructor will have a degree of knowledge of the activity ("subject matter content knowledge" in Shulman's words) and some pedagogical strategies (pedagogical content knowledge) to facilitate the learning of the activity. Usually they will have passed a ski instructor's course of some type and this gives formal legitimation of their knowledge and pedagogical expertise.

Observation of these instructional sessions for beginners will reveal that basically they conform to the traditional pedagogical form of DEP (demonstration, explanation, and practice). The instructor, usually a handsome young male or female from an exotic far-off country who speaks with a decidedly "interesting" accent, will form the class into a line, demonstrate the desired skiing technique (usually with considerable finesse) and then one by one call the learners down to slope to perform the demonstrated movement(s). Sometimes feedback is given to each individual immediately after performance, other times collectively to the class when all have finished their turn. In this context there is no problem solving or pupil centred learning attempted here. The goal is to have learners emulate the movement pattern demonstrated by the instructor.

There is no educational mission in this pedagogy. This pedagogy is in this sense "purely instructional". Of course this does not mean that the pedagogical work done in the ski lesson is benign. It surely is possible for a learner to have a negative experience and subsequently decide never to go skiing again. However, for the most part, because lessons are graded and instructors are skilled at providing learners with appropriate sequenced progressions, at the end of the day most individuals can make progress and learn this most difficult of sporting activities at least to the level of a relatively competent novice. For many, this level of performance is sufficient to reinforce their continued participation in the activity.

One of the things about skiing instruction, like golf and tennis for that matter, is that learners are clients and are paying for the privilege of the instruction. Accordingly, instructors' performance will eventually be shaped by the extent to which clients feel they have got value for money. The pedagogical work done in ski lessons will no doubt be variable but ski schools will generally be interested in maximizing retention (i.e. that people don't drop out). This is facilitated by some initial streaming (e.g. levels of grading competence such as beginners, snow-plough, stem-christie, and parallel turn) They will, accordingly take a numbers rather than an individual perspective regarding the success of their pedagogies.

The dance school

The 1997 Japanese film *Shall We Dance?* directed by Masayuki Suo is the story of an accountant who is feeling bored with his routine life that is limited to hard work and staying at home with his wife and his teenage daughter. One night, while travelling home by train, he sees the beautiful face of Mai Kishikawa (a dance teacher) on the balcony of a dance school, and a couple of days later he decides to visit the school and secretly take ballroom dance lessons every Wednesday night. However, he becomes ashamed to tell his family his secret. Meanwhile, his wife begins to see changes in the behaviour of her happier husband, and hires a private eye to investigate whether he is having an affair.

This beautiful film is, in part, about pedagogy for physical activity. To learn to dance, millions of people across the world take dance lessons in everything from Ballroom, Social, Salsa, Folk, Latin, Jazz, Hustle, Nightclub Two Step, Mambo, Boogie, Pas Doble, Tango, Rap, Hip-Hop, Fusion etc. Learning to dance "schools" are big business and cater for a wide range of people and ages. Many of the dance genres have a certain repertoire of movements to be learnt. The basic pedagogy used in dance classes is DEP (demonstration, explanation and practice) which is an almost universal pedagogy across all sites of pedagogy for physical activity. The student will practise the movement sequence over and over again, first without music and then with music. Form and style come later when the basics have been mastered. In the process of learning to dance, one's body is disciplined.

As the film *Shall We Dance?* sensitively captures, there are other things that can be learnt in the process of learning a few new dance steps. For the film's main character the pedagogical work for him included more self-esteem and a happy disposition to life. Certainly the attainment of dance competence is access to certain cultural capital. Conversely, if you can't dance then access to the social groups that exist within dance sub-cultures is limited. Like many other forms of commercial physical activity pedagogy, dance classes are strongly influenced by fashion and popularity.

Our PETE students at the University of Queensland do a unit on ballroom dancing and typically they love it. Many (most) of the students have had no experience of this form of dancing but there is now a certain social capital associated with being able to do such dances. The instructor is a retired PE teacher from a local high school and, although he uses a very strict, regimented, didactic DEP pedagogy, our students always respond positively to the lessons.

Personal trainers and gym instructors

Many of us who have been in the field of HMS for many years have at some stage been employed as a gym instructor. Perhaps a better name for this work would be exercise motivation and prescription. Anyway, in gyms all across most developed countries the gym instructors wander around fixed apparatus and free weight stations monitoring and advising paying clients on correct exercise technique, dose and general motivation. Not many of these instructors would explicitly call, or recognize, their work as that of pedagogy, but pedagogy it is.

The work of personal trainers is similarly pedagogical but there will be fewer clients at any one time and the site is not restricted to the gym. You can see personal trainers doing their pedagogy in parks, pools, the beach and basically anywhere they chose. I remember being at a conference in Long Island, New York and one day in the hotel gym I observed a personal trainer leading his client through a series of strengthening exercises for the abductor muscles of the thigh. The client, a women in her 70s, and the instructor were both lying on a gym mat with the woman mirroring the activity of the instructor. This basic pedagogical technique of mirror image demonstration is found in many sites of pedagogy for physical activity. What was missing in that particular instance was any "connection" with the client. The instructor was going through the motions while looking into the space over the client's head with a glazed expression on his face. Apparently he didn't consider that motivating his client was part of the pedagogical responsibility.

It seems that for many people, self-motivation to exercise is difficult to find and they like to be organized and "made to do it". In a local park near where I live in Brisbane there is a billboard-like sign that stands beside a popular walking track. The sign is an advertisement for a personal trainer who meets his clients at that spot every morning at 6 a.m. or other times that can be arranged. This personal trainer knows that many people need external motivation to adhere to an exercise program and he provides not only the activities, equipment and pedagogy, but also the extrinsic form of motivation. Unlike his New York colleague (above) he realizes that unless he motivates his clients he won't have a business for long.

For some inexplicable reason (to me), an increasing number of personal trainers have turned to the military to borrow pedagogical methods for their business. There are now "boot camp" sessions that are popular with some clients. These sessions are modelled on the military boot camp in which recruits are "motivated" by verbal abuse and physical punishment ("Down and do 50!"). In other words they perform to avoid negative or aversive consequences. Having survived this pedagogy when I was in the army I know that it can work to deliver a specific pedagogical intent (e.g. to get the troops fit in ten weeks). I also know that it does not work in terms of longer term fitness maintenance. Maybe its just that many young clients who choose "boot camp" to lose weight and "get in shape" are oriented to short term goals and don't understand that without systematic fading (see Cooper *et al.*, 2007) built in to the pedagogy the improvements will be lost when the motivation schedule is withdrawn (i.e. they stop the class).

It seems to me that all personal trainers and gym instructors would benefit from a closer attention to pedagogy and the pedagogical encounter. After all, at the end of the day, their livelihood will often be dependent on the subjective nature of their client's experiences. Given that some of the clients of personal trainers were turned-off school PE because they felt it to be humiliating or too demanding (e.g. Carlson, 1995) there is clearly much more we need to understand about what is happening in and across these sites of pedagogy for physical activity.

Pedagogy for physical activity in media and textual sites

Newspapers and magazines

Most of us learn to ride a bike in an informal context. Maybe we had training wheels (outrigger wheels) on a small bike that our father or mother removed when we seemed to have developed the balance and confidence necessary to ride unassisted. But it is also possible to learn about the sport of cycling, that is the organized, competitive form of that particular physical activity. Maybe that occurs by joining a cycling club, but it is also possible to learn about the sport by watching cycling events on TV or by reading about the sport. For example, in the lead-up to the 2000 Olympics in Sydney, the Australian newspaper *The Herald Sun* featured instructional inserts explaining how the events (such as cycling) worked – the rules, the history and something about what to look for as a spectator. The newspaper had a pedagogical intent, and in this sense pedagogical work was done by the newspaper. Pedagogical work was done when the reader engaged the article and came to know more about the sport in focus.

A browse around the magazine section of your local newsagency will show just how ubiquitous pedagogies for physical activity are within the pages of specialist magazines. There are magazines that specialize in such activities as surfing, triathlons, running, BMX, skiing, golf, yoga, body-building, basketball, rock-climbing, fitness and fishing. All include sections that have a pedagogical intent with regard to the physical activity that is the medium of the sport.

A scan of a golf magazine, for example, will reveal that instruction in how to play is a regular feature. These magazines, in addition to the advertising, the news of events, personal profiles of champion, technical details of new clubs etc., have a pedagogical intent and this is manifest in the provision of golf tips and instruction. The pedagogy often includes sequence photos and advice on such aspects of the game as driving, putting, chipping, playing sand-traps etc. The extent to which such pedagogies actually improve the golf performance of the reader is unknown (there is no research on this) but the magazine publishers must believe that customers want the pedagogical advice. Presumably, it helps sell magazines.

The video or DVD *as a site of pedagogy*

Over 30 years ago Jane Fonda popularized the instructional aerobics video-tape. With this instructional device, a person (often a woman who works in the home) can be led through an aerobics workout or a yoga session merely by playing the video and following the instructor. Each video is designed to bring the pedagogy for physical activity into the lounge room. And, as with so many other sites of pedagogy, the favoured pedagogical method is DEP.

There are now versions of the pedagogical resource on DVD as well as versions embedded in many "action" games that can be played through games consoles such as X Box and Nintendo. While the technology of these new devices is more sophisticated than the Jane Fonda video, the basic DEP pedagogical form remains the same.

The Internet

More recently, the Internet has proved a generative site for pedagogical advice on all number of physical activities. Golf is a perfect example. In addition to the plethora of "how to play" books and magazines on golf available in bookstores and newsagencies, a Google search for "golf instruction" unleashes a growing number of resources. Most of these are commercial enterprises that have their own patents – *VISI-Golf Modern Method of Golf Instruction* (US Patent 3,408,750, 1968) for example. There are links to videos, devices for improving putting and swing, bunker play an so on. Golf instruction (pedagogy) is a very lucrative commercial field. A search of "golf pedagogy" even turns up links to "Golf Pedagogy the Las Vegas Way" which turns out to be advice on how to choose a golf school in Las Vegas!

Interestingly, over recent years a small number of sport pedagogy researchers have focused their attention specifically on golf. Paul Schempp and his colleagues at the University of Georgia Center for Learning and Instruction have linked their work with the growing literature on the development of expertise in golf pedagogy (see for example Schempp *et al.*, 1998; Schempp *et al.*, 2007). Similar attention by sport pedagogy researchers focusing on other sports would seem to be worthwhile.

A final word

As I said at the beginning of this chapter, the examples I have given are indicative only. My intention has been to illustrate something of the range of sites in which pedagogies of physical activity are employed. Many of these sites have escaped the attention of sport pedagogy research. There is certainly more we need to know about the pedagogical work done in various sites. My guess is, however, that there will need to be something of a "fashion shift" in terms of what is seen as "of academic interest" in sport pedagogy before more attention is paid to pedagogies of specific physical activity sites in the commercial sector.

3 Pedagogies for physical education

School PE has a long history of adopting different curriculum models and, to a lesser extent, trying different pedagogies. One of the early pedagogy research efforts was the search for the best method of teaching (read "pedagogy"). The intent of this "methods research" (as it became known) was to find which pedagogy was superior. Of course superior in what sense is a key issue. There were many methodological problems with these early studies, not the least of which was the fact that "the researchers often set out to 'prove' that the innovative method was better" (Siedentop 1983, p. 39) than the traditional method with which it was compared. In the final analysis little was learned from this line of study except perhaps that we should be guarded in accepting claims that any *one* pedagogy is universally best for all children in all settings and across all subject or activity areas. As we will see later, there have been more recent attempts to compare different pedagogies and there are modest lessons to be learned from their findings.

In what follows I give an account of some of the pedagogical methods that have been used in the major curriculum models that have been adopted within school PE. I will consider also their rationales and the possible pedagogical work they might produce.

At this point I should make it clear that debates over pedagogies are not restricted to PE. In 1992 I attended a conference in Spain on "The Place of General and Subject-Specific Teaching Methods in Teacher Education". The conference had such luminaries as Lee Shulman and Donald Schön presenting a case for general considerations of teaching that were applicable across all school subjects. My own contribution was a paper dealing with some of the specific pedagogical considerations necessary in PE (Tinning, 1992b). I recognize that there are many issues and pedagogical strategies that are generalizable. For example, child-centred inquiry-based pedagogies can be found in science, English, or geography classes just as they can be found in PE. Teacher directed, subject matter centred pedagogies can be found in maths just as they can in English, physics and PE. However, for the purposes of this discussion I will limit my focus to PE, with due recognition that many of the issues have also been explored in the context of other school subjects as well.

Pedagogical methods for physical activity in schools

Teachers and instructors of physical activity can choose from numerous methods or strategies for organizing the learning environment. Interestingly, however, across most pedagogical settings (e.g. school PE classes, junior sport sessions, senior sport coaching), and across numerous forms of physical activity, from golf to tennis, from skiing to the martial arts, from rugby to basketball, there is a dominant pedagogical form used by most teachers, coaches, instructors. If you observe coaching or PE teaching sessions you will most often see the sequence of demonstration, explanation and practice (DEP) as the dominant pedagogical form. But why should the DEP model be so widespread across most forms of instruction in physical activity? Why is it the dominant pedagogical form?

There are other alternatives to the DEP model and in what follows some of these alternatives are discussed. I begin with the work of Muska Mosston (1966) who provided a useful framework for thinking about the strategy and purpose of pedagogy for physical activity. Most PE teachers learn about Mosston's spectrum of styles in their undergraduate teacher education and his framework (further developed by Sarah Ashworth [Mosston and Ashworth, 1994]) has had a central role in shaping the way in which many PE teachers think about their teaching of physical activities.

A categorization of pedagogical methods: Mosston's framework[1]

Consideration of the way in which teaching methods are classified is a useful place to begin. Although much of the literature treats teaching style as synonymous with teaching method, like Willee (1978) I consider that style is a manner of self-expression peculiar to the individual teacher, whereas methods are essentially principles in action. "Techniques and methods are available to all teachers; the way in which they are used determines the teacher's style" (Willee, 1978, p. 20). Although pedagogy in the way I am using it in this book refers to more than teaching method or instructional strategies (see Chapter 1), many researchers and scholars referred to in this chapter make no distinction between teaching method and pedagogy. When I have used the word pedagogy to substitute for teaching method I am not suggesting they are synonymous but rather I am trying to be consistent and also to recognize, even if some don't, the always interconnected relationship between method, teacher, student and subject matter.

According to Mosston (1966) pedagogical methods or strategies can be understood as representing a continuum that characterizes the degree of involvement which teacher and pupil have in creating the conditions for the learning environment. Muska Mosston was the flamboyant American whose "spectrum of teaching styles" became the most widely referenced classification of teaching methods in PE. Mosston classified teacher and pupil decisions into three main groups: pre-class decisions about subject matter, teacher role, and pupil role; execution decisions about organizational matters such as when to start activities, how long to spend practising, how the class will be arranged (in groups, pairs etc.), and the mode of communication; evaluation decisions about the use of testing devices, the use of norms, the communication of the results etc.

Importantly, teachers seldom employ pedagogical methods in a pristine fashion or according to a particular definition (they will usually teach with more of a hybrid method – a bit of this, a bit of that). It is convenient to consider three groupings of methods that, for our purposes, represent three different points on the continuum of methods. In this discussion however it needs to be remembered that these are more caricatures of pedagogies than exact replicas of reality.

When considering a teacher's role in using a particular pedagogy it is easy to slip into the belief that the pedagogy exists, as it were, independent of the teacher and it is simply to be implemented by the teacher. The extent to which the teacher can, or does, implement a range of method strategies is perceived by some as the mark of a good teacher. Of course good teaching is much more than the implementation of a set of pedagogical strategies or of a specified curriculum. It is in essence an interactive process in which the pupils and the task also play a large part in allowing certain things to happen or not happen. As Doyle and Ponder (1977) argued over three decades ago, teachers enter into a "contract" of sorts in which they trade some of their expectations (e.g. regarding task difficulty) for student cooperation. If students don't cooperate then there will be very little achieved. Different pedagogies are therefore not really a set of strategies that can be successfully or less successfully implemented by a teacher – they are more like a set of beliefs about the way certain types of learning can best be achieved. They are as much statements about ideology and valued forms of knowledge as they are about procedures for action.

At one end of the Mosston continuum is a pedagogy that is characterized by maximum teacher control over the decisions which effect what is to be taught, how it is to be taught, and how it is to be evaluated. This method has been given different labels by different authors. While Mosston (1966) called it the Command Style, Hoffman (1971) called it the Traditional Method, and Bilborough and Jones (1966) called it the Direct Method. In general, this is the method advocated for beginning teachers and for the teaching of specific physical skills. It is the method most often used to teach activities such as the throwing the javelin or a basketball lay-up shot.

Hoffman (1971) delivered a strong critique of "traditional methodology" that he believed to be the most widely used pedagogical method in PE. The method essentially consists of teacher explanation of what is to be learned, teacher demonstration (or perhaps a pupil demonstration), followed by organized class practice.

Although conjectural, Hoffman (1971) suggested that the method had its origins "not in science or even theory, but in the unglamorous realities of life" (p. 57). In other words, it is largely contingency shaped. Certainly the "unglamorous realities" of a large class of energetic, unruly children spread out across a large playing field may make the traditional DEP method look extremely attractive to the primary/elementary teacher who has to take his/ her class for PE a few times each week.

Hoffman claimed that the traditional methodology is what most learners are exposed to in their school PE classes and therefore the model of teaching that student teachers bring with them to their beginning teaching experiences. For many teachers and pupils alike, the Traditional Method of teaching PE is THE way to teach physical activity.

Although the Traditional Method is easily criticized for its "pouring-in" rather than "bringing-out" qualities; for not being sensitive to the concerns of the learners; and for establishing (or rather maintaining) a teacher/learner hierarchy, it is nonetheless an important teaching method for the teaching of certain types of physical skills. Consider, for example, the task of learning to do a back dive from a one-metre diving board. To advocate pupil experimentation would be somewhat irresponsible given the considerable aversive consequences associated with an incorrect performance. Too much rotation and the learner would land on his/her stomach. Too little rotation and the learner would land on his/her back. In both cases the result would be painful and hardly consistent with trying to build up confidence in diving. In this case, teacher direction through the structured sequencing of progressive activities would help to reduce the negative results from uninitiated trial and error learning.

Obviously the choice of pedagogical method cannot be made independent of the type of physical activity being learned. However, the purposes of PE include a good deal more than merely the development of physical skills.

At the other end of the Mosston continuum is the pedagogy characterized by maximum pupil control over the decisions that are made about the subject matter, the class organization and the means of evaluation. Again different authors refer to this method by different names. Bilborough and Jones (1966) call it the Indirect Method. This method does not follow the traditional teacher explanation, demonstration, and class practice model. In the Indirect Method the children are meant to have maximum say in the decisions such as what activity areas will be pursued in the lessons, and in essence are given a free reign to practise activities of their choice with the teacher acting as a resource for the purpose of providing feedback to the individual child with respect to her/his movement performance.

In practice, the Indirect Method is rarely used in its "pure" form because teachers do like to have more say in the outcomes (or at least the activities the children do) than this method typically allows. Besides, assuming that children always know what is in their best interests would severely limit the educational experience of the child. A PE curriculum that is based solely on pupil choice would be similarly limited. Would it, for example, be defensible to allow a child to go through school without ever learning to swim simply because the child liked to play ball games and never chose to do swimming? Teachers do have a right, and a responsibility, to teach certain things that they (as representatives of society) consider essential knowledge for children, whether the children think it's important or not.

In situations where the teacher believes that pupil choice is as important as teacher direction, the pedagogical strategy that represents a possibility for such interactive decision making is to be found in the middle of Mosston's methods continuum. The labels for the mid-ground method include: The Limitation Method (Bilborough and Jones, 1966); the Problem Solving Style (Mosston, 1966); the Guided Discovery Method (Kirk *et al.*, 1996). Essentially the decisions made in this method are shared between the teacher and the pupils, although not necessarily in equal proportions. Typically the teacher would impose some limitation on the possible activity (most likely by suggesting a particular movement problem) and the pupil would experiment within the limitations to determine their best response. Obviously there would be multiple responses to the same problem and class discussion might follow which focuses on the similarities and differences in the class responses.

Unlike with the Direct Method where the teacher expects a replication of a specific task done a certain way (e.g. a forward roll with the body in a curled shape), the Guided Discovery Method may provide many acceptable responses. The hard part for the teacher is to be able to give useful feedback to children who are making different responses to the movement problem.

For the Guided Discovery Method teacher interactions with the class are supposed to be less authoritarian, and one could expect that the class formations would be less regimented and more ad hoc than with the Traditional Method. Importantly, this method embraces more than a difference in technique – it also embraces a different view of the relationship between teacher and pupil and a different view of what is worthwhile PE. Learning specific physical skills is not the only worthwhile outcome of PE when viewed from the perspective of the Guided Discovery Method. The ability of children to respond in creative ways and to learn to compare and contrast different movement responses is also seen as important (see Bilborough and Jones, 1966).

Again it is necessary to repeat that the choice of pedagogical strategy is more than the choice of a set of working principles with respect to who makes the decisions for PE. It is intimately related to the significance that the teacher attaches to the possible objectives of the PE program. Mosston (1966) claimed that different teaching methods have differential effects on what he called the "four developmental channels" of PE. These channels consisted of a Physical Channel, a Social Channel, an Emotional Channel, and an Intellectual Channel. Although he did not specifically use these terms, he was referring to the possibility for (re)producing certain values, dispositions and attitudes. As we move from the Direct (Command) end of his spectrum of styles (methods) to the Indirect end we find (theoretically at least) greater capacity to develop all four developmental channels. To work always with a direct method of teaching would, according to Mosston, severely limit development across all channels. To this end if objectives are chosen which are located in all four channels, it would be necessary to use pedagogical strategies that have the capacity to enable all objectives to be met.

Underpinning Mosston's notion of pedagogies is the view that greater individual independence and autonomy for making decisions is the goal to which we should direct our teaching and we should employ pedagogies that are compatible with working towards this end.

Pedagogies and pedagogical work

The extract below is from Julie Myerson's (2005) book *Not a Games Person*. The account is of an experience in PE recalled from her childhood, and is not meant to represent contemporary PE classes, although sadly some are probably still like this. This anecdote is used here as an example of the perhaps unintended pedagogical work that results from a particular individual's encounter with a particular pedagogical strategy. Sometime the strategies are not productive of the desired outcomes – the pedagogical work, the effect of the experience, may not be congruent with the intentions of the teacher.

> We must take it in turns, one after another, to run forward and vault over the horse. There is no choice in the matter, no refusing. My heart thumps harder and harder as my turn approaches. Some girls do it easily. Some girls do not look worried or afraid. They just stand there with blank faces as if they're always being made to jump over things.
>
> One after another, they run and jump and vault. As each girl lands – bare feet first, knees bent – on the mat the other side, Mrs Rogers catches them around the waist and holds them for a second – 'Very good, well done!' – to regain their balance. Then she blows the whistle for the next girl to start. It's true that one or two girls only get over the horse with a little difficulty, and Pamela D nearly always winds herself, but most girls get themselves over it one way or another.
>
> 'Very nice,' Mrs Rogers says. 'Don't forget to bend your knees – that's right, up, up and over!'
>
> There are only two girls in front of me, Elizabeth A and June S. Then June goes and there is only Elizabeth. Then Elizabeth goes and the room is under-water, slow motion – this is me and the room is a place seen from above, I'm not here, my beating heart has lifted me out of the room and made it possible for me to move forward without really being me.
>
> The whistle blows.
>
> My body and I move quickly towards the trampoline and put my hands on the horse but I know from the start that there's no way I'm going over it. It's high, I'm small, my legs will not go higher than my head! Instead I do a small pretend jump, more of a bounce, then scramble

quickly over the horse on my knees and drop down on the other side. A few girls snigger, but Mrs Rogers ignores them. She holds me gently but firmly round the waist.

'It's all right Julie, never mind, let's try it again'.

I blush hard, I can feel the heat in my whole face, but I go back along the huge big room, still under-water, still slowed and dead and breathless. And I do exactly the same thing all over again. This time, Mrs Rogers holds me round the waist as if I've landed on the mat like the other girls. Except we both know I haven't.

She blows her whistle, glances at me quickly with the eye of a bird, eye of an owl.

'All right', she says. 'Next'.

The running, bouncing and vaulting continues. There are two other girls who don't get over the horse either. One is fat and one is very small, the youngest girl in the year. Each time, Mrs Rogers does the same thing. Gives another chance and then moves on.

And that is that, it's over. I don't remember that we ever did vaulting again. And maybe the other two will go on to do Bar exams, direct movies, fall in love, be chemists, have babies, work for charity, or write books like me. But one thing is certain: all three of us will progress though our school careers – our whole lives – without ever knowing how it feels to vault a horse. (pp. 73–74)

Pedagogical work of the vaulting lesson: one reading

The pedagogical strategy used in this vaulting lesson is the Direct or Traditional Method of teacher DEP. We are not actually told whether or not the teacher actually did a demonstration of the vault, perhaps one of the students did, nonetheless the pedagogy was teacher directed, in that she chose the activity (the vault), the timing (on the whistle, next), and she provided all the feedback. Mrs Rogers is sympathetic to Julie's difficulties and offers another go. But the class must move on so extended practice is not possible. Clearly the activity has been somewhat traumatic for young Julie. While she laments the fact that she will get on with her life "without ever knowing how it feels to vault a horse" this is seen as a rather minor issue.

In terms of pedagogical work we need to focus on the understandings and the knowledge acquired as a result of the pedagogical encounter. You can be the judge as to whether or not the experience has been positive for Julie in the short or long term (remembering that the benefits of doing some things are not immediately obvious). What did Julie learn about her body and her physical abilities as a result of this lesson? Could the lesson have been structured differently to avoid creating the embarrassment that Julie seemed to suffer? And does it matter anyway that one or two of the class have this negative experience? These questions become salient when we focus on pedagogical work.

If a PE teacher was given the task of teaching a tennis forehand topspin to a class of Grade 8 students there are a number of ways she could go about it. She could demonstrate a complete topspin forehand shot then arrange for the class to practise the shot in pairs on either side of the net while directing feedback to individual students and the class as a whole in the attempt to help them produce a replica of the "perfect" topspin forehand. Reinforcing the movement responses that progressively approximated the topspin forehand might allow some of the class to eventually perform the shot. This is the "do it this way" approach. In this method there is only one correct way to perform the skill – one correct technique.

Another approach would be for the teacher to pose some movement problems for the class such as "Show me a way to hit the ball over the net" or "Let's now look at the way Judy is hitting the ball and compare it with Carmina's shot" (Judy attempted a backhand in her response to the problem. Carmina did a forehand with no topspin). The teacher could then ask "What did you notice about the way they hit the ball?" and say "Try a shot like Carmina's" … "Now try to hit over the top of the ball" … "What did you notice about the way the ball bounced when you hit over the top?" etc. Reinforcing the movement responses that progressively approximated the topspin forehand might allow some of the class to eventually perform the topspin forehand. This method emphasizes problem solving and does not promote one correct answer in terms of the movement response.

The result of both these approaches might eventually produce apparently similar results in that most of the class might be soon able to do a topspin forehand. Some might be better able to topspin forehand than others; some might hit the ball harder, more accurately, with more spin; some might continue to hit into the net or out of court at the back. The "do it this way" group might do topspin forehands that look more similar than the "show me what you can do" group. But the groups have also learnt different things in the process of learning the topspin forehand. The different pedagogies used might have done different pedagogical work.

Why would you choose to teach the topspin forehand by one method rather than another? What are the advantages and disadvantages of different pedagogical strategies or methods? What pedagogical work might result from different pedagogical methods? In most texts on PE, teaching or pedagogical methods are discussed as a range of options that can be chosen purposefully in order to bring about specific explicit learning outcomes. Pedagogical methods are portrayed as if they are merely technical procedures that can be applied in given situations. The expectation is that using a given method will bring about desired results or outcomes. However, as Ennis (1992) cautions, "Although the educational process is carefully constructed, learning outcomes do not always mirror our intentions" (p. 116).

As we will see in Chapter 4, the linear model of skill learning has severe limitations and contemporary motor control researchers such as Newell (1986), Chow *et al.* (2006), and Davids *et al.* (2008) now consider skill learning from a dynamical systems model that recognizes the complexity of the relational interplay between learner, task and environment (in this case the pedagogical strategies employed).

Of course, one of the key issues with respect to comparing different pedagogies is "What are the purposes of PE which a particular pedagogy is purporting to facilitate?" In other words, it is necessary to identify the *intentions* associated with particular pedagogies. What exactly is it that the teacher wants the students to learn, both at the explicit and the covert curriculum levels? As we will see in what follows, PE has had a history of various intentions, some different and some overlapping.

School PE and the fossil metaphor

If schools were frozen in time somewhat like fossils in an old river bed, we would be able to cut through at various levels and gain some sense of the various forms of PE that existed at different periods of time. Different curriculum ideas and pedagogical practices become popular at different times for different reasons. But while we would find different fossil versions dominant at particular times, we would also find earlier versions (perhaps thought to be extinct) also present during the same period. A crude archaeological dig through schools from the early 1900s to those of today would see the following curriculum models dominant or present at various times: Swedish gymnastics, movement education, health related fitness (HRF), fundamental motor skills (FMS), sport education, TGfU (Teaching Games for Understanding) and Game Sense. Importantly, these curriculum models also embraced particular pedagogical strategies that were considered necessary for the implementation of the curriculum. In these examples, as explained earlier, the distinction between curriculum and pedagogy is often very blurred.

Considering the assumptions underpinning these curriculum models and pedagogical practices provides important insights about the changing and enduring ideas regarding what forms of physical activity are considered important to learn and how they should be taught.

In what follows I discuss contrasting pedagogical forms for PE found in the different curriculum forms of Swedish gymnastics, movement education, sport education, FMS, TGfU and Game Sense. HRF as pedagogy will be discussed in the section on pedagogies for the body. This is really a matter of emphasis since, as I have mentioned before, there really is no pedagogy for physical activity that is not a pedagogy for the body. However, in the case of HRF, the curriculum model is focused on the development of health related fitness rather than physical activity as an end in itself.

As in all attempts to categorize, my artificial categorization of pedagogies for physical activity, the body and health do not hold up empirically. The categories "bleed". Particular pedagogies for physical activity have effects on the body and health.

In a sense Swedish gymnastics should really be included as a pedagogy for the body rather than for physical activity but there is logic in considering it in the context of other pedagogies used in PE.

The pedagogy of Swedish gymnastics

Per Henrik Ling, known as the founder of Swedish gymnastics, developed a system of free-standing exercises that were based on the medico-scientific principles of the late nineteenth century. According to Bailey and Vamplew (1999), the exercises were characterized by "a specific starting position, strict adherence to set patterns of movement, and a predetermined finishing position, every movement completed to command; a demand for precision and accuracy of movement; gradually increasing degree of difficulty and exertion" (p. 4). In every sense of the word Swedish gymnastics was perfectly matched to directive pedagogy. The teacher made all the decisions.

Through its specific emphasis on educational, military, medical, remedial, recreative, aesthetic and livelihood effects, Swedish gymnastics aimed to enhance the "development and preservation, by movement, of harmony between mind and body". Ling claimed that the exercises were advantageous for several reasons: they could be performed in large groups with only one teacher and in a variety of places such as classrooms or barracks; no expenses for the purchase and maintenance of apparatuses were required; the required timing would promote control over the body; the commands would instil discipline; and free-standing movements could easily be adopted to disabilities and were more beneficial in overcoming stiffness and lack of coordination (Barker-Ruchti, 2006).

The pedagogical strategies for Swedish gymnastics are made explicit in *A Handbook of Free-Standing Gymnastics* (Roberts, 1905, p. 13) which contains over 50 pages of exercise tables and includes descriptions of the movement, the command and additional comments. One such table (shown below) reveals that each gymnastics lesson was conducted in a particular progressive sequence. A class began with general introductory movements (ordering class, taking distance, numbering and opening ranks), followed by special movements (arch-flexion, heaving, balance movements, shoulder movements, marching, and jumping) and finished with general movements (breathing exercises) that collect and fuse the specific effects (see Table 3.1).

Such scripted pedagogy seems strange in today's context, but this was one pedagogical form that was part of my own PE teacher training in the mid-1960s at the University of Melbourne in Australia. Enacting this pedagogy was rather more like delivering the lines of a play. One major exception was that in the case of the PE lesson the audience was actively involved and hence, at times, the script was interrupted. The pedagogical work that resulted from engagement with this form of PE was seldom (if ever) empirically determined but certainly its advocates such as Ling and Rogers were in no doubt of its positive benefits for participants. To some extent at least, these early advocates were something like true believers – they had faith in their system and

Table 3.1 Swedish gymnastics exercise table

(Introductory, arch-flexion and heaving exercises preceded the balance exercises)

Balance	Wing stride toe st.	Hips-*firm!* F. astride-*place!* 1, 2. Heels-*raise! Lower!* Feet together-*place!* 1, 2. *Attention!*	Weight must be kept well forward and the heels fully raised.
Balance	i. Wing stride toe st. H. turning: o. ii. Wing walk i. toe st. H. turning	i. Hips-*firm!* F. astride-*place!* 1, 2. Heels-*raise!* H. turning-*left! Right! Front!* Heels-*sink!* F. together-*place!* 1, 2. *Attention!* ii. Hips firm and left F. forward-*place!* Heels-*raise!* H. turning-*left! Right! Front!* Heels-*lower! Attention!*	For faults see Table 1., Balance, and Table 3., Head.
Balance	Reach crook half-st. 2 A. parting s., and L. stretching s.	As. forward lift and left knee upward-*bend!* A. parting and L. stretching sideways-*one! Two!* Repeat-*one! Two!* As. and F.-*change! Right!* The same movement-*one! Two! & c. Attention!*	The stretching sideways of the leg is done partly in the knee and partly in the hip joint. The movement must be slow, like the A. parting, and free from jerks.

(Shoulder, marching and lateral exercises followed the balance drills)

Jumping	Stride-jump	Heels-*raise!* Stride jump-*begin!* 1, 2, & c. *Attention-halt!* 1, 2, 3.	Jump with feet apart on 1, and feet together on 2, keeping on the toes the whole time. On the third count for the halt, the heels are lowered.
Jumping	Stride jump with facings	Heels-*raise!* Stride-jump, with facing to the left after the second jump-*begin!* 1, 2, 3, 4: 1, 2, 3, 4, & c. Heels-*sink!* Facing to the right-*repeat!*	The first two jumps are done to the front, counting 1, 2, 3, 4. The facing to the left is done "in the air," immediately before the next jump. &c., &c.
Jumping	Hornpipe step. Wing crosswise jump (2 slow and 3 quick changes.)	Hips firm and the left F. crosswise-*place!* Jumping, changing the F., 2 slow changes and 3 quick, heels-*raise! Start!* 1-2-1, 2, 3: -1-2-1, 3: & c.-1-2-*Halt!* 2, 3: Heels-*sink! Attention!*	For the slow changes, see Table 31, Jumping. The quick changes are done without any intermediate knee bending.

(continued)

(Respiratory exercises concluded a gymnastics lesson)

The following abbreviations aid in reading the above figures: A – arm, As – arms, F – feet or foot, H – head, L – legs or leg, T – trunk, Kn. – knees or knee, b – backward, d – downward, f – forward, i – inward, o – outward or oblique, s – sideways, u – upward, l – left, r – right, st – stand, pos – position.

Source: *A Handbook of Free-Standing Gymnastics* (Roberts, 1905, p. 13)

could, when requested, point to anecdotal evidence in support of their claims. Of course, such evidence would be insufficient to validate their claims in contemporary medico-scientific terms.

Swedish gymnastics was a form of pedagogy that specifically aimed at producing a docile learner who responded appropriately to direction and control. As Roberts (1905) clearly stated:

> 'Training', i.e. to bring the movement of the body under direct control of the will, and, although it may be recreative, military, or aesthetic in a subordinate sense, it is a *lesson*, and must be regarded strictly in that light. There is no need to make school drill recreative, as it is not designed for that purpose (cited in Barker-Ruchti, 2006, p. 158).

Barker-Ruchti's (2006) Foucauldian analysis of Swedish gymnastics provides an interesting perspective into this pedagogical form which, through contemporary eyes, seems little more than a "disciplinary and controlling exercise regime in which power is distributed unequally … especially so for working class children" (p. 163). However, as Barker-Ruchti points out, in addition to its claimed remedial effects of "improving posture and elasticity", there were also aesthetic effects resultant from participation in Swedish drills in unison. "Group marching in particular, was seen to have positive mental and moral effects" (p. 162). Strangely, I can personally identify with this claim in that, when in the army as part of my National Service, I found marching to be an aesthetic activity – there was something reinforcing about performing an activity in unison with many others.

Notwithstanding the claimed benefits of Swedish gymnastics, there was, however, a group of physical educators who challenged this form of PE pedagogy. Those who championed the progressive education philosophy of movement education argued that the child should not be seen as an empty vessel to be filled with knowledge or skill. Rather, pedagogies should tap into the interests of children and develop their capacities for creative movement.

The pedagogy of movement education

Movement education, sometimes called educational gymnastics, was a pedagogical form that was a PE manifestation of the child-centred educational philosophy that became popular in the 1950s (inspired by Rousseau's famous *Émile*, 1911) as a response (reaction) to the more severe forms of teacher directed pedagogy such as that of Swedish gymnastics or the skill focused German gymnastics. Rovegno and Dolly (2006) consider that movement education as pedagogy has its roots in constructivist theories based on the work of Piaget, in which the child is seen to be an active learner, explorer and discoverer. As we will see later in this chapter, constructivist theories also underpin the situated learning curriculum models of TGfU.

With movement education, pupils move in more or less unrestricted space rather than in formal lines like those of Swedish gymnastics. Children experiment with movement rather than practising a set teacher-initiated movement. According to this philosophy, children were considered to be not little adults but unique individuals – more like seeds that require watering to grow into flowers. Movement education is an approach to teaching PE that involves an analysis of movement that is based on the work of the Hungarian Rudolf Laban. This approach uses movement analysis in a pedagogical form that utilizes techniques of "individualization" and "problem solving". It privileges pedagogical strategies that are to the right-hand end of Mosston's (1966) spectrum of styles.

The 1972 film *Gymnastics in the Primary School* is a classic example of this pedagogical form. The film, produced by the London County Council, was intended to be a professional development aide for teachers. It shows two female (rather elderly) primary school teachers teaching classes in the school multipurpose room/gym. In the film the two women pose a series of movement problems for their class such as "Show me a roll in a wide shape" … "Can you do it with your legs extended?" Movement problems are organized around the main themes of Laban's movement analysis system, namely time, weight, space and flow. After the class practises the activity, the teacher then stops the class and asks certain children to demonstrate their response to the movement task. Children are then asked to focus their observation on particular aspects of the student demonstration, e.g. "Can you see how David's legs are really stretched out. Can you try one like that?" This process of problem setting, class practice, student demonstration of responses, teacher focused observation, class practice of refined task, is then repeated. The style of the teachers is supportive and non-authoritarian and "Lessons are based on problems related to the management and control of the body with the teacher guiding the children through themes" (London County Council, 1962, p. 1).

I have used this film for many years in my teacher education classes. Typically, my PETE students are divided as to whether they consider this to be "good" pedagogy or not. Some discount the pedagogy on account of the safety issues they rightly identify (e.g. no mat under a child on the trapeze); some are bothered by the fact that the women did not (perhaps could not) demonstrate to the class (in their view, a "good" PE teacher should demonstrate, and be able to demonstrate the "right way" for the class). Clearly, for many student teachers the DEP model is still the pedagogical strategy to be emulated.

Others in my classes seem less concerned with those issues and comment that they like the fact that the kids can choose their own responses rather than being required to perform a skill as chosen and directed by the teacher. Always the film is catalyst for lively discussion about the nature of "good" teaching in PE.

Whatever the merits of movement education as a form of pedagogy for PE, you would be hard pressed to find it being used in many PE lessons today. During the 1970s in particular movement education became increasingly marginalized to the more scientifically focused forms of PE (including fitness training and circuit training) on one side, and to sports and sports skills on the other. This marginalization had a strong gendered dimension to it since movement education was very much (but not solely) the preserve of women PE teachers and the science and sports focus were largely championed by men.

There have been a number of research attempts to ascertain the benefits of using movement education compared to those of traditional pedagogical methods. Most recently the Greek researchers Theodorakou and Zervas (2003) set out to compare the influence of what they call the "creative movement method" and the "traditional teaching method" on aspects of self-esteem in primary school children. They equated the creative movement method with Mosston's divergent teaching style and the traditional teaching method with his Command Style. While there are some methodological issues that were unclear, or at least unnamed, the researchers claim that while both teaching methods had a positive influence on the development of a pupil's self-esteem, the creative movement teaching method was most effective in improving pupils' general self-esteem.

Theodorakou and Zervas (2003) compared the effects of what they called the "creative movement teaching method" with those of the traditional teaching method on measures of self-esteem. Basically they tested the children (107 in all) on measures of self-esteem (using the Self-Perception Profile for Children) before and after an intervention of 24 hours with each teaching method. They found that the creative movement method was most effective in improving pupils' general self-esteem and also in specific areas of self-esteem such as the cognitive, social and physical.

It seems to me that pencil and paper measures of self-esteem such as were used as the dependent variables in this study are a problematic way to ascertain the effects of any pedagogical strategy. It's easy to get lost in the analysis of variance (ANOVA) models and lose sight of the political, emotional and movement performance aspects of the pedagogy. Significantly, any research into various pedagogies needs to address the pedagogical encounter in detail.

For example, it cannot be assumed that "treatments" are operationally consistent with the "style" under investigation. Some form of observation of the implementation of the pedagogies would seem to be necessary at least.

Bert Willee (former Director of Physical Education at the University of Melbourne), was an avowed critic of the Indirect Method and he made a telling point with respect to a limitation of this method of teaching (although in the process he exposed his own prejudices in regard to humanistic type education). He claimed that:

> non-directive methods may well arouse children's interests in and provide opportunity for, skill acquisition, and may lead children to enjoy movement in many forms. The one thing such methods rarely achieve is enthusiasm for hard work ... rarely do the so-called humanists and creativists create a demand for more oxygen (Willee, 1978, p. 229).

In this response Willee is talking about what is learned through the hidden and covert curriculum of the Indirect Method. Or perhaps, more accurately, what is not learned. Perhaps we need to remember what I discuss in Chapter 4 in relation to the development of fitness. If we think that fitness is really something which must be taken like castor oil, or if we think that there is "no gain without pain", then Willee's criticism of the Indirect Method is probably valid.

However, we know that for many children such a "no pain no gain" mentality has turned them off the process of getting fit. The pedagogical work done in many fitness lessons is often counter-productive to the explicit aim of the pedagogy. The question is how can we create both a self-discipline that can find application to task (hard work if you prefer) reinforcing while at the same time making children's experience in movement enjoyable and fun. It is possible that application to task (be it practising a physical skill or doing a fitness activity) can be reinforcing and at the same time enjoyable for children. I have certainly experienced it and have seen countless examples of children also experiencing it. Accordingly there are some serious reservations about the appropriateness of the Indirect Method for teaching PE and it is worth remembering that, as in many things, a middle ground is most appropriate.

The pedagogy of fundamental motor skills (FMS)

FMS is an approach to the PE curriculum that tends to advocate a particular pedagogical form. FMS sets out to foreground the teaching of "fundamental movement (or motor) skills" on the assumption that mastery of these "fundamentals" is a prerequisite to involvement in most sports, games and others forms of recreational physical activity.

Drawing on the work of Clarke (1995), Davids *et al.* (2005) claim that "In childhood, the development of fundamental movement skills provides a solid platform to safely and successfully perform many enjoyable and dynamic activities. These vital experiences lay the foundation for continuing adult participation in a range of exercise, leisure activities, sports and the physical pastimes" (p. 17).

Advocates of the FMS approach argue there are certain movement skills such as running, jumping, catching and throwing that are fundamental across most movement cultures (Crum, 1996). Moreover, the development of fundamental motor skills is not a necessary outcome of games and/or sports participation. In other words, if a child just plays the game of soccer, there is no guarantee that s/he will master all the movement skills necessary for successful game play. Fundamental skills, the FMS advocates argue, need to be taught specifically and independently of the pressure and contextual complexity that come from games participation. This is the conceptual antithesis of the situated learning approaches like TGfU described below.

The work of Branta *et al.* (1984), Holland (1986), Kelly *et al.* (1989) and Ulrich (1985) suggests four important assumptions that should underpin a focus on fundamental motor skills:

1   It is reasonable to expect all able-bodied people to achieve mastery of these skills.
2   The earlier fundamental motor skills are taught the more effectively intervention and correction strategies can be introduced.
3   The better (more expert) the quality of instruction the more effectively (read efficiently and correctly) these skills are learned.
4   Mastery of these skills is foundational to a long and positive association with an active or sporting lifestyle.

Drawing largely on knowledge from the sub-disciplines of biomechanics and motor learning, FMS advocates claim the benefits of a scientifically "informed" approach to teaching and learning in PE. By an analytic process in which a sport or game or activity is "broken up" into its sub-components (specific motor skills), the key instructional goals are identified. Pedagogical approaches are then tailored to skill training usually through the DEP method. For example, in tennis we could identify the serve, the forehand, backhand and volley as the key sport-specific motor skills necessary to play the game. However, the ability to run and jump and change direction quickly are also fundamental to game play.

As an example of this approach, consider the following advice to teachers given by curriculum writers in the Australian state of Victoria where a FMS approach to primary school PE was explicitly advocated in the mid-1990s. It is claimed that mastery of the overhand throw (a FMS) is to be revealed when a performer completes this skill:

•   with their eyes fixed on the target throughout the throw;
•   standing side-on to the target;

- drawing the throwing arm back (to almost straight) behind the body during preparation;
- stepping toward the target with their opposite foot during the throw;
- sequentially rotating their body in a proximo-distal form during the throw and
- following-through (across the body) with the throwing arm.

(Victorian Department of Education, 1996)

"All" the teacher needs to do is to observe the child throw and, watching for these specific features, identify any weaknesses or inadequacies in the movement pattern and offer some judicious coaching points or corrective feedback.

Of course research has long confirmed that there are some serious inadequacies in teachers' skill analysis competency. For example:

- Generalist teachers are not particularly good at doing this intricate diagnosis unless they have specialist knowledge of the activity (Biscan and Hoffman, 1976).
- Veteran PE teachers were no better at in their skill analysis competency of a front handspring than undergraduate PETE students (Imwold and Hoffman, 1983).
- Undergraduate PETE majors were no better at skill analysis capability for throwing, catching and striking than non-PE majors (Morrison and Reeve, 1988).
- Pre-service teachers were unable to accurately assess student performance on the overhand throw (Stroot and Olsin, 1993).
- The was no difference between first year PETE students, final year students and experienced PE teachers in terms of their competence in skill analysis regarding vaulting (Behets, 1996).

This identified deficit in terms of skill-analysis for PE teachers prompted Lounsbery and Coker (2008) to assert that there "is a need to revisit the priority placed on motor skill acquisition in K-12 physical education curriculum and the prerequisite instructional practice of skill analysis" (p. 263).

As with all pedagogical approaches, the pedagogical work done in FMS contains certain political consequences. In the case of the Australian example cited above, the testing of each primary school child was expected and each child's performance normalized on state test results. By this process the government had another "stick to beat teachers with" in that "under-performing schools" could be identified and presumably sanctioned in some form or other. In other words, poor performance for children in one school was presumed to be the result of poor pedagogical practice. However, as considerable research evidence supports, most likely it is the result of the interaction of a complicated set of factors and circumstances including, but not limited to, teachers' pedagogical practices.

Of course it's not the "fault" of the advocates of FMS that the curriculum model could be used for such purposes. All practices have implications. But there are other valid criticisms that need to be recognized. One concern is the gendered nature of FMS. Critics such as Jan Wright (1997) claim that the selected fundamental skills privilege competitive sporting activities that embody masculine abilities while neglecting movement attributes such as rhythm, timing, grace and flow of movement and general aesthetics.

Others are concerned that, since there is a heavy emphasis on "correctness" of technique and skill practice in a context that is stripped of meaningful connection with the activity/sport to which it is "fundamental", the underpinnings of a "situated learning" approach are violated. This is the very starting point for the advocates of the Games Sense/TGfU and sport education approaches discussed below. Perhaps this is the PE equivalent of the debate in education circles regarding the best method to teach a child to read. On the one hand there are the advocates of the whole language method (words only make sense in context) and the phonics method (breaking words up into their component sounds) on the other.

Rossi (2000) suggests that skill acquisition is not necessarily compromised by use of a child centred pedagogy. "Indeed, working beyond Mosston's discovery threshold and using models such as Games for Understanding, can provide deeper skill-learning experiences as well as being socially just" (p. 43). Rossi provides a motor learning, constructivist derived rationale for a more child centred pedagogy for PE. Notwithstanding my concern with Rossi's conflation of the socially just with child centredness, he does provide a useful bridge between pedagogies that were previously considered to be antithetical.

Meaning, connectedness and authenticity: forms of pedagogy that are underpinned by a situated learning theory

In our research within Australian secondary schools in the early 1990s (Tinning and Fitzclarence, 1992) we found that school PE was considered boring and/or irrelevant to their lives by many young people. While boredom might in itself be a significant issue to deal with, the comment that their PE experiences were irrelevant signalled a more serious problem with PE. It seemed that even though some young people enjoyed PE (especially as compared to their other school subjects), and even enjoyed various forms of physical activity beyond the school gate (e.g. sport, aerobics, swimming), they saw little connection between what they did for PE and what they chose to do outside school. PE lacked authenticity, it lacked meaning outside the context of school. Picking up on this issue, particularly as it related to sport experiences within PE classes, Siedentop (1994), in providing a case for his Sport Education curriculum and instruction model, claimed that:

Sport in physical education has typically been de-contextualized. This happens in several ways. Skills are taught in isolation rather than as part of the natural context of executing strategy in game-like situations. The rituals, values, and traditions of a sport that give it meaning are seldom mentioned, let alone taught in ways that the students can experience them (p. 7).

Increasingly, meaning, connectedness and authenticity of the learning task are being considered as necessary for good pedagogical practice. What does participation in, and the learning of, certain movement practices mean to the learner/participant? Can the learner see a connection between the learning activity and what might be important in their lives? Is the task authentic in the sense that it is part of the real world and not merely an activity that makes sense in the context of school?

The multi-activity curriculum model (Ennis, 1999) in which short units of activity (6–10 lessons) present a de-contextualized and non-authentic physical activity experience for students, has been a dominant curriculum form of PE in many countries since the 1960s. Moreover, the pedagogical form of most of the multi-activity sessions was predominantly teacher directed and controlled. It was assumed that children participating in such multi-activity curricula would develop skills, knowledge and favourable dispositions towards the activities such that they would transfer their learning to sport and physical activity contexts beyond the school gate. This was a PE example of what Lave (1997) describes in relation to cognitive knowledge and schooling. She claimed that "Schooling is viewed as the institutional site for de-contextualizing knowledge so that, abstracted, it may become general and hence generalizable, and therefore transferable to situations of use in the 'real' world" (Lave, 1997, cited in Kirk and Kinchin, 2003, p. 18). In the PE context at least, we have seen that this de-contextualized knowledge is not seen to be transferable by young learners. Young people as learners are looking for meaning and connectedness and when they don't find it they consider the knowledge as irrelevant and/or boring.

Recognition of the practical inadequacies of games teaching led Bunker and Thorpe (1982) to develop their concept of Teaching Games for Understanding (TGfU) and recognition of the shortcomings of multi-activity PE programs led Siedentop (1994) to conceptualise his notion of Sport Education. Although the initial work of Bunker and Thorpe (1982) and Siedentop (1994) was not explicitly influenced by constructivist and situated learning theories, both TGfU and Sport Education have subsequently been theorized using both these theoretical perspectives. It was Kirk and Macdonald (1998) who brought the theorizing of situated learning to the PE world when they explicated the work of Lave and Wenger (1991) from whom the concepts of communities of practice and situated learning developed.

The pedagogy of game sense and TGfU

In 1997 the Australian Sports Commission in conjunction with the Australian Coaching Council released a video titled *Game Sense: Developing Thinking Players*. The video was intended for coaches and teachers and was designed to increase the motivation of players and develop tactical and strategic thinking in addition to skill development. It was suggested that Game Sense is an approach to coaching and teaching that is game centred rather than technique centred. An accompanying workbook was also released at the time.

This video and workbook offered a particular pedagogy for a particular form of physical activity – namely major sporting games. It was conceived as a response to perceived shortcomings in the ways in which games were typically taught in school PE lessons and in junior sport contexts.

Game Sense and TGfU advocates claim that an over-emphasis on skills and drills tends to sanitize learning experiences such that the meaning of the skills and drills is lost. Game Sense puts participation in games (albeit in modified form) as the foundation from which teaching and skill refinement should proceed.

All of the following: GCAs (Game Centred Approaches); TGfU or Game Sense (Bunker and Thorpe, 1982); TGMs (Tactical Games Models) (Griffin *et al.*, 1991); and Play Practice (Launder, 2001) advocate learners playing the game (modified and/or mini) as the central organizational feature of a lesson (Olsin and Mitchell, 2006, p. 630).

The argument is that a Game Sense and TGfU pedagogy will be more enjoyable, because it is more meaningful. Enjoyment is considered a *sine qua non* for ongoing participation in the particular game and according to Werner *et al.* (1996), "the primary purpose of teaching any game should be to improve students' game performance and to improve their enjoyment and participation in games, which might lead to a more healthy lifestyle" (p. 30).

In a Game Sense and TGfU approach the considerable similarities between certain types of games are recognized and games are grouped according to their similar characteristics. There are "Invasion Games" such as football, soccer and basketball, "Striking/Fielding Games" such as baseball and cricket, and "Net/Racquet Games" such as tennis, badminton and volleyball. These classifications are considered to represent fundamentally different tactical considerations yet might require similar skill sets. This way of thinking invites teachers and coaches to see the development of "game sense" as something that involves the development of a range of fundamental principles (ways of thinking, knowledge and practices) that potentially feed into (transfer to) more than one game or situation.

In traditional PE and many junior sports coaching contexts the mastery of the basic skills should occur *before* learners progress to game situations. This conceptualization of the pedagogical progression was influenced by the principle of moving from the simple to the complex. Attempting to develop skills in the context of a game was considered ill-advised since, in game situations, players were in a far more open context (more chaotic, less predictable) that required them to process more information quickly under pressure from the opposition. Practising a skill in isolation from the game context was considered to be sound pedagogy.

There is, however, a very practical problem with the "skills then game" model. Most kids, unless they are like Julie Myerson (author of *Not a Games Person*), want to play the game NOW! Games are authentic and meaningful whereas skills practice that is unconnected to game play is not.

In Games Sense and TGfU pedagogy, the playing of a game requires more than simply picking teams and umpiring. It requires a fundamental shift in the way the teacher approaches skill development and the organization of sequential learning activities. Prominent here is a range of practical and conceptual developments, in the form of game appreciation, tactical awareness, decision making and skill execution. It is expected that PE teachers will be able to facilitate learning across all of these stages.

Successful implementation of this pedagogy would see students engaged in practices related to decision making, risk taking, problem solving, perceiving self and others (across time and space), and specific game strategies and tactics. Indeed, part of developing genuine game sense involves knowing where to be, when to be there and what to do when you get there. These are extremely difficult concepts to teach and it is argued that they are best learned in a situated learning context (see Kirk and Macdonald, 1998).

In Mosston's conceptualization, Game Sense and TGfU would involve pedagogies that move to the right-hand end of the continuum (towards problem solving).

Sport education as pedagogy

Sport education is mostly called a curriculum model rather than a pedagogy (see Penny *et al.*, 2005), however, I am interested in it as a pedagogical process. Its origins can be traced to the initiatives of Daryl Siedentop (1994) who was keen to develop "competent, literate, and enthusiastic sportspeople" (p. 4). The contextualized emphasis came from Siedentop's belief that "too often, physical education teaches only isolated sport skills and less-meaningful games" (p. 8).

Sport education comes in different forms but all have sport as a reinforcing practice at the centre of their attention. According to the advocates of sport education it has the potential to "revitalise the teaching of sport in secondary school PE" (Alexander and Taggart, 1994).

Indeed, one of the most exciting things about sport education as conceptualized in the Sport Education in Physical Education Program (SEPEP) trialled in Australia (see Alexander *et al.*, 1996) was that it has put issues of pedagogy back on the agenda of PE. Sport education is very much about pedagogy (see Tinning, 1995).

As I read comments by teachers and students about their experiences with the SEPEP (Alexander *et al.*, 1996) I was struck by the significance given to the increased independence which students enjoy and to the changed nature of the teacher's role. Teachers talked of enjoying not being centre stage but also reported that making the transition from being the central focus of all lessons to an "involved bystander" was at times difficult. Of course this shift in the decision making is not new to PE (see for example Mosston, 1966 and Hellison, 1984), however, as we saw above, Shirl Hoffman (1971) informed us in the early 1970s, through a complex set of circumstances, the teacher directed, teacher in full control, teacher as the "ring master" model has dominated PE. Indeed, the sport education model is a direct challenge to that traditional teaching method in PE. Such a challenge is both necessary and laudable.

Sport education when conceived as pedagogy and curriculum has received considerable research attention over the past 20 years. For example, Gary Kinchin's (2006) review of research on sport education in the *Handbook of Physical Education* (Kirk *et al.*, 2006) cites around 140 published papers or book chapters. Among the more sophisticated studies (in terms of measurement and experimental design) is the recent study by Pritchard *et al.*, (2008) in which the researchers demonstrated that what they called the Sport Education Model (SEM) was significantly more effective than what they called the Traditional Style (TS) in terms of improvement in game performance in volleyball. No differences were detected in terms of skill development or knowledge acquisition.

However, we might be wrong to think that it is something unique to the pedagogy of sport education that is responsible for the apparent success of these sport education "experiments". Clearly the subject matter is, for many (not all!) kids, both exciting and enjoyable and it is important to understand that the conventional PE experience of learning sports skills did not connect with the lives of most adolescent kids (see Tinning and Fitzclarence, 1992). By engaging sport in a contextualized manner (see Siedentop, 1994) the teaching space that is occupied by sport education appears to have meaning for students and hence they develop a commitment to it. But as Penny (2003) argues, there is still a need to broaden the debates regarding the potential of sport education to generate a transformative experience for young people within PE.

Applying constructivist ideas beyond the context of team games

Richard Light and Nathalie Wallian (2008) have applied constructivist methods to the teaching of swimming. They argue that while the pedagogies of TGfU cannot be readily applied to individual sports, constructivist perspectives on learning can be used to develop student centred, inquiry based approaches to teaching individual sports. In their examples of applying constructivist learning theory to teaching techniques for competitive pool swimming and for surf swimming they provide learners with the opportunity to reflect on abstract ideas (such as the feel of the water) and to generalize those ideas to other situations. They suggest that swimming as a form of physical activity is likely to involve learning at a "non-conscious, embodied level" (p. 401). Moreover, it is the "use of language in collective reflection on action that brings this learning to the level of conscious consideration" (ibid.). Citing the work of Varela *et al.* (1991), Light and Wallian (2008) refer to the Buddhist notion of *mindfulness* which might include reflection *in* action and *on* action. Mindful action, they suggest, can achieve a state in which "the mind and the body are brought together and experienced as one" (p. 401). Notwithstanding the philosophical slippage into a form of mind/body dualism that this implies, it seems to me to be a useful attempt to teach for an embodied understanding of a physical activity. In my view there is something useful here to take into considering pedagogies for many individual sports.

In terms of the future of pedagogies for PE my sense is that while there will be more theorizing and debate, and some research around the best or most appropriate pedagogies for particular purposes (e.g. the teaching of swimming or the teaching of volleyball), the possibilities for pedagogies will always be circumscribed by the foregrounded purposes to which PE is put, the nature of it being a physical/bodily subject matter and by the harsh realities of class size and available equipment. There is no Holy Grail of PE pedagogies.

Note

1 Parts of this section are based on a chapter I wrote in *Learning to Teach Physical Education* (Tinning *et al.*, 1993).

4   Pedagogy and sport coaching

Models of the coaching process such as that developed by John Lyle (1998) attest to the complex nature of the coaching role. For example, the role of the sports coach involves considerably more than instruction in the specific sport skills that form the basis of the particular game or activity. There are also some important distinctions between elite coaching, high performance coaching and coaching a junior sport team of under-12s. One is that the junior coach typically is responsible for all the skills training him/herself, whereas the elite senior coach will often have a specialist skills coach to do the pedagogy for physical activity. Another difference between coaching situations is the number of players/athletes for whom the coach is responsible. An elite level artistic gymnastics coach may have a small number of athletes in her charge whereas a junior level football coach might have a squad of 30 to work with. The pedagogies appropriate for one group of athletes might not be best for the other. In this chapter I will discuss pedagogies of youth sport and elite sport as well as comment on the ways in which pedagogy is represented in the various popular texts on sports coaching. I will then make a somewhat divergent, but I consider relevant, connection between the pedagogical focus on motor skill learning and the lessons from the HMS sub-discipline of motor learning.

Coaches' pedagogies and pedagogy for coaches

Exactly what is known about the pedagogies sports coaches employ in their role of improving the motor skills that form the basis of their particular sport focus? It was English soccer coach Eric Worthington who claimed that "the job of the coach is to improve the skill of players" (Worthington, 1974, p. 5). Surprisingly, little research has been published on the pedagogy for physical activity used by sports coaches.

Davis and Fitzclarence (1979) were early pioneers in this context with their study of the on-field training of an Australian Football team. By analyzing data collected from the observation of training sessions, Davis and Fitzclarence made judgements regarding the effectiveness of training activities. Although the study did not include an objective measure of player performance in the skill being coached, it did reveal the value of observation and recording of what coaches and athletes actually do in training. The study was a practical example of Davis' (1979) call for observation of the coach at training as part of his approach to the analysis of a coach's performance.

In the USA Tharp and Gallimore (1976) were among the first to use systematic observation methods to investigate coaching instructional behaviour. Using a ten-category instrument they developed themselves, Tharp and Gallimore recorded the coaching behaviour of John Wooden, a leading US basketball coach of the time. Data collected from 15 practice sessions revealed (among many other things) that "In direct contrast to the techniques advocated by many behaviour modifiers, praise is a minor feature of Wooden's teaching methods. ... Wooden scolds twice as much as he rewards" (p. 77). However, some 55 per cent of Wooden's scolds were what were termed "scold/reinstructions", in which information about how to do the skill correctly was given immediately following the scold or reprimand.

In a similar study, Langsdorf (1979) compared the coaching behaviour of a leading American football coach with the results of the Tharp and Gallimore study of coach Wooden. Langsdorf's coach, like Wooden, used praise only as a minor dimension of his pedagogy. Scold/reinstruction was a dominant pattern of coaching behaviour. Langsdorf concluded that praise may not be as important a motivator in high level coaching environments compared with such behaviours as the scold.

The research into coach and athlete behaviour is far from consistent and definitive. Using a specific form of systematic observation called interaction analysis[1] Avery (1978) and Rotsko (1979) investigated patterns of interaction between coach and athlete in both more successful and less successful coaching groups. They found that there were significant differences in the interaction patterns between the groups. The coach of the successful group behaved differently from the coach of the less successful group. Interestingly, yet seemingly at variance with the findings of Tharp and Gallimore (1976) and Langsdorf (1979), more successful coaches used more verbal and non-verbal praise and less successful coaches used more verbal criticism. While accurate comparisons between the studies is not possible, or at least valid, these studies reveal that by the end of the 1970s there was considerably more to know about the effectiveness of particular coaching pedagogies with different groups of athletes.

By the early 1980s researchers at the Ohio State University under the direction of Daryl Siedentop began to use systematic observation tools to investigate teaching and coaching effectiveness. One of the instruments developed and used by Siedentop and his colleagues was called Academic Learning Time Physical Education (ALT-PE). ALT was a specific form of time-on-task analysis developed for academic learning in the classroom. Adapted to physical activity settings it became ALT-PE (see Siedentop *et al.*, 1979). Using ALT-PE, doctoral student Rod Rate (1980) investigated coaching behaviour in interscholastic athletic practices including basketball, wrestling, gymnastics and tennis. Rate found that the amount of time which athletes actually physically practised task-related activities that were of "easy" level of difficulty was only 33 per cent (rounded) across all sports. That is, time practising was only about one-third of the time allocated for the training session. Such a finding was, however, rather consistent with what was found in similar studies of PE classes.

In their analysis of the literature on coaching and coach education Trudel and Gilbert (2006) distinguish between coaches' formal courses in how to become a (better) coach and actually how they learned on the job. They suggest that "For many coaches, specifically developmental sport and elite sport coaches, learning how to coach begins many years before becoming a head coach. The progression consists of observing coaches while in the role of athlete and then as assistant coach" (p. 528).

In researching the workplace of the coach as a site of learning, Rynne *et al.* (2006) used Billett's (2001) concept of workplace learning and his theorizing on the relational interdependence between social and individual agency in one's working life (Billett, 2006) to investigate how high performance coaches learn their job. Rynne *et al.*'s (2006) findings substantiate the complexity of the process of learning to be a coach and the important pedagogical work done in that process by conversations with trusted colleagues and the Internet as a source of information.

Contemporary coach educators such as Mallett (2004) and Cassidy *et al.* (2009) have called for coaches to become more reflective of/on/in their practice. Certainly, as Trudel and Gilbert (2006) point out "without this reflective process, coaches might simply accrue experience without becoming more effective coaches" (p. 528).

This call was also made 30 years ago when Barr (1978) demonstrated the potential for interaction analysis (e.g. CAFIAS) to be used as a way to facilitate coaches' reflection. Barr found that coaches trained in interaction analysis (its data collection procedures and its feedback possibilities) used significantly more questioning, acceptance and praise than control group coaches. Similar results have been found in changing the instructional practice of PE teachers (see Rochester, 1977 and Cheffers, 1977).

The conditions that facilitate coaches' reflective practice are not well understood. Certainly there have been attempts to evaluate the contribution of official coach education courses to coaches' learning. For example, Kidman and Carlson (1998) examined an action research process designed to encourage modification of coaching behaviours of coaches from a General Coaching Principles Course. The intervention included supervisory feedback, self-reflective analysis of videotapes and written responses to reflective questions based on chosen behaviours. The results indicated changes in the quality of the identified coaching behaviours. Coaches acknowledged that they benefited from participation in the action research project but also identified that the barriers that limited self-reflection and change included lack of time and limited pedagogical knowledge. The Australian Coaching Council designed a self-reflective coach education resource based on this research.

Previous inquiries into coach learning have shown that traditional means of formal coach education have been largely ineffectual and have not been highly valued by high performance coaches themselves (e.g. Cushion *et al.*, 2003; Trudel and Gilbert, 2006). In their evaluation strategy for large-scale coach education programs in Canada, Gilbert and Trudel (1999) revealed that the programs were not delivered as designed and, other than small changes in the coaches' use of course concepts in the field, there was no change in the coaches' knowledge.

A decade ago Abraham and Collins (1998) argued that research to date in assessing coaching expertise had been flawed due to its inability to adequately answer three fundamental questions: What knowledge should be taught to novice instructors? What is the optimal method of teaching this knowledge? And how should we assess to encourage learning? While they sought answers in cognitive and educational psychology, they observed that many candidates in coach education courses enter the course "with a set of beliefs about coaching before they even hear the first instruction from their tutor" (p. 71). Sound familiar? This is the exact line that we have also heard for years in PETE with respect to PE teaching.

One thing that is evident from the research on coaching and coach education is that there is a difference between types of coaching – for example between recreational, developmental (youth) and elite coaching. Their missions are different, although overlapping, and consequently the value of formal coaches' courses, experience, workplace learning and so on will be different.

Participation and performance discourses in sport coaching

A way of conceptualizing the pedagogical work of sports coaching

Lusted (1986) argues that "How one teaches [or coaches] is ... inseparable from what is being taught and, crucially how one learns"(p. 3). This interconnectedness is absolutely central. For example, focusing only on technical issues of coaching and ignoring the nature of the athlete will not produce the desired outcome. Of course the outcome is itself significant. Any analysis of coaching (or teaching) should relate to the purposes of the coaching in the first place. What are the desired outcomes? What is the intention? For many coaches the major outcomes that orient their work will be performance oriented. For many others it will be more participation oriented. Obviously they are not mutually exclusive; I am talking here about emphasis.

It is useful to think of two major discourses which orientate our work as professionals in the field of human movement. They are the discourses of performance (after Whitson and McIntyre, 1990), and the discourses of participation. Discourse is the term I am using to refer to the language, patterns of speech, metaphors, and general way of thinking about our field. It has some similarity with the concept of paradigm but is, for these purposes considered a contributor to paradigm rather than synonymous with it.

I first applied this analysis to the field of PETE (see Tinning, 1991c), then to the field of HMS more generally (Tinning, 1997) and finally specifically to sport coaching (see Tinning, 1998). A similar but more sophisticated analysis of coaching was later developed by Johns and Johns (2000).

At the outset I recognize that there are dangers in attempting to classify (or categorize) orientations for there are always exceptions and confounding, complicating factors to consider. Notwithstanding this recognition, I consider that these orienting discourses do provide a useful heuristic for thinking about pedagogies for coaching.

Performance discourses

Human movement professionals who work as elite sports coaches are essentially concerned with improving human performance, predominantly in relation to particular sports. The discourses that underpin most of their work are those of science. Science is used as the method (or means) of obtaining improved performance (the goal or the end). The main consideration with such performance oriented discourses is how can performance be improved or enhanced. Questions of means (how we can get the desired results) are dominant. I need to point out at this juncture that I am not arguing against the usefulness or use of science in sports coaching. Rather I am raising the question as to whether or not such knowledge is the most necessary and appropriate for certain sports coaching contexts (e.g. junior or youth sport).

The language of performance discourse is about selection, training intensity, measurement, survival of the fittest, competition, peaking, periodization, "no pain no gain", thresholds, progressive overload etc. In this discourse the body is viewed as a biological object that is likened to a machine to be measured and tuned. These discourses were evident in the topics covered in a conference sponsored by the UK Sports Institute (2002) on "Leadership: World Class Coaching" (see Cassidy *et al.*, 2004). Topics included: Optimising trunk muscle recruitment; Athens – heat, humidity and pollution; The pose method of running; and The performance enhancement team. According to Cassidy *et al.* (2004), these topics left "delegates in no doubt as to what sort of knowledge 'expert' coaches should have" (p. 155).

Participation discourses

I have used the label "participation discourses" to refer to the discourses that underpin the focus or orientation of that group of sports coaches (mostly junior and youth sport coaches) who consider their professional mission is to increase participation in physical activity for all the benefits (e.g. social, physical) which can be derived from such participation. Improving perform-ance, while it might be important and a significant contributor to increasing participation, is not their *raison d'être*.

Accordingly, the knowledge that they draw on most frequently in their professional practice will be that derived from the social sciences and educa-tion. The language of the participation discourses is about fun, inclusion, equity, involvement, enjoyment, social justice, caring, sharing, listening, cooperation etc.

Of course, the notions of participation and performance are obviously linked. Some might regard participation oriented ideas such as "sport for all", and even school PE itself, as of major importance because they provide a broad base for subsequent selection of the best performers for competitive sport (see Pike, 1993). While recognizing that participatory sport for all and performance sport for a select few can be mutually supportive, they can also create some tension if the performance ethic takes centre stage. The issue, after all, is what should be the *main* purpose of work in youth sport.

Favoured questions, favoured knowledge

We can learn a lot about a professional field by studying the sorts of issues it considers as problems (see Lawson, 1984). It is instructive to consider which problems are considered by the field of sports coaching to be important and which are marginalized. In what follows I provide an observation of the sorts of issues, problems and discourses that are privileged or given the majority of attention in sports coaching journals and texts. My observations are indica-tive only and are used for illustrative purposes only.

Here are the contents of one issue of *Sports Coach* (Vol. 21(1), 1998). What I have done is crudely classify them according to the discourses they privilege, i.e. either performance or participation or neither of the two.

- Editorial on the role of the coach   *(neither)*
- Interview with a professional rugby league coach   *(performance)*
- How much strength is enough?   *(performance)*
- Iron for teenage athletes   *(performance)*
- Tips for mental toughness training   *(performance)*
- The structure of team life   *(performance)*
- Coaching and the law   *(neither)*
- Legal advice on line   *(neither)*
- Body image and eating disorders   *(performance/ participation)*
- Coaching children … fundamental fun   *(participation)*
- The league coach   *(performance)*
- Reducing the risk of injury and illness   *(performance)*
- Umpires and referees   *(neither)*
- Fat loading   *(performance)*

- Coaching athletes with disabilities *(performance/ participation)*
- Research in action ... transfer of training *(performance)*
- Coaching masters athletes ... interval training *(performance)*

A tally of emphasis reveals that ten articles focused on (or foregrounded) the discourses of performance, two on a combination of both participation and performance, and only one solely on participation. A similar analysis of current issues of *Sports Coach* reveals a similar pattern. This analysis is not meant to be a criticism of *Sports Coach*. Journals have a responsibility to include articles most relevant to their readership and perhaps for *Sports Coach* this includes mostly performance oriented coaches.

Pedagogy and coaching: A belated attention

Pedagogy is central to coaching and there are many sport specific coaching books that are essentially focused on pedagogy. For example, Allen Wade's (1967) classic *The F.A. Guide to Teaching Football* is all about pedagogy (although the term pedagogy is not used). This book, and others like it from many different sports, place pedagogical strategies for teaching motor skills and tactics at the centre of their focus. In Wade's book, his pedagogies are also illustrated by numerous diagrams of various tactical drills.

There are other books that take a non-sport specific generalist approach to pedagogy of sport coaching. One popular example is Alan Launder's *Play Practice: The Games Approach to Teaching and Coaching Sports* (2001) that blurs any distinction between teaching and coaching and provides a useful chapter on what he calls the "Ps of Perfect Pedagogy". *Play Practice* is more about pedagogy for participation than performance.

Kidman and Hanrahan's *The Coaching Process: A Practical Guide to Improving your Effectiveness* (second edition, 2004) devotes considerable attention to instructional techniques including the use of demonstrations, explanations questioning, and the role of feedback. Much of this information could also be found in an introductory book on teaching. Indeed many of the ideas Kidman and Hanrahan use have come from their backgrounds as PE teachers. It is a case of the pedagogies for physical activity being transferable across different fields.

Another recent book that adapts knowledge from the field of education and PE and applies it to the context of sports coaching is *Understanding Sports Coaching* (Cassidy *et al.*, 2004). The sub-title to the book, *The Social, Cultural and Pedagogical Foundations of Coaching Practice*, is explicit in its reference to the centrality of pedagogy in the coaching process. It provides an alternative understanding of the coaching process to those that are under-pinned by the discourses of science. Within its pages we find chapters on the significance of reflection on one's coaching practice, on coaching methods, the notion of quality in coaching, understanding the learning process, and motivation. The entire book is based on Lusted's (1986) notion of pedagogy which, as I outlined in Chapter 1, is the same orientation to pedagogy that underpins this book.

The significance of pedagogy as part of the knowledge base for sports coaching is well known but until recently somewhat under-theorized and certainly under-represented compared with the scientific knowledge of the body and the biophysical and psychological aspects of the knowledge base.

One of the early texts on coaching is *Better Coaching: Advanced Coach's Manual*, which was edited by Frank Pike (1991) and published by the Australian Sports Commission and the Australian Coaching Council. Sections include: The Coach; The Athlete; Improving the Athlete; Factors Influencing the Athlete; and Planning Considerations. Chapters within the sections include:

- The anatomy of the athlete
- Measuring body physique and composition
- Physiological capacity for sports performance
- Acquisition of motor skills
- Biomechanics of sport
- Principles of sports training
- Motivation and goal setting
- Nutrition and drugs in sport
- Injury and illness
- Planning the training program
- The role of the coach.

Pedagogy and its role in coaching is addressed only marginally (though never by name) in some of the content from these last two chapters and in some of the Acquisition of motor skills chapter. The *Better Coaching: Advanced Coach's Manual* was a representation of the state of the art regarding coaching in the early 1990s. These chapters reveal a privileging of performance discourses and a perspective that much of what was important for a coach to know was to be derived from re-contextualized scientific knowledge. To be fair to this collection, it was devised as part of the resources necessary for a national coach accreditation scheme designed to improve the overall level of coaching competence within Australia. The purpose of the manual was explicitly "to provide coaches with the basic scientific knowledge underlying sports performance" (Pike, 1991, p. xi).

A book published soon after *Better Coaching*, which focused specifically on youth sport, was titled *Coaching Children in Sport: Principles and Practice* (Lee, 1993). It is instructive regarding what knowledge was then considered essential when considering coaching children in sport. In this edited collection there are chapters on:

- The importance of the study of children in sport
- Whose sport is it anyway? Adults and children's sport

- Why are you coaching children?
- Sport: It's a family affair
- Skeletal growth and development
- Children's physiological responses to exercise
- Understanding the learner: Guidelines for the coach
- Growing up in sport
- Why children chose to do sport – or stop
- How children see success and failure
- Causes of children's anxiety in sport
- Selecting the right targets
- Communicating effectively with children
- Counseling young athletes and how to avoid it
- Training young athletes
- The effects of injuries on growth
- Treating and managing injuries in children
- Healthy eating for sport
- Making sport fit for children
- Putting theory into practice – a sport example

The issues and problems covered in this text are explicitly those related to youth sports and the advice given is informed by both science and psychology discourses. Significantly however, this knowledge is re-contextualized to facilitate better participation and performance. If we were to categorize the contents into the relevant disciplines or sub-disciplines of HMS from which the knowledge was obtained (re-contextualised) we can see that child growth and development, exercise physiology, sport psychology, and sports medicine dominate. Certainly the chapters by Lee and Smith and Rod Thorpe are associated with pedagogy but, as with *Better Coaching*, there was no explicit reference to pedagogy or to the phrase "the coaching process" since these concepts only became part of the sport coaching lexicon some years later.

One recent text for junior sport coaching in the Australian context is *Junior Sport Matters: Briefing Papers for Australian Junior Sport* (2007). Similar to Lee's (1993) book, this text contains many chapters that deal with the context of junior sport, the junior athlete (growth and development, health and welfare), and coaching development and legislation relating to junior sport. However it also has a chapter specifically devoted to "Physical activity pedagogy for junior sport" (Chapter 5 by Macdonald *et al.*). Within this chapter we read of learning theory, developmental considerations, instruction for quality coaching including planning, feedback, practice, questioning and movement analysis. This information looks very like that which would be contained in a book on pedagogy of PE teaching.

Perusal of the contents of popular contemporary sports coaching books and manuals reveals that they will usually have a significant section on instruction (called variously teaching, instructional techniques, pedagogy).

Rainer Martens' *Successful Coaching* (third edition, 2004) provides a good example. In this, "America's best selling coach's guide" and official text of the American NFHS Coaches Education Program, there are five organizing sections: Principles of Coaching; Principles of Behaviour; Principles of Teaching; Principles of Physical Training; and Principles of Management. The book is pedagogical in intent since its purpose is to help coaches *learn* about the art and science of coaching. It has within it certain specific pedagogical devices such as the use of colour photographs, tables, charts, anecdotal stories and highlighted advice. In the section on principles of teaching we see specific advice on coaching using a Game Sense (centred) approach, teaching technical skills (e.g. a volleyball dig shot), teaching tactical skills (e.g. stealing second base in baseball), and planning for teaching. Within its pages this book provides advice drawn from psychology, physiology, communication, management and pedagogy.

Pedagogy and "new kids"

"Give me a lap and then down for 20"

Over a decade ago Shirley Willis (1994) wrote an article published in *Aussie Sport Action* titled "'Teaching and coaching today's kids". In the paper she told the story of a well-known experienced coach who admitted (on a radio interview) that he couldn't teach today's kids because they had a different sense of authority. They questioned things and often expected to be included in decision making. Moreover they weren't impressed by the old-fashioned punishment methods such as laps and push-ups.

A few years later Vern Gambetta (1998) lamented that "In our society free play has almost disappeared. ... Today's children are more sedentary preferring to watch TV or play Nintendo" (p. 25). He claimed that early specialization has occurred at the expense of sound [development of] fundamental motor skills, and that the problem could be addressed by reinstituting mandatory PE. This statement clearly reveals what Gambetta considers as important for school PE and the necessary link to youth sport (i.e. providing a grounding in fundamental motor skills).

Both Willis and Gambetta were bemoaning the fact that kids of today seem different.

There are many social commentators who claim that we are now living in "New Times". Their claim is that something is special about *these* times. There are many other labels also used for this contemporary period, including: postmodernity; the information age; late-modernity; and the age of uncertainty. When seeking to define these times it is common to read of the information explosion (you know how knowledge is doubling every year); globalization (the world becoming smaller through technology); information technologies; increased reliance on expert and abstract systems (e.g. global navigation systems, electronic banking); the end of permanent structures of knowledge and meaning; and a heightened level of anxiety of people living in a risk society.

In one sense, as Siedentop attests (1998), there is nothing new about members of one generation lamenting the fact that the "younger" generation isn't up to scratch in one way or another. However, Smith *et al.* (1996) and Fitzclarence *et al.* (1998) argue that we need to consider the possibility that the contemporary generational gap is the consequence of some profound social changes that characterize postmodernity and they cannot simply be dismissed as merely the age-old generational gap.

What we also know is that pretending that "business as usual" will be enough or that nothing has changed is totally inappropriate. We can make no better start towards understanding the changing world of young people than to take the time to listen to them, to try pedagogies that take account of the world beyond the playing field, the gym or the pool. In short, coaching kids in "New Times" requires more than good pedagogical skills. For the coach of young people (and perhaps of elite high performance athletes as well), the pedagogies for physical activity that they have used in the past may well be less effective with the kids of today. It is now necessary to evolve a conception of sport pedagogy that is more responsive to the ways "new kids" learn, what motivates them, and what turns them off.

De Knop *et al.* (1996) edited a book which outlined the major trends in youth sport worldwide. They concluded that the crucial problems for youth sport at the close of the twentieth century were:

* The dropout rate among teenagers (especially girls).
* Adult sport has influenced youth sport to a large extent (e.g. the rules for adults are often used for youngsters as young as eight. Specialization occurs too early and kids are looked upon as though little adults).
* Youth sport has become more serious and less playful.
* Youth sport has become too organised – different sports are competing for children's interest.
* Sport is often not equitable – especially in terms of costs.

Presumably these trends are the sort of issues or problems on which sports organizing bodies focus attention. They are probably less typically the sort of day-to-day concern of the average youth sports coach. Some of the identified problems are no doubt influenced by the particular conditions of "New Times" and there isn't much we can do about changing the cultural context. We can, however, choose pedagogies that are more responsive to the particular context. Interestingly the key problems which De Knop *et al.* (1996) identify as crucial for youth sport were *all* related to *participation*. Accordingly, answers to the problems are less likely to be found through the discourses of science and sports performance.

According to Rod Thorpe (1995) the development of movement technique tends to dominate coaching in some sports. Moreover, there is a common belief among some junior sport coaches (and perhaps some elite level coaches too) that there is a "best way" to perform a particular motor skill (e.g. a tennis serve) and the coach's role is to help the player/athlete approximate that model performance.

Regarding a coach's on-field pedagogical practice, Cliff Mallett (2004) claims that "Reproductive pedagogies are commonplace in coaching, partly because coaches tend to coach the way they were coached" (p. 147). The nature of these reproductive pedagogies is most often located at the left-hand end of Mosston's spectrum of pedagogical methods. This is characterized by demonstration, explanation and practice (DEP), with the coach making most (perhaps all) of the important decisions. It is only relatively recently that there been some interest from some sports coaches in some of the more constructivist pedagogies such as Game Sense and TGfU (see Chapter 3).

The pages of *Sports Coach*, for example, have seen numerous articles on the concept of Game Sense. According to Den Duyn (1996), the Game Sense concept is about using games to develop tactical/strategic thinking, as well as skill development. "The emphasis with the game sense approach is on developing an understanding of the 'why' of tactical play (eg., field positioning, decision making, shot selection etc). The approach is an holistic one" (p. 9). In Den Duyn's opinion, "Probably the best reason for adopting a game sense approach is that games are challenging and fun!" (p. 7). Such a pedagogy may, in turn, be more appealing to "new kids"!

Pedagogical work and youth sport

The concept of pedagogical work directs our attention to the effects/influences of particular pedagogical practices relating to ways of thinking, practices, dispositions and identities. In youth sport coaches use particular pedagogies to facilitate the learning of particular sport skills, techniques, tactics and strategies. Accompanying this learning it is also an expectation that young people will acquire such "character traits" as self-discipline, application to the task, the ability to work for delayed gratification, how to be a "good sport" and so on. We could call these educative intentions or outcomes.

MacPhail and colleagues (2003) set out to research the extent to which a local UK athletics club (Forest Athletics Club [FAC]) achieved an *educative* outcome (one of Siedentop's (1995) three primary goals of young people's participation in sport). They found that the way competition was presented to the young people was a key factor in achieving this objective. They suggest that "by and large, the coaches, club officials and parents at FAC, intentionally or not, had created a climate conducive to the development of the educative goal" (MacPhail *et al.*, 2003, p. 264). It is possible, however, that in some youth sport contexts, the way in which competition is "presented" (the pedagogy) produces pedagogical work that is pernicious. Both Fitzclarence (1993) and Fernandez-Balboa (1999) have borrowed the phrase "poisonous pedagogy" originally coined by the psychoanalyst Alice Miller

(1987) to describe some of the more pernicious pedagogical work, such as certain forms of hyper-masculinity, violence, homophobia and misogyny that may be produced in certain youth sport contexts.

McCallister and colleagues (2000) set out to identify values and life skills that coaches deem important as well as the manner in which they claim to teach for these outcomes. They also sought to examine the philosophy of youth sport coaches and the degree to which coaches implement such philosophies. In-depth interviews were conducted with 22 youth sport coaches (10 male and 12 female). The results reported were that coaches "generally" (remember there were only 22 participants) recognized the importance of teaching a wide range of values and life skills yet struggled to articulate how they do so. Despite their good intentions, coaches displayed inconsistencies between their stated coaching philosophies and the actual implementation.

Surprisingly there is little available research that looks at the nature of the pedagogies and the pedagogical work done in youth sport coaching. However, there is ample evidence that in football (of all codes) in addition to specific skills, rules and tactics (and even application to task and delayed gratification), young boys learn dominant messages about masculinity, including those which are violent, sexist and homophobic (see Fitzclarence *et al.*, 1997; Gard and Meyenn, 2000; Light and Kirk, 2000). Fitzclarence *et al.* (1997) claim that "the processes of direct teaching and coaching often engender different practice from those which are intended" (p. 72). In other words, the pedagogical work of coaching may include consequences never intended but nonetheless significant. Importantly, Hickey and Fitzclarence (1999) offer a pedagogical "way forward" in addressing the taken-for-granted development of hegemonic forms of masculinity through the pedagogical work of various football codes. They offer what they call narrative pedagogy through which boys can be taught to become more accountable for their actions and decisions.

In delivering the keynote address at the Australian Coaches Council conference in 1994, UK physical educator Rod Thorpe made the case that observational learning is a powerful learning tool. But it can be both good and bad. If kids observe the wrong things they will learn them as well as the good things you might have planned them to learn. The important concept here is that *how* a coach uses pedagogy will convey many messages, some of which were never intended. And if, as in the analysis by Fitzclarence *et al.* (1997), the unintended pedagogical work is inappropriate or even counterproductive to the central purpose or intention, then the coaching will be less than successful in the longer term.

Sport pedagogy in coaching elite athletes?

A reading of books on coaching for competitive high performance sports reveals something of the place of pedagogy within the world of elite athletics. For example, within Hannula and Thornton's edited collection *The Swim*

Coaching Bible (2001) it is hard to find anything that we might recognize specifically as "informed from the research on sports pedagogy". When attention is specifically given to technique, what is presented are some descriptors of good technique, and then a number of drills that are selected as developing specific aspects of good technique. There are also suggestions for feedback regarding specific technique faults. We get some generalized advice such as "Always try to catch your swimmers doing something good and compliment them on it, filling the air with positive feelings" (Snelling, "Applying the art of coaching" in Hannula and Thornton 2001, p. 122). But arguably this is more about psychology than pedagogy. One of the contributing authors, Bruce Mason (himself a noted biomechanist) suggests that sports scientists who can help by providing a service or carrying out applied research include: biomechanists, physiologists, psychologists, sport physicians, physiotherapists and physical therapists, massage therapists and nutritionists. There is no mention of the sport *pedagogist*!

As to the pedagogical work done within elite level sport coaching there is precious little research to illuminate. One exception is Barker-Ruchti's (2007) PhD thesis which provides an auto-ethnographical account of the often severe and punitive pedagogic methods employed by elite gymnastic coaches. Using a Foucauldian analysis of elite women's artistic gymnastics, Barker-Ruchti (2007) reveals that the dominant coaching model coerces its athletes towards homogeneity and individuality. While this might seem contradictory, Barker-Ruchti explains that while striving to force their bodies to achieve the sport's regulatory and idealistic requirements, the achievement of these standards does provide gymnasts with feelings of competence and a sense of meaning and identity. However, at the same time, ideas of female corporeal discipline and control, pleasing others through appearance and subordination are simultaneously reinforced and this limits any empowerment accompanying the development of identity and competence.

Mallett (2004) argues for the use of constructivist pedagogies that facilitate "intelligent performers" rather than passive recipients of a coach's direction. Accordingly he advocates the use of reflective journals as a device for developing thinking players/athletes.

Since pedagogies for physical activity are often reduced to strategies for the acquisition of motor skills, it is useful to consider this connection in more depth.

Pedagogy and motor skill acquisition

One way to think about pedagogies for physical activity is to think of what is needed to facilitate motor skill acquisition. There is a whole tradition in the field of HMS that has focused on attempting to understand how we learn motor skills. The application of this knowledge has been incorporated into the pedagogies advocated for the teaching of motor skills and incorporated into the practice of sports coaching and PE teaching.

Much of the thinking and theorizing about how people learn physical activities has been located within, and derived from, the discipline of psychology. Early motor learning specialists (e.g. Singer, 1968; Oxendine, 1968; Cratty, 1973) were applying the ideas, concepts and methods of psychology to understand the learning of motor skills. They were, in large part, very successful in framing the knowledge necessary to understand the learning of motor skills. Consider one example of a major textbook in the area of motor learning and control written by the American Dick Magill. His text, *Motor Learning and Control: Concepts and Applications*, was published in its seventh edition in 2003. Perusal of the Contents pages reveals sections devoted to Motor Skills and Abilities; Motor Control; Attention and Memory; Motor Skill Learning; Instruction and Augmented Feedback; and Practice Conditions. These last three sections contain information familiar to most human movement graduates. For example we see chapters on:

- Defining and assessing learning
- The stages of learning (e.g. Fitts and Posner's three stage model)
- Transfer of learning
- Demonstrations and verbal instructions
- Augmented feedback
- Practice variability
- Amount and distribution of practice
- Whole and part practice
- Mental practice

All of these issues/topics are important in understanding how we learn motor skills and the psychology of motor learning provides useful knowledge for the teacher/instructor of human movement. However, as in education before it, the bulk of the research in the field of sport pedagogy has been oriented by psychological research methods and thinking. Indeed, there have been some heated debates in sports pedagogy regarding the most appropriate forms of inquiry for the field. The "dialogue" between Paul Schempp (1987) and Daryl Siedentop (1987) represents a spirited example of two opposing views on the matter. Certainly the sub-discipline of sport pedagogy has "moved on" since these debates and now we can find work which represents both the psychologized, scientifically oriented way of knowing and the naturalistic, ethnographic way of knowing within the pages of its main journals (see for example the *Journal of Teaching in Physical Education*, and *Sport, Education & Society*). Specific discussion of research in (sport) pedagogy within the field of HMS is pursued in Chapter 11.

However, although these issues are concerned with learning or acquiring knowledge about physical activities, the approach to "coming to know" is different from that used by pedagogy. Pedagogy, in the way in which I am using it in this book, is informed by a different set of lenses – a different knowledge paradigm.

Walter Doyle (1992) explains how in education, within the USA at least, educational psychology became the foundational discipline for educational thought and research.

> This psychology, intentionally designed to mirror the forms of the physical sciences, was behavioural, experimental, and atomistic. The focus was on precise measurements of specific behaviours and the use of controlled conditions to verify scientific laws. These laws, in turn, were intended to be prescriptive, that is, they would define precisely what teachers must do in order to cause student learning. It was a science dedicated to control rather than to making sense of the forms and processes of schooling and teaching (p. 489).

A similar situation occurred with motor learning work in the field of HMS. Interestingly, in much of Europe no specific distinction is made between the sub-disciplines of sport psychology and motor learning and clearly knowledge from both these sub-disciplines can be useful in pedagogy.

However, while this is useful work and teachers and coaches do well to know it, there are real limitations when applying the findings of motor learning to the world beyond the controlled context of the laboratory. In this context Robert Singer, a pioneer in the field of motor learning (see Singer, 1968), asked a provocative question in an article in *Quest* titled "Motor learning research: Meaningful for physical educators or a waste of time?" (Singer, 1990). He concluded that attempting to answer the question was confounded by the growth of motor control and sport psychology and their relationship to motor learning; the difficulty of determining what actually constitutes motor learning research; the difficulty of judging what research is user friendly and of use to PE teachers; and who is responsible for making sense of (re-contextualizing) the research and translating it into practical advice. He suggested that progress on the practical use of motor learning research would depend on a more effective collaboration between educators and researchers. My guess is that if he were to revisit this question today, in 2009, he would be disappointed with the progress.

At face value, it does seem that after some four decades of motor learning research, the evidence base for most pedagogical practices in physical activity and sport remains thin. Tradition and convenience tend to shape physical activity pedagogy rather than the results of motor learning research.

Although Singer (1990) claims that there is much more potentially useful information to be gained from motor learning research than might be expected, he also adds that there is no "broad spectrum of convenient general principles or guidelines that can be easily applied by physical educators to all types *of learning settings, motor skills, and learners*" (p. 120; emphasis in original), He is, however, describing the scene up to and including the 1980s. My impression is that since then the interest in motor learning research has diminished and accordingly the contributions of motor learning research to practical situations in sports coaching and PE teaching have diminished.

It seems to fair to conclude that there hasn't been a steady "stream" of research in motor learning since the 1960s. For various reasons, motor learning has ceased to be popular and motor control has increasingly come to dominate. In many departments of HMS/kinesiology/sport science the focus on motor control since the early 1990s has been incredibly successful in terms of producing research grants income and scholarly publications. However, with the exception of a small number of studies, the focus of the many motor control labs has been highly sophisticated neuroscience research, and there has been little practical interest in the needs of the sports coaches and educators. This is not a criticism of the research done in the motor control/neuroscience labs, but rather a recognition that the sites of motor learning research are dwindling.

Another limitation of much of the early research in motor learning was that is assumed a linear version of the learning process. While Larry Locke's (1974) famous paper "The ecology of the gym: What the tourist never sees" and later the Doyle (1979) inspired classroom ecology model of teaching (see for example Hastie and Siedentop, 1999) were moving towards a more complex account and understanding of pedagogy, it is only recently that scholars of motor control, which is increasingly informed by theories of complexity, chaos and dynamical systems, have been focusing attention on the learner and the context in ways that have been ignored by earlier motor learning theorists (see Rossi, 2001).

Researchers such as Chow *et al.* (2006) and Davids *et al.* (2008) are now considering learning from an ecological perspective (Gibson, 1986). This perspective has some ontological sympathies with situated learning theories that underpin pedagogical forms such as TGfU. The work of Rogoff (1990) is important here for his conception of learning is based on the assumption that what is important is "relations among rather than interactions between the individual, activity and environmental factors" (Rovegno, 2006, p. 263). Importantly, this relational approach is similar in intent to the notion of pedagogy articulated by Lusted (1986) – the notion of pedagogy upon which I have based this book.

The account of pedagogy and HMS I present in this book is influenced by ways of thinking that owe more to disciplines such as sociology, anthropology and cultural studies than to psychology. Accordingly it represents a particular way of thinking about pedagogy. It is not meant to be THE way. The sort of information that learning theory might give us, while important, cannot inform us of the nature of the pedagogical work done when any pedagogical practice is enacted and experienced. This is so even when that pedagogy has been informed by the science of motor learning and control.

Conclusion

Sports coaches ply their trade in a wide range of contexts and different levels (elite, junior, recreational, developmental), and across a myriad of sports, some of which are team and others individual. The sites in which they operate also vary, from gym, to field, to rink, to pool, to track, to road, to ski fields. The variability across sports coaching is huge. Yet, no matter what their sport and context, sports coaches will be engaged in pedagogy. Most likely, however, they will devote little attention to the pedagogical side of their work.

Coaching is a complex activity and at the heart of it is the pedagogical encounter between coach and athlete. However, formal coaches' courses tend to devote limited attention to pedagogy, and there is surprisingly little quality research into sport coaching pedagogies. Moreover, there is limited quality research into sport specific motor learning that can guide the coach's work. One way forward is to encourage coaches to become more systematically reflective in matters relating to their pedagogy (see Mallett, 2004). Another is to encourage a revival of interest in motor learning research. Both of these are possible and both have the potential to contribute to improved pedagogy for physical activity in sport.

Note

1 Interaction analysis is a specific form of systematic observation technique in which data are collected on the patterns of interaction between the teacher and pupil or coach and athlete. ALT is defined as "the amount of time a student spends engaged in an academic task that the student can perform with success" (Rate, 1980, p. 3). CAFIAS (Cheffers Adaptation of Flanders Interaction Analysis System; see Cheffers, 1977) was designed specifically for use in physical activity settings.

Part III

Pedagogy for the body

5 Pedagogy and the body in HMS

Since its inception, the field of HMS (and its antecedent form, PE) has been about the body, either educating about it or working on it. When students do HMS they predominantly learn about the body as a biophysical "thing". The body is an object to be studied like any other living organism. However, human bodies also exist in a cultural context – one that is constantly changing. Of course this cultural context is itself a product of human action and in this sense there is a dialectical relationship between an individual human body and the cultural context in which it exists.

In this chapter I consider the dominant conception of the body in HMS, namely as a biophysical thing, and the pedagogies that are employed to reproduce this knowledge. I will then consider the body as a cultural "product" and the implications for HMS.

Pedagogies and the biophysical body

> Bodies have affective somatic responses as they inhabit a pedagogy's time and space. Specific to pedagogy is the experience of the corporeality of the body's time and space when it is in the midst of learning (Ellsworth, 2005, p. 4).

In most HMS courses we learn about (come to know) the body as a biophysical thing (Brockhoff, 1972), as a body IN nature. In this context the body is seen as an object for study, dissection, manipulation etc. and the privileged knowledge is propositional (e.g. the biceps brachii flex the arm at the elbow; the elbow joint acts as a second class lever). The scientific way of knowing about the body is privileged in HMS.

In very fundamental ways, how HMS graduates think about their professional mission is integrally related to the ways in which they think about their bodies. Jan Broekhoff (1972), in his paper "Physical education and the reification of the human body" makes important links between ways of thinking about the body and the forms of PE that dominated European culture in the late nineteenth and early twentieth centuries, in particular the

Ling system of Swedish gymnastics. According to Broekhoff, in the early nineteenth century, at about the same time that Per Henrik Ling was developing his Swedish system of gymnastics, the German Adolf Spiess created a system of pedagogical exercises which essentially reduced the movement possibilities of the human body to those of a marionette.

> Thus, in the nineteenth century, when man had gained the ability of looking at his own body *as if it were a thing*, and more so, when he assigned to thing-hood the label of ultimate reality, rationalized movements forms were accepted by the masses as a boon to health or a road to discipline (cited in Broekhoff, 1972, p. 92; my emphasis).

Accordingly, within HMS we have come to think about the body as an object, as a "thing". We tend to implicitly accept a body/mind dualism and we use the processes of reductionism, objectivity, and rationality to understand how the body works. We use the methods and tools of Western science and we seek certainty of knowledge and a capacity to predict and control the body through our scientific understandings of its workings.

To get a sense of how the field of HMS is integrally concerned with the biophysical dimension of the human body one only has to glance at the courses offered in typical HMS undergraduate or postgraduate degree programs. Academic courses in anatomy, physiology, biomechanics, motor control, exercise physiology, and sports medicine are foundational studies in HMS. Much of the knowledge of the body that underpins such courses is a product of what the French scholar Jacques Gleyse (1998) calls the instrumental rationalization of human movement.

Gleyse (1998) provides an intriguing archaeological approach to understanding the "evolution" of instrumental rationalization of human movement. He does this by thinking about the human body through the analogy of the factory, the heat engine and the computer. His approach is archaeological in that it uses the Foucauldian notion of analyzing the ground rules that form paradigms of thinking (in this case about the human body). He traces how the logic of the factory (evolving from the late seventeenth century) came to become the dominant paradigm for thinking about the body and how that logic spawned gymnastics exercises (e.g. Swedish gymnastics) and many contemporary forms of body-work. According to Gleyse, "The gymnasium and the structurally broken down physical exercises that emerge at the end of the 18th century in Europe are truly applications of the mill/plant model to the human body" (p. 244).

This paradigm saw a sanitized, de-reified (not godlike) human body that emphasized the "factory imposed precision motion, standardization, repetition and efficiency" (Gleyse, 1998, p. 241). Moreover, "This move towards more precision, normalization, rationalization and mechanization recurs throughout the *épistémé*[1] and notably in the field of human physical activities and discourse about the body" (ibid.). According to Glesye, it was Johan

Alphonse Borelli who in the 17th century thus opened the door for biomechanics when he "quantified with maximum precision the possible forces produced by muscles, as one would quantify work produced by machines in a factory" (p. 243). By the end of the nineteenth century, still bearing the leitmotiv of the industrial world, a new model was imposed on the conception of the human body – the steam engine. "This new model comes about via the application of theories of thermodynamics to human movement" (p. 245).

Gleyse (1998) describes how, by the 1860s, "the thesis of the body as a fuel-powered machine has become the dominant one, one that, such being the case, the entire gamut of human movements can be analysed as one would analyse a machine" (p. 247). He suggests that "the triathlon and the majority of athletic races and major road sporting events (eg., cycling) are still based on such an understanding of human movement, of corporeality" (p. 248).

The next paradigm that influenced ways of thinking about the human body also came from the next generation of industrial thinking. The invention of machines that focused on information processing (namely computers) generated a whole new cybernetic understanding of the human body. According to Gleyse (1998), "The model of the body as a biological computer replaces everywhere the previous discourses that were prevailing at that time when the industrial sector, revolving essentially around the model of man as motor, was dominant in the Western world" (p. 251). In his view "instrumental rationalization in the form of the computer has left its stamp everywhere" (p. 253). In my view Gleyse overstates the dominance of the computer analogy. This paradigm has not completely replaced previous discourse since there are still many instances of the earlier analogies in operation. Multiple discourses exist at the same time.

In Gleyse's (1998) opinion, postmodern conceptions of the body that involve a "critique of logic of modernity, of its universalist and rationalizing dominant axiologies, and a consideration of the subject, of subjectification" (p. 254) are the seeds of a new paradigm for thinking about the human body. As to whether these "seeds" will actually grow into a new paradigm we will have to wait and see.

In terms of pedagogy, it is important to understand that metaphors are frequently used as a pedagogical device and, in the case of pedagogies for the body, the dominant metaphors come from the paradigms of the industrial and post-industrial world.

Metaphor as a pedagogical device

Body as machine

Recently at my university's gym, as I worked around my modest circuit of exercises I overheard the gym instructor (a PhD candidate in adapted physical activity) giving praise to some women who had just undertaken a series of abdominal exercises. "You guys are machines" she said. The women interpreted this statement as the compliment it was intended to be.

There is little doubt that the body as machine is the most ubiquitous and powerful metaphor used within HMS. Metaphors do pedagogical work. David Lodge, in his amusing novel *Nice Work* (1989) explains, via his two characters Vic and Robyn, how metaphors work. A metaphor, Robyn explained to Vic, "is a figure of speech based on similarity. In a metaphor you substitute something like the thing for the thing itself" (p. 156). In the case of the body-as-machine metaphor it is obvious that the machine is the substitute for the body. As a machine we can understand how it is put together, how it can be tuned and maintained, how it can break down etc. And there are useful derivative metaphors that are part of the broader body-as-machine metaphor. Consider, for example, the heart as a pump, the nerves as wires, the brain as a computer. These metaphors are useful pedagogical devices and they are part of the way in which specific discipline knowledge is understood. It's not just the facts that are learned in a discipline – it's also the metaphors which are available to make sense of those facts. Good teachers will be skilled in the use of metaphor and analogy to aid student learning (Shulman, 1986).

But while the body is extremely complex, and in its specificities quite variable (your spleen for example might not be in exactly the same place as mine), metaphors that refer to the machine-like nature of the body do have their limitations. They are useful to a certain degree only. Problems arise when metaphors, such as the body-as-machine, are considered the ONLY way to analyze and understand the body. For example, believing the body to be a machine (literally) might result in unrealistic expectations for the predictability of its behaviour and function.

Like most other PE teachers and HMS graduates I was trained in thinking about the body as an object, and metaphors were useful in the process of understanding my body and the bodies of others. So ingrained is this metaphor that, even though I am receptive to and supportive of other ways of thinking about the body (see for example Tinning, 1998), I still find that the body as machine metaphor is really my default orientation to my own body. I think this is an issue for our profession in general.

While the body-as-machine (whether steam engine or computer) is a dominant metaphor for thinking about the body in the HMS field, other metaphors that align body parts with certain personalities or temperaments are also prevalent. For example, someone who is considered to be afraid, scared or lacking in courage is said to be spineless. Someone who is has little compassion might be considered heartless.

In addition to metaphors providing a powerful pedagogical tool for learning about body functioning, the place or site of learning and the machines and equipment used in the pedagogical encounter can also be important in the production of pedagogical work about the body.

Place, space, and pedagogy for the body

In discussing certain places of learning, for example museums, art exhibitions etc., Ellsworth (2005) suggests that there are "qualities and design elements that seem to constitute its pedagogical force" (p. 5).

According to Ellsworth, "Architects, artists, performers, media producers, and designers of content-based experiences, museum exhibitions, and public spaces are [acting] ... with pedagogical intent" (2005, p. 6). Moreover, they do so "in ways that emphasise non-cognitive, non-representational processes and events such as movement, sensation, intensity, rhythm, passage, and self-augmenting change" (ibid.). She suggests that "Such places of learning implicate *bodies in pedagogy* in ways that the field of education [and human movement studies] has seldom explored" (ibid.; my emphasis).

Architects of sporting venues (e.g. the gymnasium) are probably less aware of the pedagogical force that is unleashed in their works. As Bale and Vertinsky (2004) state, "The significance of space and place as central dimensions of sport is well recognised by scholars who have addressed questions of sport from philosophical, sociological, geographical and historical perspectives" (p. 1). However, little attention has been devoted to questions related to pedagogy and place. Understanding the significance of place to pedagogy requires that we first distinguish between space and place.

In their advocacy for a greater understanding of the significance of place in the pedagogy of outdoor and environmental education, Wattchow *et al.* (2008) argue that space is abstracted in the mind whereas place is inevitably lived in, first and foremost, through the body. According to Bale and Vertinsky (2004), while humanist geographer Yi-Fu Tuan notes that space is formless, "places, on the other hand, have unique faces and from this uniqueness springs a 'sense of place' that creates sites possessing meaning and memories" (p. 2). This is informative in that these memories and meanings are often embodied and result from the activities experienced in the particular place.

> To at least some extent, every real place can be remembered, partly because it is unique, but partly because it has affected our bodies and generated enough associations to hold it in our personal worlds ... and of course the real experiences of it, from which memory is carried away last much longer (Bloomer and Moore, 1997, quoted in Vertinsky, 2004, p. 22).

Vertinsky (2004) describes the War Memorial Gymnasium at the University of British Columbia that was opened in 1951 in terms of its effects on both social relations and disciplinary knowledge, and how it explicitly expressed and reinforced stereotyped gender roles in its spatial arrangements. She analyzes "space as a practiced place" by describing the power struggles that were represented in the planning, design, construction, and use of the gymnasium for the purposes of sport, training and "the pedagogy of physical education" (p. 13).

> Over the five decades of its existence the gymnasium provided a 'sense of place'; to students, faculty, staff and the local community as the changing face of knowledge and popular culture demanded accommodation, shifting spatial arrangements and acquiescence or resistance to views on how the Canadian body should be remembered and educated (p. 14).

Vertinsky describes how the gymnasium reveals the struggles that developed over attempts to accommodate Franklin Henry's vision of the various disciplines and then later fractured into the sub-disciplines of the evolving field of kinesiology (as it is known in North America). Changes had to reconcile the tensions between emphases on the professional development of teachers, scientific research and performance enhancement in sport. All these power struggles, resistances, accommodations and acquiescences were manifestations of intricate spatial and social relations that "provided a certain 'sense of place' in higher education in the second half of the twentieth century" (p. 14). Moreover, these struggles were gendered and reflected particular, though changing, conceptions of the body and the pedagogies and spaces necessary to reproduce such conceptions.

Roberta Park's (2004) analysis of Harmon Gymnasium at the University of California, Berkeley reveals a similar contestation in spatial and social relations that reflected changing attitudes towards PE of the body and the burgeoning demands of competitive sport.

How memories of the change-room reveal the power of place in the development of particular masculinities was vividly illuminated by Peter Swan (1999) in his *Three Ages of Changing*. Swan draws on the work of Grossley (1995) and Van Den Berg (1964) to argue that the physical space set aside for changing into sports attire is a site for the practice of body techniques. These techniques are embodied forms of action, often requiring specific rituals. For Swan (1999), "Boys change-rooms in school settings are like testing laboratories, proving grounds for the dominant model of masculinity" (p. 46). A similar, though female, perspective is provided by Caroline Fusco (2004) in her analysis of the female locker room.

Change-rooms are designed with a particular view of modesty with respect to the body. In many girls' change-rooms there were curtains between shower "cubicles". In the boys' change-room it was typically an open shower space. This says something about attitudes to gendered bodies. According to Rasmussen (2007),

> Symbols on toilet doors take for granted that bodies fit into two neat categories, and then proceed to sort them based on this presumption. Yet this presumption of gender binary is rarely questioned. Rather, toilets

give truth to the presumption – in effect they tell us who we are, and how we define those around us (p. 19).

Since the symbols on the toilet door are intended to reinforce a normalizing discourse with regard to gender stereotypes, they are pedagogical in intent. In this way it can be seen that the signs do pedagogical work. The change-room itself, however, while having a certain pedagogical force (Ellsworth, 2005), is a little more complicated. Earlier, in Chapter 1, I was at pains to say that pedagogical work is a consequence of the *intentions of pedagogy* and that pedagogy is concerned with processes of knowledge (re)production and also the (re)production of values, attitudes, dispositions, subjectivities and identit-ies. So where is the pedagogical intent in the change-room?

Ellsworth (1997) informs us that "pedagogy is a much messier and more inconclusive affair than the vast majority of our educational theories and practices make it out to be" (p. 8). The change-room exemplifies her point. In my view, the change-room does pedagogical work by reinforcing certain social norms (for example modesty for girls) through its architectural form. Change-room architecture (for example separate shower cubicles for women and open space showers for men) is not just a response to biological differ-ences. The architecture of change-rooms is influenced by social norms and makes concrete, both literally and figuratively, such norms. In the change-room boys and girls, men and women, come to know about their bodies in particular ways. So, although the architect(s) of the change-room did not have a "lesson plan" with specific learning outcomes, they were nonetheless engaged in a process that contained an implicit, unconscious, pedagogical intent.

Clearly this analysis of the change-room doing pedagogical work is con-jectural. However, as a consideration of the pedagogic devices examined in this and subsequent chapters will hopefully reveal, pedagogical work on the body occurs in a multitude of sites and can be very powerful indeed. An understanding of pedagogy and the body in HMS needs to also include an analysis that extends beyond the conventional sites of HM practice.

Machines, apparatus, and equipment as pedagogical devices in HMS

While architecture can create or produce indirect pedagogical force, specific machines, devices and equipment are widely used as pedagogical devices across human movement. The pedagogical purpose and the pedagogical work they do are important in an understanding of body-work in HMS.

The images in Figures 5.1 and 5.2 show different pieces of apparatus that have been key pedagogical devices at various times to discipline the bodies of young women. Although we no longer see the use of hanging beams, the ballet barre is still a ubiquitous pedagogical device in most dance studios. It is a device for disciplining the body in certain ways. There is a certain carriage

Figure 5.1 Pedagogical device for bodies of young women *circa* 1882. (Used with the permission of Bibliotech, Swedish School of Sport and Health Sciences, Stockholm.)

Figure 5.2 Pedagogical device for bodies of young women *circa* 2003. (HMS Images Archive, University of Queensland.)

of the head, a positioning of the feet, postural alignment etc. that is taught both explicitly and directly via the ballet barre. It produces a certain ballet habitus that lives on in the woman long after she finishes her ballet training. Importantly, different pedagogical devices are used for particular purposes, in these examples to produce a certain "type" of woman. Different pedagogies "make" different women.

Similarly, different apparatus and devices have been used to shape/build/ remake the bodies of young men. While we don't see wall bars (Figure 5.3) often used in school gyms today, it was a central apparatus for the pedagogies of the body from the late 1890s until the 1950s and is still used in some specific contexts.

When I worked as a Physical Training Instructor (PTI) in the Australian Army (National Service was compulsory in Australia for some males during the period of the Vietnam War) the hanging beam was used as a key training device for the bodies of young soldiers. I can still remember the commands I spoke as I managed the pedagogical encounter of the soldiers with the apparatus:

> First team under the beam READY!
> Under grip, on the beam UP!
> and it's RAISE, lower, RAISE, lower [chin ups or instep curls] and stop.
> On the ground DOWN!
> Teams CHANGE!

Figure 5.3 Pedagogical device for bodies of boys and young men. (Used with the permission of Bibliotech, Swedish School of Sport and Health Sciences, Stockholm.)

Under grip, on the beam UP!
and it's RAISE, lower, RAISE, lower [chin ups or instep curls]

These commands elicited certain responses that were intended to shape the soldiers' bodies and also their discipline. No experimentation here – just follow the orders!

The rather strange looking device shown in Figure 5.4 is used to develop the power of rugby players in the scrum and can be readily seen in operation on many rugby training grounds in schools and clubs.

Such devices produce more than leg power, for when young males learn about their bodies they also learn about what it means to be masculine. Particular forms of masculinity are intended to be produced by certain specific pedagogies. For example, there is ample evidence that high school rugby reproduces hegemonic forms of masculinity (e.g. Nauright, 1996; Gard and Meyenn, 2000; Light and Kirk, 2000; Light, 2007). As Light claims "The impact that a particular sport coaching pedagogy has on the development of young men's masculine identities cannot be underestimated" (p. 330). The "scrum machine", while used as a pedagogical device to train for power, also reinforces hegemonic masculinity. Pushing at the immovable machine with all one's might can be painful but the young man learns to subjugate pain and as a consequence develops particular dispositions to pain that in turn characterize certain forms of masculinity.

Below is a rather interesting device used for the pedagogy of swimming that nowadays we would think to be ludicrous (Figure 5.5). However, it is worthy of comment because it reveals the changing nature of pedagogy. Given the difficulties of teaching large classes in the water, early French physical

Figure 5.4 Scrum machine for rugby training. (HMS Images Archive, University of Queensland.)

Figure 5.5 Paul Beulque's pedagogic device for teaching swimming (France, *circa* 1920).

educators adopted numerous technologies intended to allow for one teacher to supervise, and hence control, all students in the class.

The device was created by Frenchman Paul Beulque *circa* 1922 by adapting a technology used for horse training and applying it to the water. It was a complex device that enabled him to control several students at a time by keeping them at the end of a moving cable. As shown in Figure 5.5, this device consisted of a platform placed across the pool for the teacher to walk upon and from there to control pupils' movements by means of cables that suspended pupils in the water.

This pedagogic device was designed to both control pupils and control their bodies. The question arises as to what pedagogical work was done in the process of being suspended from this device. Of course this could only be understood in the context of the time. Since the dispositions of young French students of the 1920s were no doubt different from that of contemporary English or American students, we can only speculate as to the effects of restrictions and limitations placed on their bodies by the apparatus. Perhaps this did facilitate the development of swimming competence, but perhaps, as the school desk produces a docile student by restricting student movement, so too this device might have produced docile students.

Figure 5.6 Exercise machine circa 1990. (HMS Images Archive, University of Queensland.)

Figure 5.7 Exercise machine circa 1890. (HMS Images Archive, University of Queensland.)

The exercise machine

Most of us are familiar with exercise stations (or machines) like those shown in Figure 5.6. They are ubiquitous in commercial gyms, sports clubs, fitness studios and even in some home garages. That such a machine is used for pedagogical purposes related to the body is clearly evident from Lindquist's (2003) account of the history of the exercise machine in his wonderful book *Bench Press*.

> Gustav Zander (1835–1920) was a gymnastics teacher in a small village in southern Sweden. He had too many pupils to be able to give them the individual tuition they really needed and therefore started constructing sets of mechanical apparatus, made of wood and with weights and levers. The resistance was regulated in such a way that the strength of each movement could be determined 'with mathematical exactitude'. Every pupil was given a personal prescription detailing which machines were to be used, for how long and at what level of resistance (p. 54).

This device (Figure 5.7) had explicit pedagogical purposes in that it could be used for training the body in a particular and systematic manner. As Lindquist eloquently describes in his book, there is considerable learning about one's body, one's self, life, politics etc. in the process of working exercise machines or doing a bench press. Such pedagogical work will not be made explicit in

Figure 5.8 Treadmill for testing/research. (HMS Images Archive, University of Queensland.)

the instruction booklets and will not be generalizable across all machine users. Nonetheless, such learning can be powerful and enduring.

The treadmill

Treadmills are now ubiquitous instruments for fitness and body-work. They were first found in exercise physiology labs and fitness gyms around the world as a device for putting the human body under known amounts of stress and then measuring the effect of that stress on certain physiological parameters such as maximum oxygen uptake (see Figure 5.8).

They can also be found in the home gym, the fitness centre, hotel and apartment gyms, and even on cruise ships! In such venues, the treadmill is used not for science, but for the specific development of aerobic fitness (although it can be used for anaerobic fitness as well) and/or for weight loss (burning up calories through demanding exercise).

Of course, unless you are on a cruise ship, there is a blizzard outside, or

Figure 5.9 Treadmill aerobics in the Cardiac Canyon (OSU). (Author photo.)

you are in a dangerous place (e.g. Baghdad) you can usually walk/run outside in the parks and on the roads. This machine, however, has a number of advantages over the walk/run around the block. Firstly, because you can set the time, speed, distance travelled, degree of hill incline, and monitor your heart rate, the machine allows for a standardized measure of the workload done. You can then compare your performance accurately with your previous efforts or with the performance of others. Secondly, you can do it in air-conditioned comfort, watch CNN at the same time and be safe from outside dangers such as the weather, automobiles, muggers, dogs, and swooping magpies! Lastly, but not insignificantly, it is fashionable to exercise on such machines.

Contemporary monitoring devices

The use of more contemporary technologies to facilitate pedagogical work is revealed in the following fictitious scenario I wrote in 1994 when thinking about the future of school PE (Tinning, 1994).

> There is a small TV camera high up on the east wall of the gym. The class come in and immediately begin to follow the instructions from the voice coming from the large flat screen TV on the western wall (placed neatly between the old wall bars). The voice belongs to Mitchell Glasson, the teacher in charge of human movement for the school. Mitchell has pre-recorded a set of instructions that are used for all class management. In the next half hour the class will be led through a workout that systematically exercises different body parts and which maintains an appropriate intensity of training. Cardio-funk music provides the rhythm and backdrop for the sessions. Each student in the school must attend three such sessions a week.
>
> Mitchell is the only PE person on staff at Grandview grammar. He is a graduate of the degree program on human kinetics at the University of Dunedin. He has no teacher training. The government, taking the lead from Britain, decided that, in order to reduce the cost of education, teachers only need to possess a good degree in the relevant subject field and could learn to teach "on the job".
>
> Mitchell, having also studied computer technologies at Dunedin U, conceived of a way to eliminate face-to-face teaching in these fitness maintenance classes. In addition to the use of video instruction, and surveillance for students mucking around, each student is required to wear a special exercise monitor belt that contains a small computer that records heart rate. At the end of each class the student is responsible for downloading their recorded information into the data bank by swiping their card through the special turnstile.
>
> The sessions are run in the gym every hour on the hour and each student chooses the appropriate sessions according to timetable options

relating to their academic studies. Mitchell has a profile of every student in his computer. He has assessed their heart rate threshold for training effect and he has developed a program that automatically graphs each student's heart rate for each session. The program also identifies students whose heart rate has fallen below threshold and issues a warning to the student. Two warnings and the student is required to pick up extra classes.

Mitchell's ideas represent the cutting edge of school practice for the year 2000.

In this vignette, the idea was to use technology to facilitate a pedagogical encounter to train the bodies of secondary school students. Of course the year 2000 has come and gone and this scenario has not eventuated in the form I describe it here. Nonetheless, teachers are making increasing use of heart rate meters and pedometers to monitor and encourage self-monitoring of students in PE lessons. Increased accountability demands will most likely create increased demands for technology that can record and measure student

Figure 5.10 Measuring the body. (HMS Images Archive, University of Queensland.)

outcomes that can be matched with teachers' pedagogical intentions. In fact, measurement has already become a central feature of much pedagogy in the biophysical sub-disciplines of HMS. In what follows I argue that much of this measurement is not benign and can produce some problematic pedagogical work on the body.

The pedagogical work of body measurement

One of the fundamental techniques used in science is measurement and we learn early in HMS courses to measure the body in various ways and with various instruments (Figure 5.10). Although less common as stand-alone courses in HMS programs today, tests and measurements-type courses lay the groundwork for subsequent measurement of physical performance, physical capacities and physical adaptations to human movement of various intensity and duration. We are familiar with such "stock of trade" measurements as Max Vo2; skinfold measures; grip strength and so on. Often we use measurements of the body to classify the body so we can locate specific training regimes or remedial exercises.

Some measurements enable us to make predictions regarding, for example, suitability to certain activities. Think of the somatotype classifications of mesomorph, ectomorph, endomorph and their distribution across athletic endeavours. The process of measurement and classification of body type (Tanner, 1964) has been useful in assisting the process of talent identification

Figure 5.11 Life's a beach. (Used with the permission of the cartoonist, Michael Leunig.)

for certain sports. Counselling a 7:1:5 individual to pursue a career as a long distance runner might be ill-advised. Other measures have also been very useful for various purposes. For example, measures of blood lactates can reveal adaptations to various training regimes while measures of posture can be used to identity children who might benefit from certain remedial movement interventions.

However, it is important to recognize that in the process of measurement and classification we normalize the body by placing particular bodies within a population of other bodies. And this process is not benign. As the cartoon by Michael Leunig (Figure 5.11) poignantly reveals, powerful meanings are often associated with classification.

When meaning is ascribed to certain classifications of bodies (e.g. talented, overweight, beautiful, ugly) this can have unpredictable consequences for individuals. HMS should understand that measurement, in addition to providing useful information, always has the potential to produce unintended "side effects", unintended pedagogical work.

Unintended pedagogical work for the body

HMS engages certain pedagogies with specific purpose(s). Learning about the anatomy of the body is, for example, an expectation of training in HMS. An explicit curriculum and pedagogy is enacted to bring about desired pedagogical work. However, the specific nature of the pedagogical work done is not always what is expected or desired. As Doyle (1992) reminds us,

> All texts [and we can think of a class as a text] are inherently indeterminate and, thus, the reader must write the unwritten part of the text, that is construct the meaning of the text. ... The same can be said for curriculum events [and we can add pedagogical encounters]. Meaning in classrooms lies with the student. Students construct meaning by interpreting curriculum events and accomplishing tasks within these events ... Interpretation and knowledge are placed at the centre of pedagogy (p. 508).

In the context of the learning of anatomy, and explicitly about the reproduction of declarative-type knowledge (e.g. the flexor carpi radialis originates from the medial epicondyle of humerus), Brian Pronger (1995) offers a provocative insight into the way in which the anatomy lab can be read as a text by the student. His story describes what he learned about the body in anatomy classes when training to be a physical educator in Canada. He was learning things not spelled out on the official explicit syllabus.

> The instructor – a mature woman, who until that moment seems more like a nice auntie whose greatest pleasure in life was baking cookies for nieces and nephews – pulled the cover from a partially dissected cadaver,

drew back the skin, lifted the abdominal muscles away from the gut and revealed the intestines of what was a rather large man. This was my first visit to the gross anatomy lab. She told me to stick my hands inside the man and move the intestines around. "The only way you really learn anatomy", she said, is "to get your hands inside and manipulate the parts of the body". While I was keen to learn about the body, I was reluctant to make such a dramatic entry. But I did it anyway and learned what I needed to know about the structure of the peritoneum. And I felt a tremendous sense of power.

Normally I wouldn't consider sticking my hands into the abdomen of a dead man, moving his organs about. I had always found the inner reaches of a person's body to be a place of mystery, to which one is given access by the living ... only under the most intimate, indeed mysteriously erotic, circumstances. Yet here I was learning something important about the living body from a dead body: The body need not be a mystery; any part of it is accessible to my probing hands, eyes, or mind. It was a rich moment, a rite of passage. Here was the confirmation of what science had always told me about the body, but which from my own experience had always rung false: The body *is* an object. In my hands, that dead man's intestines were objectified, subjected to my manipulations. That event of subjection was the source of my newfound sense of power. As a student of physical education, I realized that the power of my profession lay in its ability to manipulate the body, to make it an efficient resource. The study of gross anatomy was integral to getting to know the body in this way (p. 427).

When HMS students come to accept science as the privileged (read "best") way of knowing about the body, there is a danger that they come to believe that certain (read "most") social problems can best be solved through the application of scientific-type knowledge. This probably is not intended by the lecturers or instructors, and it most likely was not part of the official syllabus. Nonetheless, this pedagogical work manifests as a possible drift into a worldview that sees science as the only justifiable claim to truth about the world and reality. This worldview, called scientism, is an absolute belief in the empirical, or testable, and a rejection of metaphysical, philosophical or religious claims to truth.

For example, when students learn about the body as a thermodynamic machine (energy in ... energy out), this simplistic understanding paves the way for a belief that HMS, through the application of the science of exercise, can provide a solution to the "obesity crisis". Of course problems with obesity are as much sociocultural and emotional issues as biophysical and are much more complex than the reductionist body-as-machine metaphor would have us believe.

Embodied learning

> What is learned by the body is not something that one has, like knowledge that can be brandished, but something that one is (Bourdieu, 1990, p. 73).
>
> Bodily experiences are often central in memories of our lives, and thus our understanding of who and what we are (Connell, 1995, p. 53)

Learning about the body is not restricted to intellectual learning. There is more to learn about the body than what is communicated as declarative or propositional knowledge. Importantly we also learn about the body (our own body in particular) by doing things with "it". This form of learning is embodied in that the learning resides in the body itself (in the muscles, joints, neural pathways etc) as distinct from in the brain (as in mental, academic learning).[2] While it is true that there is embodied learning in experiences in the anatomy lab, as Brian Pronger (1995) so vividly described, most embodied learning in HMS occurs in and through practical classes as a result of participation in such physical activities as gymnastics, football, athletics, swimming, outdoor pursuits and so on. In this sense, all pedagogy for physical activity is also pedagogy for the body. The sites for this pedagogical work include classrooms, labs, swimming pools, gymnasia etc. and this work is done in both HMS degree programs and in school PE.

Certainly there is considerable evidence that within many degree programs of HMS there has been a gradual reduction in the amount of practical physical activity such as swimming, gymnastics, athletics, games etc. (see Locke *et al.*, 1981). As programs have been made increasingly more academic (i.e. focused on learning declarative knowledge) the curriculum time available for physical activity has been reduced. In the preparation of PE teachers this has become a significant issue since in many cases graduates of contemporary HMS degrees possess insufficient subject matter knowledge related to what it is they are required to teach (Shulman, 1986; Tinning, 1992; Siedentop, 2002). They might know a good deal about exercise science but they often have a very limited sport and physical activity background and consequently do not know how to perform certain physical activities, or how they should teach them. In other words they are limited in both subject matter content knowledge and pedagogical content knowledge (Shulman, 1986; Siedentop, 2002). There is little doubt that the embodied learning in/about human movement has been a casualty of modern HMS degree programs.

In his wonderful book *Putting Nature in Order*, Wade Chambers (1984) juxtaposes the illustration of *Frogs in a Pond* by 16th century Italian Pierandrea Mattioli with an illustration of Luigi Galvani's 1762 study of the contractions produced in the muscles of dead frogs by contact with pairs of different metals. Chambers uses the justaposition of illustrations to show two different, but equally valid, ways of 'knowing a frog'. One is to dissect it and study its pieces (e.g. the gastrocnemius muscle), the other was to study the frog in its natural habitat, as an intact organism in its natural environment (such as a pond). Both yield different types of knowledge. Both are useful and both do different pedagogical work. The "natural" habitat of humans nowadays is society. Of course society is really constructed in/ through human practices, but since most people live in societies (both small and large) I am calling society the natural habitat of humans. Societies vary in terms of their reproduced cultural practices. Some scholars (anthropologists, ethnographers) observe humans in their "natural" social/cultural habitat (context) while others (e.g. exercise scientists) tend to study humans in artificial laboratory environments. Since there is much to be learned from both, the non-holistic way of knowing that dominates the typical HMS program is limiting the potential of the field in relation to its pedagogical work in physical activity, the body and health.

Bodies IN culture

When I trained to be a PE teacher in the mid-1960s, in addition to anatomy and physiology we also did courses with the now strange titles such as Preventative Work, Body Mechanics, and Personal Gymnastics. The first two of these were focused on a scientific appreciation of the body and its normative growth and performance. Accordingly, for example, time was spent in learning the characteristics of "good" posture and the diagnosis and remediation of deviations from normal. Such practice was then a regular dimension of school PE practice (see Tinning, 2001). The course called Personal Gymnastics focused on the conditioning of our bodies through participation in a variation of Swedish-type gymnastics. I remember the course as an intense and physically exhausting experience. I have an embodied memory of those experiences. Swedish gymnastics, as Tranbaek has noted, "with its physiological and rational approach to the body made training of the body the centre of the pedagogical process" (Riordan and Krüger, 2003, p. 48). But what was the pedagogical process for? What was the purpose of the pedagogy? According to Riordan and Krüger,

> The various schools of physical exercises – associated with Jahn in Germany, Nachtegall in Denmark, Ling in Sweden, Lesgaft in Russia – developed as pedagogical, political and military instruments for building national identity. And that involved everybody: man and woman, squire and peasant, factory owner and worker. To learn to put one's body at the service of the nation emanated from a policy of acculturation of the common people in the same way as learning one's national language (Riordan and Krüger, 2003, p. 1).

This explicit connection between the forms of body training and nationalist agendas also has a long history in other cultures, as Susan Brownwell's (1995) *Training the Body for China* bears vivid testimony. What is significant here is the connection between the body and culture.

Thus, in a very significant sense, the body can be thought of as existing in nature and culture at the same time. For example, the body of the elite triathlete is well conditioned (biologically) for performance in the three disciplines of swimming, cycling and running. But the same body also exists in a social and cultural context. Being a triathlete makes sense in this context at this point in history. The triathlete's body symbolizes hard work, self-discipline and dedication and aesthetically has considerable cultural capital in the twenty-first century. Thus we can think of the body as simultaneously being both of nature and culture. Accordingly, a comprehensive HMS curriculum should provide students with the knowledge and skills to understand both the biophysical and the sociocultural dimensions of the human body (see Kirk *et al.*, 1996).

Bodies, while biological, are also culturally "loaded". They are inscribed by the dominant values of particular cultures. In Victorian England for example, having soft, non-calloused hands signified a privileged social position. Rough hands signified that one worked with one's hands and hence was of an inferior social position. Sun-tanned skin was similarly a sign of working in the outdoors and designated low social class. There is little doubt that in contemporary Western culture the body has become a crucial means by which the individual can express publicly such virtues as self-control, self-discipline and will power (Petersen and Lupton, 1996). The emphasis on physical appearance has become a signifier of worthiness. Being fat is seen to signify laziness, sloth, and even moral turpitude. It has become a social stigma to be fat. However this is not the case in all cultures, as Rebecca Popenoe (2004) reveals in *Feeding Desire: Fatness, Beauty, and Sexuality among a Saharan People*. Cultural norms vary across time and geography and what is seen to be an attractive body is not universal across time and space. The same "biological body" would be perceived, and consequently treated, differently across cultures.

French social critic and avant-garde postmodernist Jean Baudrillard (1998) suggests that the body in contemporary Western culture has become the "finest consumer object". It is worth quoting him at length:

> In the consumer package, there is one object finer, more precious and more dazzling than any other – and even more laden with connotations than the automobile, in spite of the fact that that encapsulates them all. That object is the BODY. Its rediscovery, in a spirit of physical and sexual liberation, after a millennial age of Puritanism; its omnipresence (specifically the omnipresence of the female body ...) in advertising, fashion and mass culture; the hygienic, dietetic, therapeutic cult which surrounds it, the obsession with youth, elegance, virility/femininity, treatment and regimes, and the sacrificial practices attaching to it all bear witness to the fact that the body has today become an object of salvation. It has literally taken over that moral and ideological function from the soul (p. 277).

Since the publication of Bryan Turner's important *The Body In Society* (1984) there has been a burgeoning industry in the publication of books and articles related to the body in culture. In the Introduction to their edited book *The Body: A Reader*, Mariam Fraser and Monica Greco (2005) include a number of sub-headings to bracket various content themes of the reader. They include: What is the body?; Bodies and social (dis)order; Bodies and identities; Normal bodies (or not); Bodies in health and disease; Bodies and technologies; Bodies in consumer culture; and Body ethics. This is a huge range of subject matter. The contributors to this reader come from the fields of sociology, cultural studies, social anthropology, feminism, philosophy, psychotherapy, history, communication, art criticism, and medical anthropology. The field of sociology of the body is indeed wide and varied.

Following suit, numerous scholars in the field of HMS have turned their attentions to the body in society/culture. Publications include Nancy Theberge's (1991) paper "Reflections on the body in the sociology of sport", David Kirk's (1993) *The Body, Schooling and Culture*, special issues of the journal *Sport, Education & Society*, and the edited collection *Body Knowledge and Control: Studies in the Sociology of Education and Physical Culture* by Evans *et al.* (2004).

In writing about the cultural significance of body-building, Ken Saltmann (2002) introduces us to the concept of cultural pedagogies which is useful in making sense of the body in culture. According to Saltmann, "Body-building is not merely a diversion. Easy dismissal as such would risk missing the pedagogical functions of the sport. As cultural pedagogy, sports function in a positive or productive sense. Cultural pedagogies construct public and private meanings, identities, and desires" (p. 319).

This concept of *cultural pedagogy* is important. In HMS, most of the curriculum is devoted to understanding the science of the body, with relatively little attention to cultural pedagogies which construct the public and private meanings, identities, and desires relating to the body, physical activity and health. While this is understandable from an historic perspective it does leave our graduates less than well prepared for understanding and dealing with sport and exercise as cultural practice. This has particular significance when our field turns its attention to the "obesity crisis" which it considers predominantly from a biomedical perspective (see Gard and Wright, 2003; Tinning, 2007).

Preferred pedagogies for teaching about the body

The mass lecture represents the traditional and dominant pedagogy used to reproduce knowledge of the biophysical functioning of the human body. Lectures increasingly are delivered by the lecturer/professor talking to a series of PowerPoint slides highlighting key concepts and processes. Extensive use of graphs and other visual aides is typical. The lecturer is positioned as an authoritative voice and the knowledge is considered to be factual and objective. This form of knowledge is labelled propositional or declarative knowledge. It is typically tested by means of an examination.

While the value of lectures as a form of pedagogy has been debated for many years (see for example Bligh, 1971) there is little evidence that this form of pedagogy is the best for (re)producing knowledge of the biophysical functioning of the human body. Certainly there are numerous examples of medical schools eschewing such pedagogies and using problem based pedagogies instead.

Such declarative-type knowledge is different in kind to procedural knowledge which is associated with the capacity to know how to do something.

Laboratory Two - Anthropometry
Exercise Science Technical Skills – HMST3382

Procedures for skinfold measurements
- All measurements should be taken on the **right** side of the body
- Caliper should be placed **1 cm away** from the thumb and finger perpendicular to the skinfold, and halfway between the crest and the base of the fold. This 1 cm distance should be from the edge of the thumb/finger to the edge of the calliper
- Calipers are held at **90 degrees** to the surface of the skinfold in both planes at all times
- Use fingers to pinch at the cross, therefore the callipers are placed 1-2 cm below the cross
- Pinch should be maintained while reading the calliper
- Wait 1 to 2 secs (and not longer) before reading calliper
- Rotate through measurement sites to allow time for skin to regain normal texture and thickness (approx 60 seconds)
- Take duplicate measures at each site and retest if duplicate measures are not within **5%** of each other
- Harpenden skinfolds allow for a precision of 0.1mm
- Reporter calls the number back and writes the value in the client's own lab manual. State the value in individual numerals (eg. one two point six rather than twelve point six).

Anatomical Landmarks for Skinfolds (ISAK Sites)

Triceps
The skinfold is raised with the left thumb and index finger on the marked posterior mid-acromiale-radiale line. The fold is vertical and parallel to the line of the upper arm. The skinfold is taken on the most posterior surface of the arm over the triceps muscle when viewed from the side. The arm should be relaxed with the shoulder joint slightly externally rotated and elbow extended by the side of the body. Ask the client to extend, then relax, and then take the skinfold.

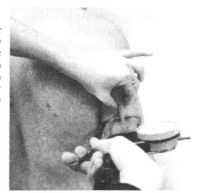

Figure 5.12 Pedagogy of skinfold measurement. (HMS Images Archive, University of Queensland.)

Accordingly, many HMS courses will also include numerous laboratory classes in which students are given hands-on experience with certain measurement techniques and tests which form the methods of scientific study of the body in physical activity and exercise. During lab classes students are given tasks (investigations) to conduct and then must write up a report of their investigations. Consider the pedagogical prescriptions to students learning how to do accurate skinfold measurements (Figure 5.12). This is taken from a laboratory manual for a course in technical skills designed for students enrolled in an exercise science program.

This pedagogy is explicit and it teaches a protocol or systematic procedures that must be adhered to for standardization and reliability issues. This form of pedagogy, which is a special form of demonstration, explanation, practice (DEP) seen so often in pedagogies for physical activity, seems to work very well in "training up" competence in the use of the measuring instrument.

Of course, as discussed earlier, once the measurements are made and translated into normative data, it is possible that students come to know their body as inferior to the "normal" body and this might have an affect on their perception of self. The conduct of skinfold measures in school PE classes can be particularly problematic in this context. I am not suggesting that accurate skinfold measures are not useful for physiological or growth and development purposes, but I am saying that measurement of the body is not benign. Like with the example of Pronger's (1995) in the anatomy lab, one will always learn more than merely how to apply the technology of measurement.

A final word

Throughout this chapter we have seen how the activities, apparatuses and pedagogies of HMS contribute to certain pedagogical work on the body. We have also seen that there are other cultural players involved in pedagogies of the body. The pedagogical work done by other players might not always be complementary to the mission of HMS, however, overall I consider the differences to be less rather than more. After all, HMS is shaped by broader regulatory discourses that impact on all society (see Chapter 9). In my view this recognition is important and it behooves us to become a little more circumspect about the contribution our field makes through its pedagogies of the body. This very idea is the subject of the next chapter.

Notes

1 According to Foucault (1980), *Épistémé* is "the historical *a priori* that grounds knowledge and its discourses and thus represents the condition of their possibility within a particular epoch" (p. 197).
2 Of course this distinction between body and brain is artificial, reflecting a particular Cartesian conception of what it means to be human. I use this distinction here for illustrative purposes only.

6 Physical education, HMS and the cult of the body

No one is free who is slave to the body.

— Seneca (4 BC–AD 65)

There is no doubt that the body (or more specifically the firm, slender body and its antithesis – the fat/obese body) has become a central focus of our field. Indeed, HMS is creating and maintaining its place as being central to the images, if not the reality, of healthy lifestyles as constructed around certain body management practices which are essentially those of the Western tradition (Tinning and Glasby, 2002). HMS degree programs and the academic/ professional field of HMS in general continue to be implicated in the reproduction of the "cult of the body" and, accordingly, there needs to be some soul searching within our field as to the limitations of its pedagogical work. We need to understand that as O'Farrell *et al.* (2000) argue, the body

> is present in a wide range of pedagogical encounters: from preschool to university and at all sites where "education" is enacted: in examination rooms, museums, theatres, cinemas, organisations – even the boudoir. The body is trained, shaped and toned to perfect tautness in minute detail at every turn and under every circumstance. This training occurs through a range of pedagogical practices (p. 1).

In this chapter I discuss this relationship in more detail and offer a response to the way our field is implicated in the so-called "obesity crisis".

PE and the slender body

> In a culture in which physical appearance is seen as an important means of claiming status, health promotion feeds into and reinforces the 'cult of the body' (Petersen, 1997, p. 200).

Twenty-five years ago I wrote a paper titled "Physical education and the cult of slenderness: A critique" (Tinning 1985). The paper created more interest than anything I have written since. Somehow it struck an accord with some members of the PE profession at the time. The early 1980s was a time when the PE profession was advocating health related fitness (HRF) and health based PE (HBPE) as a solution to the *problem* of increased sedentary life-styles and the resultant CHD "epidemic" (Tinning 1991b). In the UK Len Almond and colleagues at Loughborough were advocating HRF as the basis for school PE programs. In Australia, school curriculum materials, such as *Daily Physical Education Program* (1973), were developed as a particular form of HBPE and were underpinned by the dominant discourses of (exercise) science (Tinning and Kirk, 1991).

Two decades later it is obesity that is the targeted problem (Gard and Wright, 2001) and in Australian schools it is the school HPE curriculum that is considered as the appropriate school based "intervention" to ameliorate the problem. Rather than (exercise) science as the underpinning discourse, this new curriculum initiative is heavily influenced by the discourses of what is known as the "new public health" (Petersen and Lupton, 1996). The implications of this "new public health" will be discussed in Chapter 11.

When I used the phrase "the cult of slenderness" I was referring to the hegemony of the "look" (slim, trim, firm, taut) that within contemporary Western cultures works in many ways to reinforce unhealthy body practices such as repetitive dieting, bulimia nervosa and excessive exercising. Petersen and Lupton (1996) use the phrase "the cult of the body" to signify the contemporary content in which emphasis on physical appearance has become a signifier of worthiness and where "the body has become a crucial means by which the individual can express publicly such virtues as self-control, self-discipline and will power" (p. 25). I think that the "cult of the body" is better than "cult of slenderness" since it also includes the possibility of pedagogies to make the body bigger (in a muscular sense) as well as slimmer.

Commenting on their contemporary context, Peterson and Lupton (1996) argue that "Young people, who traditionally have been considered fairly immune to preventative health messages, are investing considerable interest and energy in behaviours that affect the looks and health of their bodies" (p. 252). They suggest that the rise in eating disorders in young people is connected to this trend and that this situation poses "a serious problem for health promoters and educators" (p. 233). In the year 2009, just as in 1985, there are significant tensions between hedonism and prudentialism that are manifested as pressures to simultaneously consume (follow one's desires/pleasures) and abstain (be prudent and avoid certain foods and practices). Unfortunately, school HPE continues to be implicated in reproducing this tension.

In my cult of slenderness paper one of the criticisms of the PE profession I raised was that school PE was failing to educate young people to become critical consumers of physical culture. A few years later Kirk (1991) claimed that school PE programs did little to address the increasing incidence of problems such as eating disorders and excessive exercising, or the stigma of obesity among young people. Moreover, he suggested that such problems might even be (in part) cultural "side effects" or unintentional consequences of the health promotion efforts of HBPE.

Contemporary school PE, according to Gard and Wright (2001) and Kirk (2006) is now considered by many "experts" to be one of the key sites in which the claimed "obesity epidemic" can be resisted. Ironically, however, the very obesity discourses that are embraced by PE actually help to produce anxieties about the body that can result in "unhealthy" eating and exercise practices even at a very early age. In this context, Gard and Wright (2001) make the provocative suggestion that

> it may be better for physical educators to say nothing about obesity, exercise and health, rather than singing the praises of slimness and vigorous exercise and condemning the evils of fat and 'sedentary' life. Failing this we implore physical educators to look underneath the surface of the discipline's cherished beliefs (p. 32).

Active mesomorphs: A selection issue?

While there are numerous reasons why young people might choose to pursue a career in the field of HM/kinesiology, one significant factor is that they tend to be active mesomorphs who enjoy sport and physical activity. A career in HM is seen as a way to continue to be involved in the things they enjoy doing. Most likely their mesomorphic habitus (see Chapter 9) contributed to their enjoyment of such pursuits.

Let me elaborate. When a young person enters a program of HMS they have usually self-selected in the first instance. Sure they need to get the necessary grades (usually high) for entry, but they actively choose to study about the body and physical activity. Often, and more often than not, they are physically able and have, to some reasonable degree, achieved success at sports or other physical activities. They are the active mesomorphs and in general they find participation in physical activity reinforcing and affirming. Like so many of my HMS colleagues around the world, I too was such a young person.

With specific reference to PE teaching, Macdonald and Kirk (1999) suggest that the overwhelming historical legacy influencing what it means to be a good teacher in this field is that "one must, literally, look the part – mesomorphic, able-bodied, physically capable and physically fit" (p. 132). Moreover, whether PE teachers like it or not, their lifestyle and their bodies are constantly under surveillance by the community and the students alike. This is especially the case in smaller communities such as in rural towns (see Macdonald and Kirk, 1996).

David Brown (1999) makes a compelling argument that PE teachers are complicit in reproducing dominant forms of masculinity through their own embodied identities. As a result of "long-term personal investments into the dominant masculine arenas of PE and sport, their identities are strongly engrained with these characteristics by the time they begin Initial Teacher Training" (p. 155). I would argue that this is also the case for most HM/kinesiology students as well. In the words of singer/songwriter Ruth Aplet, "And the culture comes down".

Part of that culture is "transmitted" by/through one's body. But what exactly do PE teachers and exercise advocates transmit or communicate through their mesomorphic physical selves without saying a word? It has long been thought that the mesomorph is characterized as being insensitive to the needs of others, particularly those who find it difficult to learn physical skills or who find sport and the movement culture in general less than enjoyable. As Hargreaves (1986) claimed, mesomorphs are more likely than ectomorphs or endomorphs "to be unsympathetic to those who are perceived to be thin, fat or physically incompetent and are more likely to be conformist and authoritarian" (p. 170).

Hargreaves (1986) also suggested that "the mesomorphic image resonates strongly with ideologically conservative notions concerning achievement, drive and dynamism, discipline, conformity, cleanliness, efficiency, good adjustment, manliness and femininity" (p. 170). Mesomorphism as ideology (Tinning, 1990) accepts muscularity and slimness as "good" and assumes that such a body shape actually represents control, efficiency, discipline and health.

Although it is always risky to generalize, various researchers have identified a cluster of attitudes and temperamental traits associated with mesomorphs. According to Carter,

> Such traits as assertiveness of posture and movement, love of physical adventure, need and enjoyment of exercises, love of dominating, bold directness of manner, competitive aggressiveness, physical courage for combat, and Spartan indifference to pain may readily be observed in many physical education teachers (cited in Whiting *et al.*, 1973, p. 127).

Certainly representations of PE teachers as portrayed in literature are less than flattering (see Nettleton, 1985).

McCullick *et al.* (2003) provide a more contemporary though no less chastening account of how PE teachers are portrayed in movies. Their research shows that in American films PE teachers are portrayed as being synonymous with coaches, as incompetent teachers, and as drill sergeants and bullies who enjoy humiliating students. Male teachers are portrayed as buffoons devoid of "masculine" leadership qualities and female teachers as butch or lesbian. In the classic UK film Tess, the PE teacher (actually called the games teacher) shows similar characteristics and has a solid mesomorphic body with balding head and a thick neck. In all, not a pretty picture.

Like most HM professionals, since I too am implicated within the cult of the body and am reinforced by my own physicality I have had to work against my own prejudices. It is only by moving outside the comfort zone afforded by the sub-culture of the active mesomorph to listen to and read the voices of others as they negotiate their own bodily challenges that I have become more understanding (e.g. reading Susie Orbach's [1978] *Fat is a Feminist Issue* and Roberta Pollack-Seid's [1989] *Never Too Thin: Why Women Are at War with Their Bodies*).

In the case of the PE teacher the prejudices that tend to be reinforced within the active mesomorph sub-culture are lived out in pedagogical practice. There is plenty of evidence to confirm that many PE teachers give more attention to the students who are most like themselves – namely the active mesomorphs who find success within physical activity (see for example Martinek *et al.*, 1982; Dodds, 1993; Hay, 2006). For the junior sports coach it might mean neglecting the kids who are less able while giving a disproportionate amount of time to the talented kids. For the exercise scientist it might mean preferring to work with elite athletes rather than with physical activity programs for elderly citizens.

Of course, to be fair to PE teachers, maybe teachers across all disciplines are influenced by recognition in their students of certain shared attributes. Consider, for example, the English teachers who favour the good readers, the maths teachers who favour the mathematically gifted, or the drama teachers who favours the students who can act. However, while recognizing there is a possibly broader problem, I think the fact that the body is so central to PE and that the body is such an obvious display of athletic possibilities mean the issue will always be rather more serious for PE teachers.

Having said all this, I hasten to add that I know that there are many PE teachers who are exceptions to the PE teacher caricature. However, if we take a profession-wide view, the image of the PE teacher is not a positive one. So, in terms of the cult of the body and its reproduction via school PE, it would seem that Brown (1999) is correct when he argues that PE teachers might not have much choice when their own embodied identities are part of the problem. So is change possible and what can be done?

HMS programs and the cult of the body: Possibilities for change?

Simplistically then, we have recruits coming to HMS with a particular habitus shaped by, and inclusive of, their mesomorphy, their physicality, their attitudes and dispositions to the body, physical activity and sport and health. While it would be possible to select students who do not possess mesomorphic bodies and perhaps who do not have a love and passion for sport and physical activity, that would be crazy. However, selection of more individuals who enjoy different forms of movement culture other than team sports might be interesting. Like it or not, the active mesomorph is going to continue to be the dominant group in all HMS programs. The challenge, therefore, is to use pedagogies that critique and disrupt the taken-for-granted assumptions and beliefs that tend to be associated with such physicality.

Just because young people come into programs of HMS/exercise science and PE with particular dispositions, values and embodied histories with regard to their bodies, sport and physical activity, this does not mean that they cannot change.

Giddens (1991) argues that in contemporary times the self "is seen as a reflexive project, for which the individual is responsible. We are, not what we are, but what we make ourselves" (p. 75). But this is not a simple task. Moreover, since the reflexive project calls for the "ongoing reconstruction" of our identities, our ontological security may be threatened. Ontological security is important. If we need a reminder that unintended pedagogical work can have damaging effect on our ontological security the story of Spanish PE teacher-educator José Devís-Devís and his student Guillem provides a powerful example. It is worth retelling.

The story, published in the *European Physical Education Review* (Vol. 5(2), 1999), tells of how Devís-Devís, working at the INEF in Valencia, set a number of books for his PETE students to read. One expressed a liberal view of sport, another a subjective and participatory view of an athlete, and the third a more socially critical perspective on sport in society. On reading Brohm's *Sport, A Prison of Measured Time: Essays* which presents the Marxist critical perspective on sport, Guillem, a student who was described as having a strong athletic identity (Brewer *et al.*, 1993), was so challenged that he experienced a serious *identity* crisis. As he admitted, "sport is my way of being and on this I have built my life" and after reading the book he said "I didn't feel happy with myself. I knew that [the reading] had subconsciously left me devastated" (Devís-Devís and Sparkes, 1999, p. 139). The symbolic reaction to this crisis saw Guillem actually burn the book as an act of resistance and denial. Of course many people may first resist that which challenges their cherished beliefs as a first stage in coming to change. The issue with Guillem was the severity of his resistance and the emotional consequences this produced. Devís-Devís and Sparkes (1999) suggested that

> The case of Guillem reveals how the simple act of being confronted with views that challenge one's taken-for-granted assumptions about the world, one's cherished beliefs, preferred identities and sense of self can be an excruciating experience for some students, who experience it in the form of a crisis (p. 147).

The link between a student's identity and what they learn from (and about) the socially critical curriculum is clearly demonstrated in this example. The potential "slippage" between what is intended to be learnt and what is understood (Lusted, 1986) is clearly evident. In terms of research in pedagogy, understanding the impact of the pedagogical strategy (reading a book) requires a research paradigm (and method) such as personalistic and critical inquiry.

We need to be very careful of using pedagogical encounters that embarrass or degrade students' values, choices and commitments. Kenway and Bullen (2002), as a result of their research into popular culture, schooling and young people, argue that "students do not tend to appreciate teachers [or professors] who make them feel ashamed about their choices and lifestyles all in the name of helping them" (p. 165). Indeed, "deconstruction may have an emotional fallout" (ibid.). With similar sentiment about the limits of critique, Crowdes (2000) claims that in many classes in which critical pedagogies are used, students "are often left with their fairly extensive sociological vocabularies and socially aware minds detached from their bodies and agency in matters of conflict resolution and change" (p. 25). Accordingly, she argues for the use of pedagogic strategies that join *somatic* and *sociological* perspectives. In both school PE and in HMS more generally, when we do engage in critical pedagogies it is usually rather strong in the sociological and rather weak in the somatic.

Kimberley Oliver's activist research work in engaging adolescent girls in critical inquiry on the body provides an example of how our earnest attempts to lift the ideological blinkers off our students (in her case adolescent girls) are not always straightforward. Oliver (2001) reports that "despite the pedagogical possibilities of using images from popular culture to engage adolescent girls in critically studying the body, there are also many struggles involved in this type of curriculum work" (p. 161). Oliver wanted the girls to "begin to name and recognise some of their unassumed beliefs about the body" (p. 146) and this would seem a useful process. However, in a later publication Oliver and Lalik (2004) "wonder whether learning critique alone might not leave adolescents with feelings of frustration and helplessness" (p. 22).

Gard and Wright (2001) argue that far from providing a critique of the cult of the body, the PE profession remains deeply implicated in the reproduction of healthism values through its active and uncritical construction of obesity as a problem to be "attacked" through the school curriculum. Healthism as an ideology in HMS/HPE is premised on the assumption that PE contributes to better health because exercise = fitness = health (see Kirk and Colquhoun, 1989; Tinning, 1990). This linear relationship is seldom problematized or questioned by the "true believers" in field of HMS.

Moreover, it is considered that failure to maintain a slim healthy body is an individual failure. Fitness and health are seen to be the individual's responsibility alone. Such is the strength of this belief for many HM professionals that they consider physical activity to be *the* major factor contributing to better health.

New curriculum initiatives in some countries (for example, in Australia, the *Queensland 1-10 HPE Syllabus* (Queensland School Curriculum Council, 1999) now offer opportunities for PE teachers to tackle issues related to the "cult of the body" and to educate students as critical consumers of physical culture. However, many PE teachers face a dilemma in operationalizing such opportunities since they often have considerable investments in the "cult of the body" through their own subjectivities and embodiments as sport and exercise devotees and this can render them blind (or at least myopic) to the possible cultural "side effects" of their PE practices. Moreover, most PE teachers are not personally equipped with the skills of cultural critique that are necessary to create the pedagogical encounters necessary to develop such skills in their pupils. As a pedagogical "way in" to developing such skills, Jan Wright (2004) provides a useful account of how analyzing media texts can be used to develop in students a critical disposition to problematic representations of male and female bodies in various media.

So it seems that there are grounds for believing that, even with "enlightened" curriculum frameworks to guide teachers' practice, PE continues to reproduce values associated with the cult of body. We need to understand why HPE continues to be ineffective (or even counter-productive) in helping young people gain some measure of analytic and embodied "distance" from the problematic aspects of the cult of the body.

In the program of HMS for which they are selected, the typical undergraduate will be schooled in certain ways of thinking about the body. They will come to *know* the body in particular ways. Sometimes the theoretical ways of knowing confirm what their personal experience has taught them – but sometimes there are tensions. The heavy emphasis on science is understandable given the history of PE as a field of study and its constant struggle for academic status, but it does have its limitations. It tends to focus attention on measures of performance and ignore *meaning*.

Such is the significance of meaning that Scott Kretchmer (2007) argues that it should be part of a new research paradigm for our field, one which "places meaning on a level playing field with muscles, cells, genes and other movement related phenomena" (p. 373). However, in the typical HMS program today there is a dominant emphasis on intellectual knowing about the body. There has been a gradual decrease in the importance of the experience of physical activity in contemporary programs. Sometimes students can graduate without ever having their "movement boundaries" challenged. In other words they come with a certain set of experiences (e.g. in ball games) and never have to confront the difficulties, challenges and feelings associated with mastering unfamiliar activities such as gymnastics, dance, inline skating or rock climbing. When we consider the history of the movement culture across various countries such as Sweden, Germany and Britain (see for example Riordan and Krüger, 2003) we can see that the embodied dimensions of participation and its *meaning* for the participants have been more significant than the science that might attempt to explain or direct it.

In pursuing the mission of HMS to understand physical activity and to advocate for increased participation in the movement culture, the hegemony of science as the way of knowing, and coming to know, will always provide a limited, restricted view of participation in the movement culture. It is therefore necessary that our undergraduate degree programs in HMS make more use of sociological, philosophical and experiential understandings to disrupt common understandings and taken-for-granted assumptions regarding movement culture and the cult of the body more specifically.

Giving voice to alternative discourses of the body in HMS

Importantly, not all the contemporary interest in the body is underpinned by Cartesian dualism, nor is it all dominated by the objective rationality of Western medicine. Lupton (1994) argues "Western societies in the late twentieth century are characterised by people's increasing disillusionment with scientific medicine" (p. 1) and that people are searching for other ways of healing, maintaining, and thinking about their bodies. If HMS is really to help students as future citizens negotiate "healthy lifestyle" practices in the "risk society" then it must open itself up to the challenges offered by other ways of knowing about the body and health.

One example is the Confucian inspired East Asian tradition of thought "emphasises the constantly changing nature of reality" (Nisbett, 2003, p. 174). The world is not static but dynamic and changeable. Although this thinking is now far more acceptable in contemporary Western culture with the appreciation of the implications of chaos and complexity theories, many Western HMS students continue to have faith in the "certain" knowledge of exercise science and have an aversion for the "uncertain" knowledge of disciplines such as sociology (see for example Macdonald and Brooker, 2000).

In our HMS programs is any credence given to ways of thinking about the human body other than through the paradigm of Western science? Although we see the increasing presence of Tai Chi and yoga in "health club" offerings, what do we do in our training to help students seriously engage such different perspectives from practical, experiential and theoretical perspectives?

It is true that alternative voices are now being heard, but they are still marginalized in terms of column inches devoted to them within the programs of HMS and PETE and in our school PE programs. Although there are scholars, thinkers, writers from many different disciplines and backgrounds in the West who have been calling for new ways to think about the body, health, education, and the world in general (e.g. Wright, 2000; Lupton, 1996; Chopra, 1993; Heron, 1981), few if any of these alternative thinkers appear on the HMS reading lists in most Western universities.

It is, however, encouraging to note that there are some PE and HMS scholars in the West who are engaging with other ways of thinking about the body in the context of our field (e.g. Armour, 1999; Oliver, 2000; Evans *et al.*, 2003). Much of this new work is challenging to those who were trained through the discourses of science in which the body-as-machine metaphor and its technocratic rationality is the only explanation available or legitimated.

Jan Wright (2000) contends that we "should play close attention to the kinds of body-work that we foster and the forms of embodiment we pro-duce" (p. 39) when we privilege practices that are underpinned by the body-as-machine metaphor. Wright contends that through an examination of alternative movement practices (such as the Feldenkrais method), exist-ing mainstream practices that (re)produce the discourses of the "cult of the body" can be challenged. In my view it behooves us to begin to seriously consider alternative ways of thinking about the body and about health more generally.

Some of those alternative ways of thinking about the body are outlined by Norman (1995) in an article titled "Zen and the art of body maintenance" in which she discusses "bodywork", "a 90's blend of exercise, therapy and spirituality" (p. 22). Norman reports that in Australia it is the fastest growing area of alternative health care. Maybe we should be skeptical of such body-work. However, an informed skepticism should be built on first engaging with the "truth game" of the discourse. Consider the following example of one body technique that has had a long connection with PE.

The Alexander Technique "is referred to as a re-education [of the body] rather than a therapy" (Brennan, 1991, p. 4). Alexander was an Australian whose ideas about posture were embraced by many significant people throughout the world. Advocates of this practice have included George Bernard Shaw, John Dewey, Aldous Huxley, John Cleese, Paul Newman, Roald Dahl and countless actors, singers and, more recently, athletes. According to Brennan (1991),

> The way in which we think is as much part of Alexander Technique as the way we move. In essence the Technique is a way of using our minds in a conscious manner so that we are able efficiently to direct our bodies in order to keep them as stress-free as possible (p. 10).

Alexander was convinced that the mind and body were an inseparable whole and treating only the physical symptom of a "body problem" was both ill-informed and unproductive. He was actually in good company since millions of Asians have a similar philosophy (Nisbett, 2003), however, according to Edward Maisel (1970) this placed Alexander

> in opposition to the orthodox physical medicine of his day, as well as the unorthodox (osteopathy, chiropractic etc). All of them in his view concentrated with lopsided emphasis on the body alone. Still later this organismic approach of his would set him apart from the burgeoning psychoanalytic movement which, in its exclusive pre-occupation with factors of the psyche, he regarded as equally unbalanced (p. xvi).

Interestingly, Ernest Jokl, a noted South African physical educator of the 1950s and 60s and an advocate of orthodox physical medicine and the "sci-entific principles" of PE, published a scathing attack on Alexander's work.

Unable to receive a retraction, Alexander sued Jokl for libel. The conflict was taken to court and settled in favour of Alexander. People like Alexander who confront the dominant paradigm often have to contend with strong forms of opposition. At least he wasn't burned at the stake!

One contemporary form of body-work that has attracted the attention of some physical educators in the USA is "somatic education". *The Journal of Physical Education, Recreation & Dance* has published a number of articles since the early 1990s that basically argue for bringing somatic education (as a form of body-work) into PE (see Linden, 1994). One particular technique was to perform exercises using large inflatable balls (45–95 cm in diameter) to develop somatic awareness (see Green, 1992; Gomez, 1992).

HMS pedagogies should be one among the assemblage of bio-pedagogies (Harwood, 2008) within the educational landscape in which holism is not just advocated, it is embodied. We should pursue with vigour the search for the limitations of our current thinking and begin to consider the wisdom of multiple ways of seeing the world. The ideas of people like Mathias Alexander or Paul Linden should be considered in our curricula alongside the ideas of exercise scientists such as Ken Cooper and Per-Olof Aostrand.

However, while multiple paradigms should be considered from an intellectual perspective, we should recognize that intellectual truth games do not, and cannot, provide all the answers. Sometimes it is only through experience that we can come to know something. Accordingly we also need to begin to allow ourselves to experience some other possibilities that exist beyond the football field, the netball court or the aerobics gym.

As an example, my own commitment to engaging, if not necessarily embracing, alternative discourses regarding health and the body has not been simply an intellectual exercise. Like many sufferers from lower back pain I have used the regular routine of sit-ups as a form of specific muscle strengthening for the abdominal muscles to help ameliorate my condition. This conventional science based exercise treatment to ameliorate lower back troubles was not a panacea for my situation. In desperation I sought alternative modalities and in the process experienced the Alexander Technique. I had to suspend my intellectual skepticism and experience the modality at an embodied level. Like the sit-ups, it didn't fix the problem, but I consider it made a positive contribution in terms of my ongoing kinaesthetic "feel" for my posture. My point here is simply that sometimes the actual experience of a modality can offer us new ways of knowing that although it might not "fit" with our intellectual ways of seeing, it can nevertheless be useful.

Challenging the cult of the body ideology in HMS

> Being conscious … is not simply a formula or a slogan. It is a radical form of being.
>
> (Paulo Freire, 1978, p. 24).

According to Evans and Davies (2004), theory can be used as a vehicle for "thinking otherwise"; being conscious of other possibilities. This is rather like the idea of the sociological imagination which Giddens (1993) defines as *"being able to 'think ourselves away' from the familiar routines of our daily lives in order to look at them anew"* (p. 18; emphasis in original). Moreover, as Shilling (1993) informs us, the body "can be conceptualised as occupying a place at the centre of the sociological imagination" (p. 22).

Importantly, the sociological imagination allows us to "make the familiar strange" which potentially challenges orthodoxy and provides the possibility of disrupting the cult of the body. However, there is always the danger that we might slip into assuming that if we can just get our thinking straight (by applying the "right" theorizing), if we get our curricula right (the right curriculum development), and if we do our pedagogy right, then the miseducative pedagogical work of the cult of the body will be ameliorated or even eliminated. The shadow of the "cleaving to order" (Law, 1994) may be always lurking. In applying the sociological imagination to PE and HMS we need to be mindful that ways of theorizing do not become forms of a new orthodoxy.

In what follows I suggest that a "modest critical pedagogy" (Tinning, 2002) might offer a way forward for addressing the cult of the body in HMS.

The notion of a modest critical pedagogy is an *orienting way of thinking* about how we might engage HMS students in self-examination of beliefs and dispositions in the process of becoming PE teachers, exercise scientists, health promotion workers or sports coaches. It is not a prescription for pedagogical strategies.

Importantly, while there would be many forms of a modest critical pedagogy (just as there are critical pedagogies) they would share a certain circumspect disposition in their *claims* to know. A modest critical pedagogy would not assume that there is a set of pedagogical procedures that, when found (discovered or invented) will lead to certainty with regard to the "delivery" of certain outcomes (emancipatory or conservative). A modest critical pedagogy would take seriously Bauman's (2001) claim of the contemporary importance of "tertiary learning" that relates to the capacity of the learner to unlearn and adapt to uncertainty.

According to social analysts such as Giddens (1991), Beck (1992) and Bauman (2001) and many others, certainty *is* illusory in contemporary times and there seems little doubt that we must to learn to live with uncertainty (see Kelly *et al.*, 2000). In this context Bauman (2001) offers a caution that has particular relevance to students of HMS:

> If they expect to find a cohesive and coherent structure in the mangle of contingent events, they are in for costly errors and painful frustrations. If the habits acquired in the course of training prompt them to seek such cohesive and coherent structures and make their actions dependent on finding them – they are in real trouble (p. 125).

A modest critical pedagogy would recognize the limits of rationality as a catalyst for change. It would seek to develop emotional commitment in students to challenging the ideology of the cult of the body. It would necessitate a recognition that emotional commitment is embodied (Dowling, 2008). It would not privilege left-brain intellectualizing – it would also embrace subjectivity and the creative right brain (Heron, 1981). A modest critical pedagogy would recognize, and try to work with/from, student and teacher embodied subjectivities. Of course, since they already have a strong embodied engagement with the ideology of the cult of the body through their own mesomorphic habitus, helping them develop an emotional commitment to change is a difficult task.

According to Carlson (1998), in academic discourse it is necessary to find something to say, to find a voice or rhetorical style in which to say or write it, and to join in a conversation or "truth game". By truth game he is referring to the Foucauldian notion of a "discursive practice that establishes norms regarding who can speak, what they can speak about, and the form in which they speak" (p. 541). Significantly, different truth games produce different truths. Since the dominant truth game regarding the body is that of science, in attempting to disrupt the ideology of the cult of the body it is necessary to seek other rhetorical styles that help convey different truths. The three rhetorical styles that form the basis of Plato's dialogues provide a useful framework for thinking about the discourses that could be employed within a modest critical pedagogy for HMS to challenge the ideology of the cult of the body. They include:

> *Logos*, the analytic voice of critique associated with the truth games of science and philosophy;
>
> *Thymos*, a voice of rage against injustice from the perspective and position of the disempowered, the disenfranchised, and the marginalised; and
>
> *Mythos*, a personal voice of story telling, cultural mythology, autobiography, and literature (Carlson, 1998 p. 543).

A modest critical pedagogy for HMS that is oriented through this framework might allow for the development of commitment to challenging the ideology of the cult of the body (through *thymos* and *mythos*) within a context that, while giving voice to *logos*, avoids making certainty the object. There would be many pedagogical possibilities that could be used to give voice to *logos*, *thymos* and *mythos*. Working with a modest critical pedagogy would enable HM academics/professors to become something like Carlson's (1998) new postmodern academic who speaks with

> a hybrid voice that crosses borders, one that interweaves voices of *logos*, *thymos*, and *mythos* and that shifts back and forth from analysis to

anecdote, from theory to personal story-telling, from principled talk of social justice to personal and positioned expressions of outrage at injustice (p. 543).

It is instructive to consider the rhetorical styles privileged in the way in which HMS graduates engage the "obesity crisis". Given the significance of science within HM it is little wonder that it is the voice of *logos* that is privileged. In practice *logos* has gradually become the lingua franca of our field and when we engage the obesity issue the voice of *logos* dominates. We hear of BMIs, intervention studies, epidemiology, calorific expenditure, skinfold measures etc., and the purpose of this discourse is to facilitate prediction and control of human capital.

Too often members of our field are quick to position the overweight and obese of the world as "losers". Influenced by the ideology of healthism, there is often a lack of respect and sympathy for the circumstances that impact on the lifestyle choices many people make. In human services professions like exercise science and PE there is a need to recognize and respect the multiple realities that are the lived experiences of people. Listening to the voices of *thymos* and *mythos*, in addition to that of *logos*, could help us gain a more informed and sensitive position when engaging the dilemmas of our field.

In my view, connecting students with different perspectives in thinking about the body should be approached by use of the voices of *thymos*, *mythos* and *logos*. The voices of *mythos* and *thymos* have greater potential to elicit emotional responses to, and connection with, the problematics of the cult of the body than the voice of *logos* (see Dowling, 2008).

Here are some examples of the sorts of texts that could be engaged for each of the rhetorical styles.

For *mythos* (a personal voice of story telling):

- Sparkes, A. (1996). The fatal flaw: A narrative of the fragile body/self. *Qualitative Inquiry*, 2(4), 463–494.
- Fussell, S. (1991). *Muscle: Confessions of an Unlikely Bodybuilder.* London: Cardinal.
- Lindqvist, S. (2003). *Bench Press* (S. Death, Trans.). London: Grant Books.
- Bale, J., Christensen, M., and Pfister, G. (Eds.). (2004). *Writing Lives in Sport: Biographies, Life-Histories and Methods.* Aarhus: Aarhus University Press.
- Denison, J., and Markula, P. (Eds.). (2003). *Moving Writing: Crafting Movement in Sport Research.* New York: Peter Lang.

To give voice to *thymos* (rage against injustice):

- Edut, O. (Ed.). (2000). *Body Outlaws: Young Women Write About Body Image and Identity.* Toronto: Seal Press.

- Pollack-Seid, R. (1989). *Never Too Thin: Why Women Are at War with Their Bodies*. New York: Prentice Hall Press.
- Orbach, S. (1978). *Fat is a Feminist Issue*. New York: Berkeley Books.
- Klein, N. (2000). *No Logo*. London: Flamingo.

To engage the analytic voice of *logos* (the voice of reason and science):

- Gard, M., and Wright, J. (2005). *The Obesity Epidemic: Science, Morality and Ideology*. London: Routledge.
- Blair, S., and Brodney, S. (1999). Effects of physical inactivity and obesity on morbidity and mortality: Current evidence and research issues. *Medicine and Science in Sports and Exercise*, 31(11), 646–662.
- Stearns, P. (1997). *Fat History: Bodies and Beauty in the Modern West*. New York: New York University Press.
- Howell, J., and Ingham, A. (2001). From social problem to personal issue: The language of lifestyle. *Cultural Studies*, 15(2), 326–351.

Gard and Wright (2001) implore us to "look beneath the surface of the discipline's cherished beliefs" (p. 32). Some of these resources would help us to respond to this call. Of course, merely reading a book and discussing it in class will not produce predictable pedagogical work – such as an emotional commitment to challenge the ideology of the cult of the body. As we saw with the Spanish student Guillem (Devís-Devís and Sparkes, 1999), challenges to our understanding of "which way is up" (Connell, 1983) are often resisted, and student reaction will always be variable and unpredictable.

At the end of the day, since knowledge is not what is intended but what is understood, the success of a pedagogy in disrupting the ideology of the cult of the body will be an individual matter for each student. Enabling HMS students to come to their own understandings through the multiple voices of a truth game is probably all we can hope for.

7   The body in school PE and sport

It is stating the obvious that school PE and sport are fundamentally concerned with bodies and hence with pedagogies of/for the body. There is now a plethora of accounts, both scholarly and popular, of recalled experiences of the body in school PE and sport (see for example Kanpol, 2002; Myerson, 2005; Gard and Meyenn, 2000). Exploring the range of experiences we read on the one hand of Julie Myerson's negative experiences and her self-definition of being "not a games person" and on the other hand of Barry Kanpol's positive experiences in which sport offered him an education that stood in marked contrast to a repressive disciplined academic classroom context. And somewhere in the middle are the experiences of countless young people.

As I previously mentioned, pedagogies of/for physical activity are also pedagogies of/for the body. Importantly, however, not all pedagogies of/for the body are pedagogies of/for physical activity. There are many ways in which we learn about our bodies that do not come through participation in physical activity. But there is no denying the fact that schools have been a central mechanism of society for disciplining young bodies (Kirk, 1993).

One thing about PE and sport is that what the body looks like and what it can do or can't do is very much on display. Typically, it is those with a mesomorphic body-type that are most suited to the type of physical activity demanded in school sport and PE. Exceedingly skinny and or fat bodies are usually less suited. Importantly, as Bourdieu (1990) has argued "What is learned by the body is not something that one has, like knowledge that can be brandished, but something that one is" (p. 73). So when the body goes on display in PE, it is oneself that is on display. Moreover, if, as Caddick (1986) argues, "We are our bodies and only in and through them do we know ourselves and our relationships with others" (p. 60) then our participation in PE class (with our bodies) might be central to our developing relationships with our class mates. In other words the PE lesson is a powerful and potentially vulnerable space.

The PE teacher's body

HPE teachers teach about physical activity, the body and health. In so doing it is not only the pedagogical activities they create that do pedagogical work. The fact that the teacher is an embodied person, as distinct from a robot or a textual message, carries with it special power. For example the teacher's body itself does pedagogical work related to the gendered body. David Brown (2002) recognized this embodied complexity in his research and found PE teachers to be "living links", acting as a "cultural conduit" in the process of transmission and maintenance of gender relations in sport and PE. His research adopts a relational view in which "patriarchy in the classroom is embedded within the minds *and* bodies of teachers and pupils themselves, sharing a social presence and influencing one another's actions by using the culturally specific gender 'norms' as a point of reference" (p. 2; emphasis in original).

In other words the PE teacher's body by virtue of its materiality does pedagogical work *without a word being spoken*. There is a rather dated "experiment" that is worth relating here because it highlights something of the complexity of HPE and the pedagogical work done regarding the body.

Some 20 years ago two American researchers, Melville and Maddalozzo (1988), set out to investigate whether the size of the teacher (read "appearance of body fat") made any difference to children's learning in relation to the exercise intentions of high school students. What Melville and Maddalozzo did was to show 850 high school students two 20-minute videotapes. The first half of each tape focused on the importance of flexibility to health and sports performance while the second half focused on body composition and the role diet and exercise can play in controlling body composition. The difference between the videotapes was the physical appearance of the teacher. The same teacher taught the two lessons, but in one he was his normal slim mesomorphic self, whereas in the other he wore what was called a "fat suit" that made him look considerably fatter. After the lesson all students were given a content examination and a questionnaire to assess their knowledge and attitudes. According to Melville and Maddalozzo (1988), the results supported the hypothesis that appearance of fatness in a physical educator does affect the teaching of exercise concepts to high school students.

> Also, data showed them to be very aware of the different fitness levels of the instructor in the tapes and strongly intolerant of the seemingly poorly conditioned person. They did not think he was an appropriate role model, they tended not to like him, they did not perceive him to be particularly knowledgable, and they indicated that they would be less influenced by his message to exercise (p. 351).

Not withstanding some research design issues, such as the absence of pre-intervention measures, at face value there is something going on here

– something troubling. Of course the idea that the PE teacher (or HM professional more generally) needs to "look the part" is not new. Back in the 1940s James McCloy (a leading physical educator at the time) claimed that "the example of the teacher is another potential factor in the mind-set of the pupil. Does he [sic] look the part? Does he look healthy, vigorous, and alert or is he fat and pudgy?" (McCloy, 1940, p. 158). Similar sentiments have been expressed by other leaders of our field:

> Physical fitness must become a way of life for all of us. How can we expect anyone to listen to what we have to say about the benefits of fitness if we are overweight and in poor physical condition ourselves? (Johnson, 1985, p. 34).

> How can we be effective in promoting health and fitness if our bodies are not living testimonies of our commitment? What we are communicated more than what we say (Wilmore, 1982, p. 43).

The troubling aspect of this sentiment is that it seems to make sense along the same lines as the argument "Would you listen to advice to stop smoking from a doctor who smoked?"

Moreover, I have to admit that personally I cannot unequivocally say that the message underpinning this role model sentiment is anathema to me. Sure, the rational me that reads social critiques of the obesity debate recognizes that there is considerable "collateral damage" (less than desirable pedagogical work) that can be associated with this sentiment when it is enmeshed in the dominant contemporary culture in which health, self-identity and consumption are increasingly entwined (Bunton and Burrows, 1995), but I still can't discount the common sense observation that there is some truth in role model theory.

The teacher's performing body

The issue of the teacher's body always becomes a topic of debate when I show students a film titled *Gymnastics in the Primary School* (*circa* 1972) as a catalyst for discussion of different pedagogical methods. You might remember that I introduced this film in Chapter 3 when discussing pedagogical methods. In the film, two infant-grade teachers teach lessons in movement education. Neither is young. Neither is athletic and certainly neither would fit the active mesomorph image discussed above. Both teachers wore "street" clothes rather than track suit or PE kit, and both move very little throughout the lesson. Consistent with the movement education approach, they set movement problems introduced with, for example, "Show me a roll in a curled shape". They do not demonstrate what a forward roll *should* look like. The children are free to make a movement response within the bounds of their imagination and physical capabilities. The teacher, having observed the various responses then selects certain students to demonstrate what they have done and asks the class to observe certain differences or similarities between the responses.

In class discussions, certain PETE students react very strongly and argue that the women are "not real PE teachers". When pressed they suggest that they don't fit the image they have of a PE teacher (the active mesomorph in PE kit) and that they don't (and probably can't) demonstrate! Others in the class (always the minority) defend the teachers by saying that for the particular pedagogical method they do not need to demonstrate and hence their own body and its physicality is not an issue. Lively discussion regarding the purpose of teacher demonstrations in the context of what makes a good teacher of PE follows.

Of course the teachers in the film were generalist teachers rather than PE specialists and this was part of the message of the film – that the "average" classroom teacher could teach PE. Certainly it is expected that specialists have much more subject matter content knowledge than their generalist colleagues with respect to PE, and one manifestation of this knowledge (in its practical form) is the ability to demonstrate to the class in order to facilitate their learning of the activity.

Bresler (2004), in writing on dance in the curriculum, claims that

> Expertise in the subject matter of dance is *key*. The perceptions and repertoire of movement activities of teachers not trained as dancers is limited. They are less likely to be aware of the cognitive and expressive possibilities embodied in movement. Furthermore, those with little dance experience are less likely to be touched or inspired by it (p. 147; my emphasis).

While I have a sympathy with this perspective, I still consider that personal demonstrations by the teacher might be a useful pedagogical device but are not absolutely necessary for teaching PE (see Tinning, 1992). I understand that there is knowledge about movement that can only be acquired through participation in movement, but it is not clear to me whether or not such knowledge is absolutely essential to teach movement. Knowing what it feels like to do a back-dive might be useful in communicating to pupils what it might feel like when they launch themselves backward off the one-metre diving board, but often those feelings are idiosyncratic and notoriously difficult to articulate in a way that makes sense to others. The key question here is whether having the teacher perform a given activity necessarily facilitates better learning for the student. For some members of a class, a competent teacher demonstration might be seen as another opportunity for the teacher to take an ego trip. For others, they might think "Well that's OK for him but I'm simply not that capable."

A key issue for PE is the nature of the practical knowledge that is required for teaching. Arnold (1988) distinguishes between weak and strong senses of practical knowledge. Practical knowledge in the weak sense is where an individual can perform an activity (is physically able to do something) but cannot articulate or describe how it is done. Practical knowledge in the weak sense is thus characterized by embodied knowing. It requires a "measure" of physicality and a body that is capable of performing such movement tasks. A question arises as to whether an embodied knowledge is all that is needed by the teacher. Practical knowledge in the strong sense is where an individual can physically perform an activity or skill, and can also articulate/describe how it is done. Being able to identify and articulate how a performance is done is essential to the strong sense of practical knowledge.

Certainly it is possible to possess knowledge of how a movement is performed without being able to perform it oneself. One only needs to look at sports like gymnastics to recognize that coaches often do in fact possess extensive knowledge about particular movement skills without being able to perform the movements themselves. Being able to also perform the skill might be a bonus rather than a necessity. It is, however, expected that PE teachers will possess the ability to both perform and to describe the particular movement skills that form the basis of the taught curriculum.

In most PETE programs there is some effort to develop practical knowledge in the strong sense of the student teacher. This is usually done through movement labs and practical classes (call them what you will). In my view, in a PETE course a student teacher should have practical and hence embodied – as distinct from abstract and theoretical – experiences in the various movement activities that constitute the school PE curriculum, but the requirement for "performative competence" (Arnold, 1988) is, in my view, not absolutely necessary.

In my own training in the 1960s considerable time was devoted to developing our movement competence so we could demonstrate across a wide range of sports and physical activities. Development of such movement competencies were predicated on the assumption that it would be necessary to demonstrate to be an effective teacher. Movement education approaches challenged this assumption and this was one of the factors that drew resistance from advocates of traditional methods, such as Willee (1978). The training necessary to develop such competencies was also an efficient form of disciplining the body (Foucault, 1986) and long after the ability to perform the competencies has left me, the disciplinary power of the process remains with me in an embodied sense.

Corporeal pleasure in pedagogy

The ideas of Erica McWilliam (1996) on pleasure/risk/desire in pedagogy provide some interesting insights into teacher demonstrations. McWilliam (1996) makes the case that "the body of the teacher needs to be remembered in writing about teaching and learning, because it produces desire in pedagogical events, for good as well as ill" (p. 367). She contends that it is important to understand the desire to teach and learn as embodied, that is "residing in the materiality of students and teachers, not simply in their minds". Some interesting work relating to these ideas is contained in the edited collection *Taught Bodies* (O'Farrell *et al.*, 2000).

McWilliam (1996) is interested in "re-configuring a model of pedagogical instruction that engages quite specifically with materiality of classrooms and bodies" (p. 373). Since we know that their own bodies are central to the teaching of many physical educators (see for example Sparkes, 1999), I wonder what this re-configuring might look like in the PE context. Thinking about the role of the PE teacher's body in enacting demonstrations (e.g. of skilled movements), McWilliam's (1996) words are informative:

> In performing knowledge acts for the student gaze [for example a demonstration of a particular movement skill], we ought to be able to acknowledge what Deutscher (1994, p. 36) calls 'the elating sensation of a physical carnation of one's body as a teacher ... the overt pleasure produced by the possibility of one's own performance as empowered subject knowledge, the seductive effect of instantaneity between teaching and learning body' (p. 310).

What might this desire to perform mean for teacher receptivity to less teacher centred pedagogies? What messages are conveyed in teacher demonstrations? What messages about the body? What pedagogical work for reproducing the cult of the body is done in such demonstrations? Andrew Sparkes' (2004) account of his heartfelt frustrations when injury prevented him from receiving the "confirmation of self" he had usually received from physically demonstrating to his PE class is illustrative of both the potentially affirming properties of the student gaze and also of the commonly held belief that teacher demonstrations are an essential part of effective PE teaching: "No gasps. No confirmation of me. Good PE teachers 'do' it. Show don't tell. Shit! Where does that leave me? Time to go" (p. 165). Physicality, manifest as a bodily instantiation of competence, is part of the embodied identity of many (most) PE teachers. But not all teachers do demonstrations.

Bodily lessons

At this point I want to relate a story that I wrote about a student teaching experience that I endured back in the late 1960s. The story, while true, is about non-demonstration and represents something of a caricature of the PE teacher, reinforcing those negative images/memories that have been so damaging to PE. Of course there are good stories out there that might have been more applicable and that have a more positive message, but this one has a special place in my memory bank. The scene is the swimming pool of a wealthy, elite private school.

As soon as they were changed into their bathers (swimmers, togs) the boys moved rather sheepishly into the gym and stood shivering beside the pool awaiting their instructions (yes, the school had a gym and its own indoor pool!). Year 8 boys of all shapes, sizes, and sexual development were displayed immodestly in all their fleshiness by the brevity of their swimming uniform. (Years later I think of Billy Connolly's story of swimming at Aberdeen in the Scottish summer).

I sat at the poolside with my university folder ready and prepared to take notes while observing the head PE teacher "take a swimming lesson". As a first-year student teacher I was eager to learn about "how one taught". Although the specifics of the "lesson" have faded from memory over the years, I still vividly remember the "essence" of this pedagogical act.

Still shivering (although it was an indoor pool) the boys lined up on the command from Bill (a pseudonym, just in case he is still alive). A brief roll call was my responsibility and when all were checked and present Bill proceeded with "the lesson". He lined all the boys up behind the one-metre diving board and announced the task: "I want you to do a forward somersault off the board and I'm looking for any talents that you might have for diving." Although I intuitively realized it at the time, years later I would recognize this task as one of considerable risk, uncertainty and ambiguity (see Doyle, 1972).

That being the extent of the "instruction" the first boy shuffled along to the end of the board and, after considerable hesitation and some words of "encouragement" from Bill, he launched himself into the air in the vain hope that gravity would be kind and deliver him gently onto the water. It is unclear as to what mental picture the boy had of a forward somersault but his performance was more in the racing dive (belly whacker) category than the somersault category. Shocked and stinging from the ungainly entry, the boy swam to the side as Bill advised the rest of the class that "you have got to turn over in the air".

There followed a procession of boys launching themselves in lemming-like fashion from the end of the board in attempt to approximate a forward somersault. Naturally the first boy to actually rotate all the way over to his feet was presented to the class as a model by Bill: "Beaudy, Mark ... I hope you all saw what he did." For those boys who were huddled nervously half way down the line it was difficult to see exactly what was happening at the end of the board so the "demonstration" was lost.

As the boys landed on the water in various ungainly and painful positions Bill responded with raucous laughter. The odd boy who achieved something like a reasonable entry on completion of a somersault was duly congratulated by Bill as he made his (short) list of prospects for the school diving team.

I remember sitting watching this spectacle wondering if this really was

PE and thinking that parents were paying big money for the privilege of having their boys so treated!

What pedagogical work might have been done in this lesson? Of course it is hard to predict all the unintended pedagogical work but these are some of the features of this lesson that might have been problematic:

- The public display of their bodies on the diving board and their skill or lack of it was clearly embarrassing for many of boys.
- Given his raucous laughter it was evident that the teacher clearly received (and displayed) pleasure at the pain and discomfort of some of the boys in the class.
- The subject matter of the "lesson"was scary, dangerous and given scant recognition by the teacher.
- There was clearly no student responsibility (except for their own performance) and no negotiation of the activity.
- Since in the entire lesson each boy only got to have three "goes" at the activity there was little opportunity for the boys to practise the skill. Of course this might have been a blessing for most of the boys.
- The teacher gave the boys no mental picture of the dive to work from. This could have been facilitated by a teacher demonstration, demonstration by a student who could do the activity, by means of diagrams, film loops etc.

It seems reasonable to assume that for some boys, perhaps many, their experiences in the lesson might have left them sympathetic to the view that "PE is one of life's great levellers, a uniquely ruthless aspect of school experience which shapes us all and leaves its traces in unexpected and lingering ways" (Publisher's note, Dust cover, Myerson, 2005).

Certainly, this "lesson" has all the hallmarks of what Juan-Miguel Fernandez-Balboa (1999) has specifically called poisonous pedagogy in relation to some PE practices. The term poisonous pedagogy was first coined by psychoanalyst Alice Miller (1987) to refer to the negative parenting practices passed down from generation to generation that do damage to successive generations. In the context of student teaching, I was the next generation of teacher that was supposed to learn from Bill. But certainly the boys in the class would also be the "beneficiaries" of the poisonous pedagogical work resulting from the diving "lesson".

On a more positive note, over the past 20 years or so there has been considerable analysis of the ways in which certain PE pedagogical practices actually have poisonous consequences for some young people. Pat Dodds' (1993) analysis of the pedagogical practices that perpetuate the "ugly isms" typical in many PE lessons in the USA schooling system provides an early example of the poisonous pedagogies that relate to body knowledge and PE.

Scholars who have contributed to the identification or naming of poisonous pedagogies within PE and who have invested in doing academic work toward social justice most often locate their theoretical position under the "big tent" (Lather, 1988) of critical pedagogy. Critical pedagogy scholars have been extremely important in the process of exposing inequities and inequalities related to PE and health in schools. We know a good deal about how miseducative PE can be. However, while these scholars (myself included) have been successful in their critique, by and large critical pedagogues have been short on offering alternative practices (see O'Sullivan *et al.*, 1992). Moreover, as we saw in Chapter 6, the success of critical pedagogies in helping emancipate young people from the tyranny of the cult of the body has been far from successful (see Tinning and Glasby, 2002).

The physically literate and competent body

Some time ago Brian Nettleton (1976) argued that physical competence should be an educational objective. Apart from within the debate over the characteristics of the physically educated individual (see Siedentop, 1994; Tinning, 2000), the idea of physical competence was never really picked up by physical educators in arguing the case for their particular contribution to education. Thirty years later it again joins the discussion as a dimension of Whitehead's (2001) physical literacy.

The notion of competencies has received a good deal of criticism in educational discourse (see for example Collins, 1993; Schwarz and Cavener, 1994; Smyth and Dow, 1998), much of it is well deserved. But Nettleton's (1976) conception of physical competence was not a simplistic one, such as the ability to perform a certain movement task. In discussing physical competence he suggested that students should have the opportunity to develop their individual feeling of self-worth through building an acceptable image of the performing self. For Nettleton, good PE programs should involve intense experiences, improvement of performance, and participation in intimate, small groups with opportunity for autonomy and independence. They should provide the opportunity for students to experience joy in movement and to develop social relations. One could imagine that such programs could just as easily be built around skateboarding as they could around the game of soccer.

The competent physical-self (Nettleton, 1976) in large part depends on developing certain physical competencies that are valued by the young people themselves. In thinking about physical competence we need to ask what particular competencies are needed for participation in the movement culture and if there are any that should be considered essential learning for all kids as part of their developing physical literacies. As we saw in Chapter 4, some physical educators consider that there are, for example, certain fundamental motor skills that should be developed through primary school PE (see for example Walkley *et al.*, 1993). And, while there might be many secondary PE teachers who lament the situation that some students come to them from primary schools without having developed what they consider to be the necessary physical competencies (e.g. to throw and catch), the development of physical competence is not the sole responsibility of the primary school.

Physical competence in the way I am conceiving it is even broader than Nettleton's offering. It also includes the ability to use the body in a physical sense. For the moment I won't open the can of worms regarding the philosophical argument regarding mind/body dualism represented in claiming a "physical" sense. Take for example, being able to do a chin up, to climb a rope, to competently be able to traverse a monkey bar, to move with rhythm, or to know, through experience, the limits of one's physical endurance. These are also aspects of physical competence and all represent valued capital in certain contexts.

Physical competence as capital

When physical competence is valued by a particular group of people, developing self-worth is a by-product of that developing physical competence. That value is attached to certain displays of physical competence is a cultural fact. Horse riding in Mongolia might be different in form from hip hop dance in California but for many young people each represents considerable "street cred" amongst their particular peer group or cultural tradition. We can think of this value attached to physical competence as capital (Bourdieu, 1991) in the sense that it represents a "tradable resource". The capacity to perform certain physical activities may afford an individual a certain creditability, peer respect or status in a particular sub-culture (e.g. with other young kids in school or the neighbourhood). For example, skateboarding competence may serve as capital for some kids in a certain part of town but across town where tennis or rugby are highly valued it has little exchange value. Physical competence therefore has capital in particular circumstances with particular young people. It is worth considering this fact when we develop school PE curricula.

Shilling (1993) introduced the term *physical capital* which has specific relevance to PE. He argues that in modern societies the body has become a source of physical capital that has considerable exchange value beyond that associated with the capacity to do physical work. So, in addition to the capacity (capability) to perform certain physical skills (e.g. throw and catch) we can also think about the appearance of the body as a dimension of physical capital. Particular bodies (e.g. six-pack abs) are valued more than others. I remember being in the gym at the Aarhus University in Denmark when a small group of young men entered the gym. What amazed me was that while I pedalled the exercise bike for 20 minutes and then worked through my modest regime of exercises (another 30 minutes), these students worked through a series of ab crunches, sit-ups, all solely focused on their abs! How they walked the next day I don't know but it seemed to me that this was a powerful testimony to the physical capital ascribed to the look, rather than the function, of six-pack abdominals.

For some young people the physical capital they acquire in demonstrating certain physical competence, and/or in displaying a certain body shape, is vital to their developing sense of self (see Wright and Burrows, 2006). Of course, as discussed in Chapter 6, in the pursuit of certain physical capital there are often problems associated with pedagogical work that reinforces the cult of the body. Some insightful and generative work has already been done in PE with respect to Bourdieu's notion of capital (see Hunter, 2004; Brown, 2005; Hay and lisahunter, 2006).

Significantly, one of the places where young people can acquire some of the physical competence that can bring them physical capital is within school PE. In different words this is the essence of Nettleton's (1976) argument and, accordingly, it is worth thinking about the significance of physical competence as an educational objective. It is also worth considering the folly of assuming that acquiring physical competence is equally significant for all young people. For example, boys who self-define as "Emos" are unlikely to be attracted to the physicality of PE. Stereotypically presented in the media as being hard-core punk, emotional, sensitive, and angst-ridden, Emos purposely stay thin and weak as a cultural statement against hegemonic masculinity.

The bodily pedagogical encounter

In making his case for the development of the competent physical-self, Nettleton (1976) suggests that emphasis should be placed on how PE teachers go about their work rather than on what they teach. In thinking of the diving "lesson" described above it is easy to see how that it is the attitude, awareness and sensitivity (or lack of) of the teacher to the needs and interests of their heterogeneous students that is more important than the activity itself. As always, it is the *pedagogical encounter* between the learner, the subject matter and the teacher (Lusted, 1986) that is significant in influencing the sort of experience, and the sort of learning that takes place.

Within this pedagogical encounter what seems axiomatic in regard to good teaching is the desire of the teacher to *connect with* young people in and through their experiences in movement (Azzarito and Ennis, 2003). But what does "connect with" really mean? We know for example, that the skills-drills approach to developing physical competence that has characterized much of our pedagogical practice in PE does not work for many young people. In the contemporary postmodern context pleasure is increasingly a key factor in young people's leisure choices and is a key issue in their experience of school (see Hay and lisahunter, 2006). They seek pleasure and are increasingly demanding relevance.

While being careful not to slip into the trap that games and sports are reinforcing for all young people (remember Myerson's (2005) *Not a Games Player*), it is true that we do have the pedagogical possibilities to connect with what many young people regard as enjoyable and pleasurable. We now know about the importance of situated learning (Kirk and Macdonald, 1998) in PE and sport and have seen how innovations like sport education (Siedentop, 1994), TGfU (Werner *et al.*, 1996) and Game Sense (O'Connor, 2006) can develop certain physical literacies while engaging learners in meaningful and enjoyable ways.

In all of these innovations, understanding something of the meaning young people attribute to their bodies and the place of physicality in their lives seems important. In this regard it is also important that PE teachers understand that all pedagogical encounters in physical activity are at their core, bodily encounters. The pedagogical work of PE will always have an embodied dimension and that will often be the most significant thing that young people take from PE.

Part IV

Pedagogy for health

8 HMS and discourses on health

Health, physical activity and public policy

There is now a substantial body of evidence to demonstrate that regular physical activity improves and sustains good health (Hardman and Stensel 2003; Paffenbarger *et al.*, 1983; Paffenbarger *et al.*, 1986) and that the increasingly sedentary lifestyles of urban dwellers in developed countries is contributing significantly to the burden of ill-health (Powell and Blair, 1994; Hardman, 2001).

In response to the decline of physical activity in these societies, a model based on biomedical discourse has emerged that transforms human physical inactivity into a risk factor that, if allowed to persist, will inevitably expose individuals to the possible loss of functional capacity and increase their morbidity and mortality. The physiological and epidemiological research upon which this model is based has attempted to understand the forces that influence physical activity in order "to provide information that will allow us to intervene more effectively" (Sallis and Owen, 1999, p. 110).

The results of this line of inquiry have shown that it is plausible that inactive childhood lifestyles that persist into adulthood may be one of the factors that have contributed to the development of numerous contemporary diseases (Armstrong *et al.*, 1996). Consequently, paediatric exercise science is now recognized as an important area that investigates the implementation of strategies to reduce risk by increasing health related physical activity. There is now a specific journal devoted to such research, the *Journal of Paediatric Exercise Science*. Understandably, schools are considered to be the appropriate institution to educate future active healthy citizens (Tinning and Glasby, 2003) since school PE programs are mandatory for most children and in such programs they are involved at some level in regular physical activity (Sallis and McKenzie, 1991).

In order to accomplish increased levels of activity for school aged children, biomedical knowledge has been re-contextualized into a pedagogical construction (Bernstein, 1996; see Chapter 9 in this volume for elaboration of this concept) to provide a theoretical basis for the transformation of school PE. This knowledge is derived from "biological, behavioural and health sciences ... which now constitute largely taken for granted 'regimes of truth among teachers'" (Evans and Davies, 2004, p. 4). Unfortunately, proponents of this biomedical approach including researchers, epidemiologists, health professionals and policy makers have so far been unable to achieve a consensus for prescribing appropriate amounts of physical activity or a way of incorporating such health related physical activity into PE programs on a scale that will impact on the targeted youth populations (Johns, 2005).

Johns (2005) argues that the biomedical model that has been re-contextualized in HMS/HPE pedagogy establishes a hegemonic discourse as official policy that "valorizes its own claims and has the effect of marginal-izing other discourses and in doing so creates its own barriers to successful implementation" (p. 71). He also suggests that there is difficulty in establishing "useful prescriptive guidelines for teachers when individual responses to physical activity are dependent on individual hereditary and developmental factors that make it difficult to construct a guideline that will be useful for all students" (ibid.). Lastly he claims that the biomedical model is "extolled as a moral imperative" that in turn "reduces the chances of capturing the interests or meeting the needs of modern youth" (ibid.).

Notwithstanding these reservations, in Australia, the National Guidelines for Physical Activity recommend that children engage in at least 60 minutes of moderate to vigorous physical activity (MVPA) per day (DHAC, 2004). The recent *Healthy Kids Queensland Survey* (Abbott *et al.*, 2007), consistent with findings worldwide, highlighted that a significant proportion of children and young people in Queensland was failing to meet these recommendations. With this in mind, and the knowledge of the importance of physical activity for overall health and wellbeing, Education Queensland recently announced their *Smart Moves* program (EQ, 2007). This initiative directs primary schools to allocate 30 minutes of curriculum time per day to moderate physical activity and also to increase the use of "incidental" physical activity across the curriculum.

At the time of writing this chapter there was an example in the news of a Queensland School caught between competing discourses and school policies. Belgian Gardens State School in Townsville, as a response to a heightened concern over possible risks involved in the playground, banned the performance of cartwheels in the school grounds. The press and the public were quick to point out the irony of this act in the context of the *2008: Year of Physical Activity* celebration by the Queensland Government that was all about encouraging more incidental and formal physical activity in schools.

The not-so-new mission of HMS

Over the past two decades, the field of HMS/kinesiology has progressively aligned itself more closely with "epidemiological and biomedical research [about health] to legitimate its research agenda [and] its presence in the curriculum and pedagogical practices" (Gard and Wright, 2001). This transition has served to privilege modern experts in exercise science and has had the effect of constraining alternative views and discursive practices that influence physical activity. Increasingly, as new policies regarding physical activity and health are "rolled out" by government authorities it becomes harder to sustain a debate over the "truth" claims on which the policies are based.

Currently I work in the School of Human Movement Studies at the University of Queensland (UQ). The School began as a Department of Physical Education located in the Faculty of Education in 1941. The Department remained as part of the Education Faculty until the 1990s when, in recognition of its increasingly science based orientation, it moved into the Faculty of Biological and Chemical Science (BACS). The funding level per student was better in BACS than in Education. By the end of that decade it was apparent that HMS had a better "fit" with the mission and orientation of the Faculty of Health Science than BACS and another move was initiated. I arrived at UQ in 2000, and the first year of HMS was located in Health Science. Below is a sample of some of the publications that have come from HMS since its location in Health Science. They provide testimony to the increasingly central focus on health within the School of HMS.

- Hay, P. (2006). Pursuing HPE outcomes through physical education. In R. Tinning, L. McCuaig, and lisahunter (Eds.), *Teaching Health and Physical Education in Australian Schools* (pp. 159–164). Frenchs Forest: Pearson Education Australia.
- Austen, S., Fassett, R., Geraghty, D.P., and Coombes, J.S. (2006). Folate supplementation fails to affect vascular function and carotid artery intima media thickness in cyclosporin A-treated renal transplant recipients. *Clinical Nephrology*, 66(5), 373–379.
- Brown, W.J. (2006). Individual or population approaches to the promotion of physical activity ... is that the question? *Journal of Science and Medicine in Sport*, 9(1–2), 35–37.
- Brown, W.J., Mummery, K., Eakin, E., and Schofield, G. (2006). 10,000 Steps Rockhampton: Evaluation of a whole community approach to improving population levels of physical activity. *Journal of Physical Activity and Health*, 3, 1–14.
- Galvão, D.A., Nosaka, K., Taaffe, D.R., Spry, N., Kristjanson, L., McGuigan, M.R., Suzuki, K., Yamaya, K., and Newton, R.U. (2006). Resistance training and reduction of treatment side effects in prostate cancer patients. *Medicine and Science in Sports and Exercise*, 38(12), 2045–2052.
- Heesch, K.C., Masse, L.C., and Dunn, A.L. (2006). Using Rasch modeling to re-evaluate three scales related to physical activity: Enjoyment, perceived benefits and perceived barriers. *Health Education Research: Theory and Practice*, 21(S1), i58–i72.
- Johns, D.P., and Tinning, R.I. (2006). Risk reduction: Recontexualizing health as a physical education curriculum. *Quest*, 58(4), 395–409.
- Wright, J., O'Flynn, G., and Macdonald, D. (2006). Being fit and looking

healthy: Young women's and men's constructions of health and fitness. *Sex Roles*, 54, 707–716.

Some current government funded research grants with the School of HMS include:

- A randomized control trial to compare the efficacy of a home based and "centre" based resistance training program in terms of outcomes relating to functional status and health in older Australians.
- Assessment of physical activity patterns and arthritis management strategies among men and women with evaluation of government agency initiatives under the Eat Well Be Active: Healthy Kids for Life Action Plan 2005–2008.
- Understanding and influencing physical activity to improve population health.

This brief story is one of many played out around the world as the field of HMS responds to changing contexts, both politically and institutionally. What is implicit in this shift of "home faculty" is a perspective on the mission of HMS. In the case of UQ, the current explicit mission is "to promote health and wellbeing, and optimal physical performance, of individuals and populations of all ages" (HMS Research Report for 2006–2007).

We can also see an increased focus on health in the course offerings at both undergraduate and postgraduate levels:

HPRM1000 Physical Activity & Health
HPRM3000 Health Promotion: Perspectives & Practice
EDUC3009 Educating for Better Health
HMST3362 Exercise Prescription & Programming
HMST3052 Sports Medicine of Physical Activity
HMST3740 Exercise Prescription & Programming for Musculoskeletal & Neurological Conditions
HMST3741 Exercise Prescription & Programming for Ageing, Metabolic Disease & Cancer
HMST3742 Exercise Prescription & Programming for Cardiorespiratory Disease
HMST3617 Ergonomics in Occupational Health & Safety

So, HMS is explicitly about producing and reproducing knowledge related to physical activity, the body and health. The purpose of this section is not to debate whether such a mission is appropriate or not. Rather this section focuses specifically on the pedagogies HMS employs for health. In doing so it needs to be reiterated that pedagogical work for health is also done when the focus of pedagogy is on bodies and/or on physical activity.

Historically of course, our field has always been focused on developing healthy bodies (now healthy citizens). As Roberta Park describes in her engaging chapter "For pleasure? Or profit or personal health? College gymnasia as contested terrain" (2004, in Vertinsky and Bale, 2004), in the late nineteenth and early twentieth century "physical education was a topic of interest to an impressive number of educators, social reformers and medical doctors" (p. 181). As a consequence of this interest the University of California at Berkeley established a Department of Physical Culture in 1888, and in 1879 Dudley Sargent MD was appointed as the Director of the new Hemenway Gymnasium at Harvard. The explicit purpose of these initiatives was to improve the health of their undergraduate men.

Hal Lawson (1993) presents an excellent analysis of the origins of PE (aka the field of HMS/kinesiology) as a serving profession in the USA and in particular the part that Dudley Sargent played in this history. In his analysis Lawson claims that Sargent and many of his contemporaries in the late nineteenth century believed that "ordinary people were inherently weak and feeble, needing to be protected from their own folly and rashness" (p. 3). These early human movement professionals were worried (and rightly so) about the ill-health caused by industrialization and the consequential lifestyle of ordinary people (read "the poor working class") and they advocated, with evangelist zeal, "exercise programs aimed at restoring and maintaining the bodily health of the masses" (ibid.).

Lawson goes on to tell us that "Sargent, like so many others in our field, believed that without compulsion and regulation, persons needing these [exercises] the most would not experience them." Moreover, Sargent believed that "Without professional regulation, the health, lifestyles, and lives of ordinary people will be adversely affected" (p. 4). This *circa* 1900 discourse about health and lifestyle sounds very similar to the discourses that dominate our field in this shallow end of the twenty-first century (apologies to Chris Bigum). There is, however, an important difference between the techniques employed to govern around 1900 and those of today, as I will discuss below. But first it is necessary to outline something of the contemporary context in which HMS "plies its trade".

To understand something of the contemporary social context it is useful to have some grasp of certain theoretical concepts that allow us to see behind the obvious. I am talking here about providing an orientation to thinking about the circumstances in which contemporary HMS is practised. This orientation is underpinned by what Giddens (1993) called the sociological imagination which "necessitates, above all, being able to 'think ourselves away' from the familiar routines of our daily lives in order to look at them anew" (p. 18).

Knowledge about health and healthy living

How, what and where do HMS professionals acquire knowledge about health and healthy living? Certainly health is fundamentally connected to the body and, as we have seen in Chapter 6, knowledge about the body is central to the curriculum of all undergraduate HMS programs. In this chapter my intention is to provide a broader context for how we come to know about health. This will entail providing some theoretical frames that enable us to get a sense of why particular versions of health are dominant and taken for granted, and why now.

"Risk society" and the "new public health"

The field of HMS is intimately connected to the notion of healthy lifestyle. Indeed, it is an orienting concept embedded in the mission statement quoted above. Importantly, central to contemporary conceptions of healthy lifestyle is the notion of "risk society" as conceptualized by the German social theorist Ulrich Beck and British sociologist Anthony Giddens. In *Risk Society*, Beck (1992) suggests that there is a sense that in the last half of the twentieth century [and now in the beginning of the new millennium], "we are eye witnesses to a break within modernity, which is freeing itself from the contours of the classical industrial society and forging a new form – the (industrial) 'risk society'" (p. 9). These processes signal a "demystification" of the roles and functions of "science and technology in classical industrial society" (ibid.) and the creation of doubt and uncertainty in the domains of "work, leisure, the family and sexuality" (p. 10).

Giddens (1991) argues that the conditions of "radicalised modernity" are marked by processes in which claims to certainty in knowledge production – the very bedrock of Enlightenment thinking – become intensely problematic. Further, the intensification and globalization of reflexively produced knowledge, results in a "runaway world" of "dislocation" and "uncertainty" (p. 3). For Giddens, human existence is not necessarily more risky under contemporary social conditions, but rather, the origins of risk and uncertainty have changed. He argues that "manufactured risk is the result *of* human intervention into the conditions of social life and into nature" (p. 4; emphasis in original). Moreover, "what was supposed to create greater certainty – the advance of human knowledge and 'controlled intervention' into society and nature – is actually deeply involved with this unpredictability" (p. 3).

The uncertainties and opportunities that are a consequence of the advance of *manufactured uncertainty* are largely new and the human body itself has become a repository for the expression of these uncertainties and opportunities. For example, biochemistry, genetics and scientific "truths" about exercise and diet in effect are taken "on-board" in an embodied way and reinforce a need for intensified self-management and regulation of the body. In this context individuals are having to constantly revise their lifestyle activities in light of these new knowledges and accordingly the body is reconfigured as, for example, the "fit body", "beautiful body" or the "healthy body".

In "connecting the dots" (Klein, 2001) between *risk society* and the discourses of health, fitness and the body, we can see that fitness is widely promoted as an opportunity to avert several of the risks to selfhood present in modern society. This requires that individuals constantly monitor their body practices such as diet, sleep and consumption of such unhealthy products as tobacco, alcohol and fast foods (Petersen and Bunton, 1997). However, given the central importance of physical appearance in our culture, such monitoring, which is central to health promotion, "feeds into and reinforces the 'cult of the body'" (Petersen and Bunton, 1997, p. 200).

In their introduction to their book *The New Public Health: Health and Self in the Age of Risk*, Petersen and Lupton (1996) note that the focus of public health has shifted from the control of filth, odour and contagion generated when the growth of nineteenth-century cities outpaced adequate infrastructure such as water and sanitation to the social and personal factors of risk that have arisen from changing lifestyles.

This new perspective they term the "new public health" and it coincides with how modern societies are increasingly characterized by responses to the potential hazards of "risk society" and how these are managed (Beck, 1992a, 1992b). In some sense it is possible to consider Dudley Sargent's concern over the lifestyle practices of "ordinary people" in early twentieth-century industrial America to be an early example of the spirit of the new public health.

Since the early 1990s, the new public health discourse has generated a new sub-discipline in HMS. Exercise scientists and epidemiologists specializing in health related physical activity as a form of health promotion at the population level have now coalesced in the sub-discipline of "physical activity and health". Underpinning this new sub-discipline is the belief that physical activity "should be the cornerstone of contemporary public health" (Bouchard 2001, p. 347).

While the benefits of physical activity are a central message of the new public health, precisely how much more activity is required to offset the risk of disease is currently being debated among researchers and no exact prescription has yet been provided (Bouchard and Blair, 2001; Bouchard, 2001). The only agreement that has been reached among the experts is that physical activity *should* be promoted among the young as part of a new public health agenda (Johns and Tinning, 2006).

However, health pronouncements are concerned with more than just physical activity. We are also cautioned to "Lose weight!"; "Avoid fat!"; "Stop smoking!"; "Reduce alcohol intake!"; "Get fit!"; and "Practise safe sex!" and these representative public health messages have created the conditions in which the health status and vulnerability of the body have become central themes of existence in contemporary Western society (Petersen and Lupton, 1996). According to Petersen and Lupton (1996),

> Everyone is being called upon to play their part in creating a 'healthier', more 'ecologically sustainable' environment through attentions to 'lifestyle' and involvement in various collective and collaborative endeavours. All these concerns, expectations and projects come together in, and

are articulated through, an area of expert knowledge and action that has come to be known as 'the new public health' (p. ix).

As Howell and Ingham (2001) argue "More and more, public issues became defined as personal troubles and problems of lifestyles. Self-discipline was the means to the good life in all of its connotations" (p. 331). Moreover, since the new public health involves prescriptions about *how* we should live our lives individually and collectively there is a moral agenda at work here (Petersen and Lupton, 1996). In the rush to create healthy citizens who can participate in the "good life", moral questions relating to conceptions of the "good life" and the nature of a good society are frequently ignored or reduced to technical issues stripped of their moral values.

Interestingly, Gard and Wright (2001) argue that in the context of the so-called obesity crisis of the early twenty-first century, many scientists slip from their empirical evidence into a moralizing discourse which frequently places the blame on individuals for their poor lifestyle choices.

Moral values are socially constructed and vary across different cultures and different historical periods. For example, according to the Danes Hansen and Kayser-Nielsen (2000), in the eighteenth-century views of health were linked to virtue and respectability:

> The category of health was above all a category of morals which determined the 'right way to live' in the broadest sense of the expression. This meant that the clergy and philosophers alike influenced to a great extent the debate on health and were viewed as experts in this field (Hansen and Kayser-Nielsen, 2000, pp. 21–22).

Contrast this with the situation in the nineteenth century where "the fear of living an unhealthy life" and "The question of health or lack of it is now concentrated wholly on the body whereas previously the question of health was only concerned with matters outside the sphere of the body" (p. 22). Moreover, "the relationship between the view that was held of the body and medicine in general during 'The Modern Advance' is to a great extent influenced by an intermediate link between medicine and the common body culture, the link, to be more precise, being physical education" (p. 21). This identification of PE as the link between medicine and body culture, takes us back again to the work of the Department of Physical Culture at Berkeley and Dudley Sargent at the Hemenway Gymnasium at the turn of the twentieth century.

Discussion of lifestyle in the new public health is unlikely to engage with ethical arguments such as Peter Singer's (1993) *How Are We To Live?* Rather, the "good life" is seen as an instantiation of a particular lifestyle that is increasingly a manifestation of late capitalism (Howell and Ingham, 2001). But lifestyle is not a term that has become popular simply because it represents a particular conception of health risks and avoidance practices.

Lifestyle has become inextricably linked with consumerist culture. Indeed, "The language of lifestyle has been fuelled by a do-it-yourself consumerist health economy, and its heavy advertising campaigns have educated the public in ways that no government agency could have" (Howell and Ingham, 2001, p. 342).

While admonishments, pronouncements and even "rational" discourse about how we should live our lives are part of the governmental process (see below), individuals soon recognize that "choosing" a "healthy" lifestyle is not as easy as it might seem. Nor is it appropriate for some populations, given the particular Western/Eurocentric conceptualization of a healthy lifestyle that underpins the new public health discourse (see Macdonald *et al.*, 2008).

Governmentality, bio-power and bio-pedagogies

Returning to Lawson's discussion of Dudley Sargent again, the essence of Lawson's argument is that, at least in the early twentieth century, the human service professions like PE set out to regulate the lives of people in their own best interests. There was a mix of paternalism, evangelicalism and arrogance at work here. It was (and is) experts (professionals) who "know" what's best for people and also they alone who can provide the right cure. As Lawson tells us, the idea of regulating the lifestyles of others with systematic physical exercises or with advocacies such as "Physical education and sport for all" cannot be considered in isolation from the larger pattern of regulation by a host of other human service professions.

With the advent of the Industrial Revolution and the mass migration of "unruly populations" to the new industrial cities in Europe, new problems arose as attempts were made "to tame and govern the undesirable consequences of industrial life, wage labour and urban existence"(Rose, 1993). Accordingly, the governing of individuals, families, markets and populations became increasingly problematic.

Governmentality is a theoretical frame (Rose, 1990) that comes from the work of Michel Foucault and offers a generative way of analyzing what he termed "the conduct of conduct". Governmentality is useful in helping us understand pedagogies for the making of healthy citizens. Foucault considered government to be all the deliberate "endeavours to shape, guide, direct the conduct of others" and includes those strategies where one is "urged and educated to bridle one's own passions, to control one's own instincts, to govern oneself" (Rose, 1999, p. 3). Indeed McCuaig (2008), taking the lead from Rose (1996) and Lupton (1995), claims that public health regulation provides an exemplary paradigm of the deployment of governmental strategies that seek to shape the conduct of individuals and collectives.

Bio-power and bio-pedagogies

Governmental technologies are essentially pedagogical devices that are employed in the process of governing. In this context Foucault's notion of *bio-power* is a particularly useful concept to help understand pedagogies of the body and of health. Bio-power as a concept specifically captures the intersections between the life and health of a nation's citizenry and the governmental strategies endeavouring to maximize them (McCuaig, 2008). As McNay (1994, p. 116) explains,

> biopower focuses on the individual human body as a machine and tries to extort from it greater efficiency, productivity and economy of movement. On the other hand biopower takes as its target the biological processes of the collective social body by attempting to increase life expectancy, birth-rate, levels of health.

Valerie Harwood, in *Biopolitics and the 'Obesity Epidemic': Governing Bodies* (2008), provides a useful account of the connection between pedagogy and bio-power as embedded in the concept of bio-pedagogies. She claims that

> Across a range of contemporary contexts are instructions on *bios*: how to live, how to eat, how much to eat, how to move, how much to move, how to look. We are told what to eat, what to do, what to avoid. In short, an extensive pedagogy is aimed at us, a pedagogy of *bios*, or what can be termed 'biopedagogy'. In Greek *bios* refers to life, yet as a biopolitical concern, this takes on new meanings and implications. When we are told messages about what or what not to eat, we are experiencing biopedagogy, a biopedagogy premised on a conflation between *bios* and health that has far more at stake than simply 'being well'. Following Michel Foucault's work on biopower, *bios* is a concern of the state: *bios* is biopolitical.

It is this notion of bio-power that has particular relevance to an analysis of the pedagogies of health in the field of HMS. Indeed, bio-pedagogies are about both health and the body simultaneously. Importantly, pedagogies of the body and of health are often used as governmental technologies to serve the particular interests of the state. The pedagogies employed by HM professional prototypes such as Dudley Sargent at the beginning of the 1900s in an attempt to *regulate* the lives of people in their own best interests were a form of governmentality. These pedagogies were, however, rather ponderous and heavy-handed and over the past century there have been shifts in the forms of governance away from the heavy arm of the state to self-regulation that is facilitated through the pedagogical work done by a range of private and government agencies. Modern political rule has gradually become conceptualized as a matter of acting upon the conduct of individuals and populations "in order to increase their good order, their security, their tranquillity, their prosperity, health and happiness" (Rose, 1999, p. 6).

One of the ways in which our profession attempts to regulate lives is through the state institutions of mass schooling. Schools are a significant site for PE in this regard. Kirk and Spiller's (1993) social history of the development of PE in schools in the Australian state of Victoria from the beginning of the last century to the 1950s is informative in relation to PE's contribution to the regulated life of school children. They show clearly how there were various influences on the exercise curriculum which, in most explicit ways, were intent on regulating the lives of school children for their own best interests. The influence of Swedish gymnastics and then military drill were the most obvious.

Sometime late in the 1970s Australian school children were given a "daily dose" of PE as a means of regulating their bodily activity for health oriented purposes (see Chapter 10). The particular governmental technology employed in this bio-pedagogical work was the 1973 Daily Physical Education program (DPE) and it represented a form of face-to-face preventative medicine intended to "make" healthy future citizens. Thirty years on and the Key Learning Area (KLA) of Health and Physical Education in Australia, and a similar curriculum manifesto in New Zealand, does its governance not through prescription (as did the DPE program) but rather by means of articulating certain key learning outcomes that do pedagogical work designed to create *self-regulating* healthy citizens.

The pedagogies of contemporary HPE are intended to help young people identify risks to healthy living (their own and that of others), and to make rational decisions with respect to participating in some activities (e.g. sport) and avoidance of others (e.g. taking drugs).

Bio-pedagogies of other players

In recognizing that any functioning coherent society requires some regulation, we can easily understand how schools play a vital role in the construction of a regulated life. Certainly most societies tell their youth what's good for them and attempt to regulate their lives accordingly. That is one reason why adolescence is such a frustrating time. But what happens when people leave the institutional controls of school? How does the state continue its influence on a regulated life? Well, it's rather complicated but it does get significant help. More and more we are seeing a shift of influence from schools to more general cultural forms, in particular mass culture. It is here that the connections between school PE and the field of human movement become very significant.

According to Kirk (1993) many of the institutional forms of control and discipline that characterized life in the early 1900s have been replaced by individualized forms. We now act as our own police in certain matters of control and discipline. The care of the body is one such example. No one forces me to go to the gym or ride my bike to work. I am influenced, often in ways that I don't always fully understand or recognize, by the discourses relating to physical activity as an important part of a "healthy" lifestyle, and by the discourses on the body as an icon portraying desirability and attractiveness. I also happen to find such activity pleasurable and recognize its non-physical contributions to reducing anxiety and stress, and generally helping me to better balance my emotional life.

Thus we can consider that diverse agencies such as the school, the family, the mass media, parliament, the legislature and the police force, as well as less obvious agencies such as the Anti-Cancer Council and the National Heart Foundation, all set out to regulate people's lives in certain ways.

These governmental agencies use a vast array of regulating "devices" or technologies of governance. Some examples of these technologies are rather obvious, for example road rules, traffic lights and mobile breath testing units regulate the behaviour of motorists; curriculum documents, ministerial policies, and the size and shape of classrooms regulate teaching behaviours. Some are less obvious. For example, daily newspapers and television news perform governmental work by informing us of potential risks (e.g. traffic accidents, a fall in the Dow Jones or Nikkei indices, or even just the Bureau of Meteorology predicting a storm approaching). Specifically related to the regulation of bodies in "risk society" we can recognize governmental technologies such as the HPE syllabus, the Ottawa Charter, the health promoting school, healthy food charts, national fitness norms, and the Body Mass Index (BMI) as some of the technologies of the new public health.

Many of the preferred bodily practices that are intended as outcomes for HPE relate to abstinence, or at least moderation, in the consumption of certain foods. However, most of the highly visible, entertaining, and powerful advertisements (e.g. Coke ads) that are the economic lifeblood of commercial media have a different purpose. They are invitations to consume. Thus the bio-pedagogical work of HPE will often be in conflict with, or at least in tension with, the bio-pedagogical work done by media advertising. This is a key issue when we are concerned with the effectiveness of the HPE curriculum in the making of healthy citizens.

In considering the governmental processes at work in producing citizens who choose "healthy" lifestyles (rather than "unhealthy" ones) it is instructive to recognize HPE as being part of a regime of power and knowledge oriented to the *regulation* and surveillance of bodies for particular ends (Foucault, 1986). The contemporary notion of "risk society" is central to this process.

In this sense, if a mission of the field of human movement is to educate people to take care of their bodies and to engage in "healthy" lifestyle pursuits, we must realize that much of the work in regulating life beyond the institution of compulsory schooling is done by the media and others with vested interests in the body and or physical activity. So people police their own bodies and lifestyles (with a lot of help from the media) and the field of HMS/kinesiology shares the economic benefits when thousands of men and women seek our professional services in the gyms and pools around the country. What the benefits of this trend for HMS professionals are, however, is a much more complex issue.

Expert knowledge and certainty

There is little doubt that the role of the expert (and of expertise) is crucial in modern societies. According to Nettleton (1997), "The techniques and practice of experts in the human sciences (psychology, sociology, medicine etc. [human movement studies] are critical to the possibility of contemporary forms of health and welfare" (p. 209). It is, however, a relatively new phenomenon for since the 1970s there has been a proliferation of expert knowledge on aspects of lifestyle conducive to health and ill-health (Petersen and Lupton, 1996).

Much of the HMS and HPE literature is part of this new discourse. In the "old PE" regime for example, the teacher's expertise was in the administration of an exercise regime at the face-to-face level. In the "new HPE" teachers' expertise is needed in facilitating children's connection with abstract expertise as represented in the resources that inform the rational decisions considered necessary to reduce risky lifestyle practices.

For example, expert knowledge about food and exercise is crucial to the HPE learning area. In a world of increased manufactured uncertainty (Giddens, 1991) experts (particularly those trained in abstract intellectual forms of knowledge) are meant to help us reduce uncertainty and help us gain a more secure foothold on an uncertain world. However, since experts serve to reshape the "aspects of social life they report on or analyse" (Giddens, 1991, p. 14), "the penetration of this expert knowledge about lifeworlds, into these lifeworlds is constitutive of the manufactured uncertainty that characterizes contemporary settings" (Kelly *et al.*, 2000, p. 290). Importantly however, expert knowledge about food and exercise can serve to increase our anxiety about how we live our lives. Have I eaten too much saturated fat today? Will I be able to get my exercise session in today? Worry worry. Such anxieties can be understood in the context where "Many health promoters [and HPE teachers] would wish to "turn people into calorific and cholesterol counting machines. In this respect, they are closer to missionaries than to the disinterested scientists that they believe themselves to be" (Petersen and Lupton, 1996, p. 41, citing Metcalf, 1993).

In the context of "risk society" students of HPE/HMS must learn to manage their lifestyles such that risks are avoided or reduced. Indeed, risk identification and management is a key tenet in the conception of the new public health that increasingly underpins the professional training of new HPE/HMS professionals.

Further, although much of the new public health discourse which underpins contemporary university HMS/kinesiology and school HPE is presented with a mask of certainty (Gard and Wright, 2001), Giddens and Beck tell us that certainty is precisely what is unattainable within postmodern "risk society".

> Patterned professional regulation of people's lives and lifestyles at best presumes that professionals have the right answers for these questions. All too frequently, however, the questions themselves are neglected or ignored (p. 15).

Central to the bio-pedagogical work of HMS is expert knowledge. Expert knowledge about the body, physical activity and health are essential to the governmental technologies marshalled to create the healthy citizen. However, other cultural players also marshal particular bio-pedagogies in relation to health and accordingly this assemblage will have unpredictable outcomes.

Changes in how we come to think as we think about our field

As explained in Chapter 5, how we think about HMS is integrally related in very fundamental ways to the ways in which we think about our bodies. For example, the exercises for posture maintenance and development contained in school syllabi such as the 1933 *Syllabus of Physical Training for Schools* and the 1946 *Grey Book*, and also those contained in other pre-World War 2 PE books such as *The Teaching of Body Mechanics* (1936) by I. S. Howland, were all heavily influenced by an increasingly scientific way of thinking about the body. Significantly, this scientized conception of the body and its associated body-as-machine metaphor is now so widespread among the HMS field that it has become an ideology. Ideology in this sense is a taken-for-granted set of ideas, belief system, or way of thinking about something (e.g. reality, the body, health, society, politics). Ideologies are often used to justify and sustain the position and interests of powerful social groups (e.g. patriarchy).

It is important to understand that shifts in thinking and in curriculum emphasis in our field do not occur in a vacuum. They are profoundly influenced by the ways in which experts think about the field. The work of Goodson (1987) and Kirk (1992) has demonstrated this with considerable force. One thing that is apparent is that most, maybe even all, of the textbooks used in contemporary HMS courses are oriented towards, or based on, a particular worldview of health and the body. In particular they represent a Western rationalist perspective with respect to the body and health. Of course this seems entirely reasonable given that we are part of the Western intellectual and cultural tradition. Moreover, Western science and medicine has been exceedingly successful in eradicating disease and in increasing the lifespan of those of us who live in developed Western societies. However, it's not quite that simple or straightforward.

As Beck (1972) has pointed out, we are now facing manufactured risks that are the direct result of our industrialized life, and our conventional Western "remedies" (read "drugs") are as much part of the problem as they are part of the solution to these risks and their consequences on our health. In this regard, according to Elliott (1996), "the central modernist dilemma [is to] attempt to reach some kind of personal balance between security and risk, opportunity and danger" (p. 7). In HMS the "advice for wellbeing" tends to be that of the exercise sciences and the solution to some young people is seen in ever more work on the body through exercise and diet regimes. However, there is advice from other sources and other paradigms of knowledge regarding the body that can offer real contributions to achieving a better balance.

Aristotelian and Confucian thinking about health and the body

It was the Dutch born American physical educator Jan Broekhoff (1972), who argued that "Rationalised movements" (such as PE) "can only emerge in a society when man has gained the capability of looking at his own body as if it were a thing"(p. 88). So we can see that the conception of Western PE and HMS in general is underpinned by a particular way of thinking about the body as an object. Importantly, considering the body as an object, as a biophysical "thing", is a technocratic way of thinking (see Whitson and Macintosh, 1990; McKay *et al.*, 1990; Tinning, 1991c), which is well characterized by the man-as-machine metaphor. Moreover, it is underpinned by the same ontological and epistemological foundations described earlier when I discussed the dominant form of research and practice in PE pedagogy.

According to Nisbett (2003), medical scholars in the West have been dissecting the human body for over 500 years (give or take a few when it was outlawed) and surgery has been a fundamental part of Western medical treatment for far longer than that. By contrast, Chinese medical treatment did not engage in dissection until it was introduced by Westerners in the late nineteenth century. Moreover, "In all of Chinese history, surgery has been a great rarity"(p. 22). Nisbett argues that the Chinese reluctance to use surgery can be understood in the context of their views on holism and relationships. Each part of the body is interconnected with other body parts and this vast array of interconnections is at the basis of acupuncture. To remove a diseased part of the body without attending to its relations with other parts of the body would be, in Nisbett's words, "too simple-minded for the Chinese to contemplate" (p. 23).

In the Aristotelian tradition, Western cultures have a preference to categorize (by applying the rules about properties) as a way to see and understand the world. This intellectual tradition of categorization, classification and taxonomy is object focused and it underpins Western science. Categorization represents a search for order and certainty, and although this fits nicely with the Aristotelian Greek belief in stability, significant social analysts such as Giddens (1991), Beck (1992), Bauman (2001), and many others explain that in contemporary times certainty *is* illusory.

Asian cultures, on the other hand, understand the world more by rela-tionships than categories (Nisbett, 2003). They learn about the world more through verbs rather than nouns. According to Nisbett (2003), "Easterners today have relatively little interest in categories, find it hard to learn new categories by applying rules about properties, and make little use of them for purposes of induction" (p. 148). The Confucian inspired East Asian tradition of thought on the other hand "emphasises the constantly changing nature of reality" (p. 174). The world is not static but dynamic and changeable. Although this thinking is now far more acceptable in contemporary Western culture with the appreciation of the implications of chaos and complexity theories, many Western PE/HMS students continue to put their faith in the "certain" knowledge of exercise science and have an aversion for the "uncertain" knowledge of the disciplines such as sociology (see for example Macdonald and Brooker, 2000).

Chinese philosophical thought developed a form of dialectic that is quite different from the Western Hegelian notion of the dialectic. In the Hegelian tradition, which underpinned Marxist materialist analyses of society, and later critical theory and critical pedagogy, dialectic implies a thesis, followed by an antithesis, that is then "resolved" by a rational process of synthesis. The ultimate goal of this process is to resolve contradiction. The Chinese dialectic on the other hand "uses contradiction to understand relations among objects or events, to transcend or integrate apparent oppositions, or even to embrace clashing but instructive viewpoints", and as such, "Dialectical thought is in some ways the opposite of logical thought" (Nisbett, 2003, p. 27).

Although it seems that Asian students are well placed to live with what Westerners might regard as contradictions, in my experience at interna-tional conferences and in reading the HMS academic literature, most Asian researchers in our field have been reluctant to engage with the ideas of criti-cal pedagogy and postmodernity. Perhaps the reason for this can be found in Nisbett's (2003) contention that theorizing and "big picture" thinking is not a feature of Confucian modes of thought.

It is worth pondering on how, or if, the different views of the body as represented by Aristotle and Confucius can be reconciled within our field. Is any credence given to ways of thinking about health and the human body other than through the paradigm of Western science? Although we see the increasing presence of Tai Chi and yoga in commercial "health club" offer-ings, what do we do in our undergraduate HMS programs to help students seriously engage such different perspectives on health and the body?

We do not know much (perhaps anything) about whether Asian HM professionals experience any cultural dissonance when learning their profes-sion in Western universities or from engaging pedagogies and curriculum texts derived from the West. We do know, however, that the body (or more specifically the firm, slender body and its antithesis – the fat/obese body) has become a central focus of our field. Indeed, HMS is creating and maintaining its place as central to the images, if not the reality, of healthy lifestyles as constructed around certain body management practices which are essentially those of Western tradition (Tinning and Glasby, 2002). The possible implications of this are seen in the relationship between healthism and the so-called contemporary obesity crisis.

Western lifestyles, healthism, and obesity in East Asia

There is now ample evidence that many young people in East Asia are overweight or obese (see Johns, 2005) and there is no doubt that a significant health problem associated with this trend is confronting the governments of countries such as China, Japan and Korea. This problem has been largely imported from the West in the form of better living standards for many urban Asians and the attendant increased emphasis on consumerism in the increasingly market oriented economies of these countries. Unfortunately, it is to the West that Asian governments appear to be turning for solutions to this growing problem.

Aaron Lynch, in his book *Thought Contagion: How Belief Spreads Through Society* (1996), provides an interesting and provocative possibility here. Lynch argues that actively contagious ideas across many fields of knowledge are called *memes* (pronounced like "teams") and that their propagation can be studied by the new science of memetics. He talks of "the epidemiology of ideas" (p. 9) and the "self-propagating idea" (p. 2). Lynch gives very brief mention of *memes* relating to diets, exercise and sport, and it seems to me that applying these ideas to questions of education and physical culture might provide some generative insights for our collective understanding.

In regard to obesity, however, the solutions the West offers are themselves implicated as part of the problem. This can be understood by a consideration of the concept of *healthism*. Although I discussed healthism in Chapter 6, it is worth briefly explaining again this concept that was first coined by Crawford (1980) to describe the tendency for health problems to be defined as essentially individual problems. Healthism is a set of ideas that includes the unquestioned assumption that exercise = fitness = health; that the individual is solely responsible for his/her own health; that body shape is a metaphor for health, and that it is through the physical that health is manifest. Healthism is a Western construct. It is a manifestation of Western ways of thinking and it fails to take into consideration the dialectical relationship between the individual agent and the structures of society (for useful critiques of how healthism as ideology operates within PE and the field of HMS see Kirk and Colquhoun, 1989; Tinning, 1990). The fact that healthism as ideology is increasingly underpinning policy and practice in many East Asian countries is a serious concern and has only recently received attention from scholars such as David Johns (2005) and Herman Chan (2008).

In my view issues related to overweight and obesity will not be solved by a reliance on Western thinking alone. This is a clear example of the folly of appropriating Western ideas while ignoring local Eastern ideas. The reductionist logic of the "energy in, energy out" equation is a simplistic explanation for a very complex problem. Maybe there are more sensitive understandings to be found in the Confucian traditions that privilege holism, harmony (everything in balance), collectivity and connectedness. Maybe Chinese dialectism would allow a more appropriate understanding of the roles of the individual and the state.

Importantly, however, taking a different view of the assumptions that underpin the thinking of our field need not lead to a synthesis. Confucian dialectical thinking is not aimed at synthesis; it would allow for contradictions and can embrace clashing but instructive viewpoints. In my view that would be a positive direction to take.

As I suggested earlier when discussing pedagogies used to disrupt the ideology of the cult of the body (see Chapter 6), allowing the voices of *mythos* and *thymos* to be heard, in addition to the voice of *logos*, would be a generative way to provide HMS students with critical, informed and emotional accounts of how pedagogies work in relation to health and our field. In applying the rhetorical styles of a modest critical pedagogy to the discourses of health, HMS students could read the following:

For *mythos* (a personal voice of story telling):

- Delorme, D., Kreshel, P., and Reid, L. (2003). Lighting up: Young adults' autobiographical accounts of their first smoking experiences. *Youth & Society*, 34(June), 468–496.
- Siegel, B. (1990). *Love, Medicine and Miracles*. New York: Quill.

To give voice to *thymos* (rage against injustice):

- Day, P. (2001). *Health Wars*. Tonbridge, Kent: Credence Publications.
- Pronger, B. (2002). *Body Fascism: Salvation in the Technology of Physical Fitness*. Toronto: University of Toronto Press.
- Glassner, B. (1995). In the name of health. In R. Bunton, S. Nettleton and R. Burrows (Eds.), *The Sociology of Health* (pp. 159–176). London: Routledge.
- Pollack Seid, R. (1989). *Never Too Thin: Why Women Are at War with Their Bodies*. New York: Prentice Hall Press.
- Orbach, S. (1978). *Fat is a Feminist Issue*. New York: Berkeley Books.

To engage the analytic voice of *logos* (the voice of reason and science):

- Callan, M. (2004). "Lifestyle" and its social meaning. In G. Albrecht (Ed.), *Advances in Medical Sociology: Volume 4*. Greenwich, CT: JAI Press.
- Lupton, D. (1997). Consumerism, reflexivity and the medical encounter. *Social Science and Medicine*, 45(3), 373–381.

- Stearns, P. (1997). *Fat History: Bodies and Beauty in the Modern West.* New York: New York University Press.
- Chopra, D. (1993). *Ageless Body, Timeless Mind.* Sydney: Random House.
- Nestle, M. (2003). *Food Politics: How the Food Industry Influences Nutrition and Health.* Los Angeles: University of California Press.

The point of including "alternative" sociologically oriented discourses about health and the body is to help students begin to see somewhat differently the things they take for granted. If science helps us to understand strange things (such as the "workings of the body") and make them familiar, a sociological orientation can help us to make the familiar strange and in so doing see the world though new eyes.

9   Pedagogies for health in HMS

From biomedical science to pedagogy: Knowledge (re)production and health

When a personal trainer devises a specific exercise program for a client who desires to lose weight and tone up; when a strength and conditioning coach works with players to develop leg strength; or when a PE teacher incorporates health related fitness activities into the curriculum, they are all involved in a process in which appropriate biomedical (and other) knowledge produced by research is re-contextualized as a pedagogical discourse and then reproduced via a pedagogical encounter.

By this I mean that the knowledge that informs these instances of professional practice is knowledge produced by experts somewhere else (in the lab or other esoteric place) and made more user friendly for particular pedagogical purposes. This re-contextualizing process is necessary because the particular scientific biological knowledge that underpins a particular exercise intervention (in the local gym, football club or school) is, in its "original form", probably quite esoteric and certainly not immediately useful for informing practice. It is, therefore, useful to distinguish between the production of knowledge and the re-contextualization of knowledge. The reproduction of knowledge (for example via HMS pedagogies) cannot take place without its re-contextualization (Singh, 2002).

Consider, for example, the knowledge that muscles can stretch more following a contraction. This phenomenon is based on the physiological process known as reciprocal innervation and has been incorporated into contemporary books on stretching such as *The Flexibility Manual* (Peters and Peters, 1995) and *Science of Flexibility* (Alter, 2004). It is also taught in most courses on applied exercise physiology. Reciprocal innervation was first hypothesized by René Descartes in the seventeenth century and the underlying neuro-mechanisms were conceptualized a century later by Charles Sherrington. Later experimental work confirmed Sherrington's conceptualizations (e.g. Blackburn and Portney, 1981). In this example the scientific knowledge was generated by researchers/scholars and later made understandable and practical by others (e.g. Peters and Peters, 1995 and Alter, 2004). In other words the scientific knowledge was translated into user friendly information that can be incorporated into practice. This re-contextualizing is part of the process of knowledge (re)production and is of central importance to the process of pedagogy.

In attempting to understand pedagogies for health in HMS I will draw on some features of the framework provided by sociologist Basil Bernstein (1996) of the process of knowledge (re)production. It is hard to lift the lid on Bernstein's work without being somewhat overwhelmed by its complexity. What I want to do here is give a very brief explanation of some of his useful concepts so that I can use them to discuss the pedagogy of health in HMS. My explanation no doubt will be insufficient for serious Bernstein scholars (such as Evans and Davies, 2004) but hopefully it will provide just enough detail so readers who have little or no background in sociology (perhaps exercise science folk) might grasp the basic logic of the framework that explains how the re-contextualizing process is central to knowledge (re)production and therefore to pedagogy.

The pedagogic device

Bernstein (1996) conceived of what he termed a *pedagogic device* as part of an elaborate theorizing of how discourse becomes pedagogical. According to Bernstein, a pedagogic device regulates pedagogic communication by legitimizing certain meanings through the application of certain internal rules. These rules are tacit and although relatively stable, they are not ideologically free.

Bernstein (1975) conceived of three different fields of knowledge production, namely primary, re-contextualizing and secondary. Knowledge production in the *primary field* of knowledge occurs when knowledge workers in universities, research institutes and the like produce knowledge through research (as in the example of stretching mentioned above). This knowledge is then reworked or translated by other expert knowledge workers into textbooks, curriculum documents, policies, interventions strategies and the like within the *re-contextualizing field*. Typically in this process expert knowledge is made more understandable for the non-expert; it is rendered pedagogical. Teachers, for example, in the *secondary field*, eventually use this re-contextualized knowledge as the basis for their curriculum content for particular lessons. Using a number of pedagogical strategies, teachers are expert knowledge workers who bring the rules of engagement to play, and thus reproduce this re-contextualized knowledge.

The pedagogic device is what operationalizes the production, reproduction, and transformation of culture (Bernstein, 1996). It provides the intrinsic grammar of pedagogic discourse through three different but interrelated rules: distributive rules, re-contextualizing rules, and evaluative rules. It is worth considering distributive rules and re-contextualizing rules in a little more detail.

Distributive rules

Distributive rules "mark and distribute who may transmit what to whom and under what conditions" (Bernstein, 2000, p. 31) and in so doing they endeavour to set the outer and inner limits of legitimate discourse. Distributive rules distinguish two different classes of knowledge, thinkable and unthinkable knowledge. We can think of the Copernican idea that the sun, rather than the earth, is the centre of the universe as unthinkable knowledge in the late fifteenth/early sixteenth centuries. Indeed, because this was against the teachings of the church, Copernicus was considered to be a heretic and was fortunate not to have been burnt at the stake. According to Bernstein (1996), in all societies there are at least two basic classes of knowledge; one is esoteric and the other is mundane. However, the content of these classes of knowledge varies historically and culturally, and the principles generating both classes are also relative to a given period. Esoteric knowledge may become mundane knowledge in different periods. Copernicus' esoteric unthinkable knowledge of the fifteenth/sixteenth century is today both thinkable and mundane. As such, "distributive rules mark and specialize the thinkable and the unthinkable" (Bernstein, 1996). In general, the distributive rules are concerned with the production rather than the reproduction of discourse. Re-contextualizing rules on the other hand are generally concerned with the reproduction of discourse and therefore central to pedagogy.

Re-contextualizing rules

Bernstein (2000) defines pedagogic discourse as a rule that embeds two discourses: (i) a discourse of skills of various kinds and their relations to each other; and (ii) a discourse of social order. The discourse that creates specialized skills of one kind or another and the rules regulating their relationship to each other is the *instructional discourse*. The moral discourse that creates social order, relations and identity is the *regulative discourse*.

In all pedagogic devices the regulative discourse is the dominant discourse because it is the moral discourse that creates the criteria that give rise to the character, manner, and conduct of the social order. Moreover, the regulative discourse produces the order in the instructional discourse. "There is no instructional discourse which is not regulated by the regulative discourse" (Bernstein, 2000, p. 34). This is because any theory of instruction "contains within itself a model of the learner and of the teacher and of the relation" (p. 35) that is a manifestation of certain regulatory discourse.

Pedagogic devices that are intended to (re)produce knowledge about health and bodies, for example through the instructional discourses used in an HPE lesson or an exercise science lecture, are underpinned by a regulatory discourse that is hidden within the instructional discourse. As we will see in more detail in Chapter 10, a hidden regulatory discourse that operates within much of HMS and school HPE is *healthism*. The fact that it is hidden allows the health knowledge reproduced in these pedagogic devices to be considered to be free of values and ideologies.

Let's now see how this process of knowledge (re)production operates in the context of some specific examples from the field of HMS.

Coming to know about health: Expert knowledge, discourse, pedagogy and the school health education lesson

One of the features of pedagogy is its reliance on expert knowledge and the role of the expert. Think for a moment about a "simple" health lesson that is part of the formal HPE curriculum (at least in Australia and New Zealand). Let's say the lesson is about food, nutrition and diet. Increasingly, such a lesson will have the pedagogical intent of increasing the knowledge of students such that they might make better choices and hence lead an increasingly healthier lifestyle, thereby ameliorating the "obesity crisis".

In arguing that the HPE curriculum is a particular governmental technology employed in the making of a (certain) healthy citizen, the HPE teacher becomes implicated as an expert in the process (Tinning and Glasby, 2002). The preferred healthy citizen is to be a self-regulating, informed, critically reflective citizen capable of constructing their own healthy lifestyle and managing risk such that the health threatening dangers of contemporary living are minimized. It is here that the HPE teacher offers expertise (usually via instruction) as one of a range of experts (including doctors, health promoters, psychologists, dieticians, etc.) on matters concerning bodies, health and lifestyle.

Consider the following example from the HPE curriculum in the Australian state of Queensland. Table 9.1 shows the core learning outcomes for the *Promoting the Health of Individuals and Communities* strand of the HPE syllabus (Queensland School Curriculum Council, 1999) that students are meant to acquire across Years 1–10. Level 4 outcomes are meant to be more sophisticated and demanding than those of Level 3 and so on.

The kind of knowledge outcomes that are expected from this strand in relation to nutrition and health are all based on rational decision making. The HPE teacher is the expert in pedagogy and is expected to arrange the learning experiences for students such that they acquire the relevant knowledge that is consistent with these outcomes. Most teachers will have the required expertise to do just that. But the expertise is limited for it tends to privilege particular rationalist ways of knowing about health and nutrition. While it is possible that the HPE teacher might discuss the power of emotion in influencing our eating behaviours (for example, comfort food, pleasure food, desirable food – see Lupton, 1996) and perhaps even the conflicting signals to consume and abstain that characterize much contemporary advertising related to food and the body, the mandated HPE curriculum does not expect such questioning. The science of nutrition is seen to be the most important knowledge to develop in young people. This is somewhat ironic

Table 9.1 Core learning outcomes for the *Promoting the Health of Individuals and Communities* HPE syllabus strand in Queensland

Level 1	Level 2	Level 3	Level 4
1.2 Students recommend healthy eating practices and demonstrate making healthy choices from a range of goods.	2.2 Students explain the benefits of eating a variety of nutritious foods and plan ways to increase the range of nutritious foods in their diets.	3.2 Students explain how eating behaviours affect health and take action on a food-related goal which promotes health.	4.2 Students develop and implement strategies for optimising personal diet based on identified nutritional needs for growth, energy and health.

since the HPE curriculum is supposedly based on and advocates a social view of health.

Using the Bernstein framework we can trace the re-contextualizing process that works in/through this health lesson. Let's say that this lesson is part of a unit on "The food we eat" and the aim for the unit is to make kids aware of the "food pyramid", the importance of a balanced diet, and the need to reduce the amount of saturated fats we eat. Versions of this same health knowledge can be also found in many university and college courses related to diet and exercise. Although increasing use is made of the Internet to access knowledge resources, the content knowledge on which the teacher bases the lessons in the unit will usually be drawn from a textbook called something like *Health Education for Secondary Students*. The textbook is a re-contextualization of the latest scientific knowledge regarding health and the section on food and diet is up to date in its information about the increased prevalence of obesity and overweight in children and young people.

Some of the information that is included in the textbook is re-contextualized in a way that eliminates some of the uncertainty and caveats that were contained in the original scientific papers from which the knowledge was derived. For example, when scientists outline the limitations of their research and provide cautions regarding generalizations because of limited sample size or whatever, such caveats are rarely reproduced in health education textbooks. In the re-contextualizing process, the knowledge becomes condensed, sanitized, and made more digestible. In this process it also becomes less uncertain.

Further, textbook authors, and some experts in the primary field, sometimes go "beyond the data" and add a bit of moralizing as well. As Gard and Wright (2001) have convincingly shown, this has been particularly prevalent in the discourse on the "obesity epidemic". A textbook is a pedagogical device for reproducing certain truth claims. Teachers, in good faith, use textbooks as a major source of their content knowledge and, given that many textbooks also contain student learning activities (e.g. quizzes, extension activities), they are used for pedagogical content knowledge as well. Typically, teachers will be looking for certainty, something they can tell their students that is correct, factual and "evidence-based". Limitations, ambiguities and uncertainties are not convenient for many pedagogical strategies. Moreover, young people, while they might be more skeptical than previous generations, also have a desire for certainty – something on which they can hang their ontological hats.

It is unlikely, however, that the content for the unit will come solely from the textbook. Rather, the unit of work on "The food we eat" becomes a convenient assemblage (Leahy, 2008) of information taken from the textbook and other sites of information such as the Internet, the popular press, television shows, and advertisements about food, diet and health that are ubiquitous in contemporary Western culture. Of course, while not all the "knowledge" that is re-conceptualized and reproduced by these information sites is derived from authoritative experts, it nonetheless all becomes part of the complex contemporary assemblage of bio-pedagogical processes involved in school health education.

The bio-pedagogical strategies enacted in the health lesson on food are intended to produce certain curriculum prescribed outcomes. As Leahy (2008) demonstrates, "the development of 'bio-pedagogical strategies' are a range of expert knowledge drawn from fields of education and health. As lesson planning continues each bio-pedagogical strategy is located within a 'scaffold' which means they rub against each other in an attempt to coherently lead students towards demonstrating the lesson outcomes" (p. 3).

She goes on to argue that "The dominance of expert knowledges here is not surprising, given that many scholars [in particular Dean, 1999; Rose, 1989] have highlighted the significance of expertise in governing populations" (p. 3). Leahy comments that it is interesting how various knowledge discourses converge and morph and that "expert knowledges in health education … tend to become hybridized as they are mobilized in classrooms, by teachers and students alike" (ibid.).

According to Berman (2000), in order to understand contemporary concerns such as the "obesity crisis" it is necessary to recognize the impact of corporate commercial culture on education, sport and modern living. Berman suggests "the values and ideology of marketing and consumerism managed to overwhelm America in the twentieth century" (p. 115) and a strong case can be made that this same ideology has also overwhelmed the field of education (see Kenway and Bullen, 2001). Steinberg and Kincheloe (1997) argue that as the distinctions between education, entertainment and advertising diminish, the influence of corporate-media culture and the corporate pedagogues has increased. Significantly they have observed that education takes place in a variety of social sites including, but not limited to, schooling, and that corporate pedagogues have become postmodern society's most successful teachers.

In this context, Nicholas Rose (2000) argues that "schools have been supplemented and sometimes displaced by an array of other practices for shaping identities and forms of life" (p. 1398). He suggests that advertising, TV soap operas, and lifestyle magazines have become the new regulatory techniques for the shaping of the self, thereby replacing much of the traditional authority of education. This has huge implications for the field of PE and health. We can think here of the impact of corporate sport and lifestyle advertisements on the developing "active" identity of young people.

In simple terms, school HPE is competing for the hearts, minds and bodies of young people against increasingly sophisticated corporate pedagogues who focus their energies on tapping into young people's notions of pleasure. According to Kenway and Bullen (2002), it is important to recognize the connection between consumer culture (as a significant element in popular culture) and the non-rational self. They use the French word *jouissance*, which means "playful, sensual pleasure", as central to their argument:

> The *jouissance* which children derive from consumer culture is designed to ensure that they unreflexively consume rather than interpret such texts. *Jouissance* is about producing a surge affect, not the reflexive pleasure of knowing about what is happening as it happens. By its very nature, children's consumer-media culture seeks not to operate at this level of rationality (p. 75).

In response to this understanding, Kenway and Bullen argue for developing pedagogies of the popular and the profane. They argue for discovering the "power of pleasure" and the "pleasure of power". This talk of pleasure opens a window into the power of the visceral, corporeal and non-rational. Importantly, in PE and health much of the pedagogical work done relating to such issues as food, sex and drugs is heavily focused on risk management and consequently emphasizes avoidance or abstinence while giving little or no consideration to pleasure. The pedagogies used in health education lessons continue to privilege the rational re-contextualized knowledge of bioscience and ignore the embodied, sensual and non-rational dimensions of experience.

The point that bio-pedagogies are very much articulated by emotion and the non-rational is significant. In this context, as Harwood (2008) reminds us, attempting to understand bio-pedagogies solely as an enactment of expert knowledge would be to oversimplify the complexity involved. Leahy (2008), citing Ellsworth (2005, p. 6), points out that bio-pedagogies are by nature "a social relationship that gets close in. It gets right in there in your brain, your body, your heart, in our sense of self, of the world, of others, and of possibilities and impossibilities in all these realms." Bio-pedagogies are thus "explicitly designed to permeate and creep into students' ways of thinking and being" (Leahy, 2008, p. 8).

The process of (re)production takes place in pedagogical encounters that entail a complex interaction between subject matter (knowledge), the learner and the teacher (Lusted, 1986). Learners come to know about health through the regulatory and instructional discourses of the official school health education curriculum and through the pedagogical work done in and through the assemblage of other bio-pedagogical agents. While recognizing that all "teachers" are not necessarily flesh and blood humans, the particular individual biographies of both learners and teachers render the outcomes of such pedagogies both complex and unpredictable.

Leahy (2008) gives examples of how teachers of health are complicit with their students in enacting a pedagogical assemblage that mobilizes "the affects of shame, guilt, pride and disgust alongside expert knowledges" (p. 12). This is powerful stuff and the pedagogical work done by these assemblages cannot be known in advance. School HPE health lessons then, as a governmental technology, produce many effects well beyond those articulated as outcomes in official curriculum documents. Typically, experts who determine the outcomes for HPE can map only some partial truths – those that typically reproduce re-contextualized truths that are founded on rationality and science. Maybe, just maybe, they map the least powerful and least significant effects of the assemblages of bio-pedagogies.

Expert knowledge, discourse, pedagogy and exercise science: The exercise science textbook

The undergraduate student of exercise science will usually study exercise physiology as a compulsory subject. Most certainly they will also do a course in advanced exercise physiology as well. Predominantly they will obtain their new knowledge from lectures, from laboratory classes, from textbooks and increasingly from CD-ROMs. I obtained a copy of one of the popular textbooks used in many such courses. The book, the third edition of *Physiology of Sport and Exercise* by Wilmore and Costill (2004) is over 720 pages and is heavy. Its weight and its price afford it a sense of gravity. It is a book that is primarily pedagogical in purpose. In addition to the written text there are numerous diagrams and graphs that are used as pedagogical devices to convey knowledge. The knowledge is declarative or propositional and is typically tested by means of examinations.

The authors, Jack Wilmore and David Costill were (they have both now retired) respected exercise scientists. Their status as experts is affirmed by their impressive biographies revealing that they having published some 750 papers and chapters across their illustrious careers, and held many prestigious posts such as President of the ACSM (American College of Sports Medicine).

In setting out to produce this pedagogical device, Wilmore and Costill engaged in the re-contextualizing process. In referring to the findings of their own research and the research of others, they attempt to assist the student/reader to come to know how the body functions in response to the demands of exercise and sport. Readers would seldom challenge the knowledge presented in such a book. It is authoritative and it appears unbiased and scientific. However, in the re-contextualizing process there is considerable "smoothing" done. Many caveats, limitations and cautions that might have appeared in the original published studies were most likely not included for the sake of clarity and readability.

One of the chapters in Wilmore and Costill (2004) is worthy of analysis in this regard. Chapter 21, "Obesity, diabetes, and physical activity", re-contextualizes contemporary scientific knowledge related to the contribution of physical activity to the "lifestyle diseases of obesity and diabetes". Overall, I'm sure the chapter does a good job in presenting the agreed wisdom relating to this issue. However, I present one example of "smoothing" that reveals it as a problematic practice. In the chapter there is an explanation of Body Mass Index (BMI) including what it measures and how it is determined. There is also the reproduction of the 1997 World Health Organization BMI classi-fication system (pp. 670–671) used to categorize individuals as overweight or obese. According to Wilmore and Costill, "This classification system has made a major contribution to our understanding of the *true* prevalence of overweight and obesity" (p. 668; emphasis added). All fine? Not quite. BMI is a measure not without its critics.

Gard and Wright (2001) in their book *The Obesity Epidemic: Science, Morality and Ideology* provide a detailed account of the criticism of BMI. They report that "BMI is a highly problematic measure of fatness. At best it accounts for between 60 and 75 per cent of the variation in body fat content of adults. It does not account for the differences in percentages of body fat for the same BMI in different ethnic groups, nor for variation in human physique (size and amount of fat, muscle and bone)" (pp. 92–93). BMI, they claim, "is not a 'gold standard' for measuring human fatness or obesity" (p. 93) and accordingly, "all statistics on the levels of obesity in human population need to be interpreted with a great deal of caution to avoid science fiction being represented as scientific fact" (p. 94).

In Wilmore and Costill's (2004) textbook there is no mention of these criticisms. What they present is just one side of a rather serious argument. Arguing that the book would need to be twice as long if they had bothered presenting both sides of such disagreements is not appropriate. It would be better to have two volumes that presented the contested nature of the truth game than one volume which effectively masks the contested nature of truth.

Part of the pedagogical work done by such textbooks is that students sometimes come to believe that science is more certain than it actually is. For example, in the case of exercise prescription and health, for all the empha-sis on physical activity as a contributing factor to good health, the precise formulation of the type, frequency and intensity of activity that is necessary to reduce health risk continues to baffle exercise scientists. Precisely how much more activity is required to offset the risk of disease is currently being debated among researchers and no exact prescription has yet been provided (Bouchard and Blair, 2001; Bouchard, 2001). The only agreement that has been reached among the experts is that physical activity *should* be promoted among the young as part of a new public health agenda (Johns and Tinning, 2006).

But just as with the health education lesson, the bio-pedagogies of the exercise science textbook join with other bio-pedagogies from an assemblage of sources such as the Internet, TV, DVDs, magazines etc. The student of exercise physiology will inevitably learn about health not only from the textbook, but also from the bio-pedagogies devised and operationalized by other cultural players.

The ABC of/on health

The Australian Broadcasting Commission (known as the ABC) offers a number of radio and TV shows that focus on health. Many of these focus on physical activity and health. As the national broadcaster, the ABC carries a certain imprimatur of authority – and often seriousness. *The Health Report*, presented by Dr Norman Swan (a medical doctor), presents information on certain key health issues, such as exercise and diabetes. The show is well researched and Dr Swan offers useful reviews and distillations of evidence and advice. In the process of preparing the show Dr Swan and his team are involved in the process of re-contextualizing knowledge for particular pedagogical purposes. *The Health Report* is intended to educate, inform and therefore is avowedly pedagogic.

During the show reference is often made to the ABC website http://www.abc.net.au from which you can "drill down" to specific information about health, healthy living and fitness at http://www.abc.net.au/health/healthyliving/fitness/default.htm. A scan of that site is informative. There is information about such things as: How to chose a gym; Sports injuries and how to prevent them; Beat the bulge, drop the drugs; The great weight debate; How to avoid cancer; Fat, fit and living longer; Mediterranean diet, lifestyle and mortality; and many more. There are Health Quizzes, and an Exercise Guide that asks "What moves you? We'll help you find the best kind of exercise to suit your needs." There are connections to videos, transcripts and audio of *The Health Report*. There is also a link to "Fitness stories" elsewhere on ABC. On the day I visited the site these included: The knee files – part one (*The Health Report*); Triathletes warned about early season heat (*Science Online*); Treatment for acute lower back pain (*The Health Report*); and The health effects of exercise (*The Health Report*).

The reason that I have outlined some of the details of the ABC's offerings related to health, healthy lifestyles and physical activity is to show something of the extent of the pedagogical intent of other cultural players who operate in an overlapping way with the subject matter of the field of HMS. They are part of an assemblage of bio-pedagogies (Leahy, 2008).

Now of course the ABC's mission is to entertain as well as inform and it needs to be understood that, as mentioned earlier, for many young people who live a highly technology-mediated lifestyle, the distinctions between education, entertainment and advertising are increasingly blurred (Steinberg and Kincheloe, 1997). Negotiating what is meant as entertainment and what is meant to be "truth" can be a difficult task.

Importantly, this occurs in other fields as well. Business shows on TV and articles in the *Financial Times* etc. do pedagogical work in relation to finance and business. They are not meant to replace professional advice from financial counsellors/advisors but they nonetheless serve a function in helping the public to come to know more about business and financial matters. In this sense they are, to paraphrase Foucault, not necessarily bad or good, but possibly dangerous.

Another dimension to the way we come to know about health is through the marketing of the pharmaceutical companies and other commercial interests in the health industry. As Howell and Ingham (2001) have suggested, the advertising campaigns of the health industry "have educated the public in ways that no government agency could have" (p. 342). Pharmaceutical companies, for example, have a pedagogical intent and the pedagogical work their advertisements do is part of the assemblage of information/knowledge that the "innocent" learner/citizen must decipher in order to make the "right" decisions regarding their health.

Conclusion

To return to the question of the connection between the field of HMS and pedagogies for health, as I claimed at the start of this chapter, HMS has a mission that is clearly aligned with research and teaching about health. However, we are not alone in this "game". There are competing claims to truth "out there" and knowing what other claims there are and the power of their pedagogical device(s) might be a very important professional knowledge to have.

Those of us who work in universities or colleges that prepare future HMS professionals typically produce, re-contextualize and reproduce knowledge about physical activity, the body and health. Some will do more of one than the other but there will always be some dialectic interplay between what one researches and what one teaches. Through this process of knowledge (re) production we need to ensure, as much as possible, that our graduates leave our programs with the requisite knowledge applicable to their future professional accreditation and practice, and also with a sensitive "crap detector" that can be applied to arguments, evidence and claims from both sides of an issue. Being skeptical about claims to truth is a characteristic of good scientists, good journalists, good professionals, and, I would argue, good citizens. Understanding and recognizing the legitimacy and authority of all claims to truth is a feature of good "crap detection". Claims to truth will always be messy when we recognize that knowledge is always connected to human interests (Habermas, 1972).

10 Pedagogy and Health Oriented Physical Education (HOPE)[1]

For the purposes of this chapter most of my comments will be related to the practice of PE in schools, with particular reference to Australian primary schools. While the specific initiatives I discuss may be particular to the Australian context, the context that spawned these initiatives has been generally similar in other Western countries such as the UK, USA, Canada, New Zealand etc.

Within our schools, PE is generally organized around four elements or themes: sports, consisting of competitive individual and team activities; health related activities such as aerobics, running, and circuits; recreational pursuits such as canoeing, archery, orienteering and the like; and sports science knowledge which consists mainly of the teaching of biophysical knowledge about the body and physical activity. The emphasis given to each of these elements varies from school to school depending on many context-specific factors. However, since the early 1970s PE has been strongly influenced by a "new health consciousness" that, in many primary schools at least, was the impetus for an increased emphasis on the element of health related physical activities within the PE curriculum; what I have called Health Oriented Physical Education (HOPE). The acronym HOPE is meant to be a pun, for my argument is that these programs and initiatives are based on hope rather than a sound understanding of the significance of context in all educational endeavours.

In Australia, Great Britain, Canada and the United States the new health consciousness was manifest in a number of curriculum innovations that collectively can be grouped as HOPE. Two such innovations were Health Related Fitness (HRF) in Britain and Daily Physical Education (DPE) in Australia. The HOPE movement, which sees PE as a site for the promotion of a healthy lifestyle, was at the centre of the DPE initiatives of the 1980s and is also at the centre of the anti-obesity role advocated for PE in 2008. I will first focus on the 1980s and then describe how HOPE is alive and well in contemporary pedagogical practices of HPE in the early twenty-first century.

HOPE, in all its various forms, is a specific response by the PE profession to a perceived problem or cluster of problems. It is considered a solution to a problem. As Kirk and Colquhoun (1989) found in their study of daily PE in Queensland primary schools, daily PE was considered by teachers to be something of an "antidote" to the problem of the perceived sedentary life-styles of children. But where did the problem come from? Who defined or set the problem as a problem?

According to Lawson (1984) "problems are not just 'out there' like objects of nature; they are socially constructed" (p. 49). They are socially constructed in the process of what he calls problem-setting. Problem-setting involves a form of social editing where some possible problems are eliminated from consideration and other possibilities are foregrounded and become the focus of attention. Problem-setting is a political act which is intimately linked with power, control and what counts as legitimate knowledge in the culture or profession. It is significant not only in what it defines as a problem but also in what it chooses not to define as a problem. Why, for example, has the PE profession not argued for a greater emphasis on the aesthetics of movement or the development of appropriate sporting behaviours as its "lighthouse" objectives?

To understand HOPE we must have some knowledge of the sociocultural context in which the problems, to which HOPE is a response, were defined or set.

The new health consciousness and PE

The roots of the new health consciousness lie back in the early 1970s when there was a developing awareness of the increase of diseases associated with what was known as Western affluence. Some medical researchers of the time labelled the group of diseases including stroke, and coronary heart disease (CHD) in its various forms as the "hypo-kinetic diseases". This group of diseases, as the label suggests, is associated with a modern lifestyle that is increasingly sedentary. Associated with decreased physical activity, modern Western lifestyles were also characterized by abundance of food (at least for those who were not among the millions of poor that exist in the most afflu-ent of Western countries), an increase in stress, and an increase in cigarette smoking. Accordingly, it was during the 1970s that "lifestyle" became a key concept in the discourses of PE and health.

CHD, the most common form of these diseases, became a national "prob-lem" associated not just with personal loss and tragedy, but also with loss of productivity in the nation's work force. One significant Australian govern-ment response to the problem was the establishment of the National Heart Foundation that has sponsored research into heart disease prevention and the promotion of what they considered to be healthy lifestyles. Similar initiatives occurred in most other developed countries.

One of the projects of the National Heart Foundation that had direct influence on many Australian primary schools children of the time was Jump Rope For Heart (JRFH). This project (borrowed from an American project of the same name) introduced skipping to schools as a form of physical activity which was rhythmic and vigorous and which had the potential to improve the fitness of children and youth. Of course skipping had long been a recognized PE activity but now it was formalized, standardized and given a specific instrumental purpose.

The links between this new health consciousness and the development of the PE curriculum occurred in a number of ways. An important factor that provided a background for such links was the increased scientization of the training of future PE teachers and curriculum developers (see Kirk, 1990). By the early 1970s universities and colleges in Australia that were responsible for preparing teachers of PE were increasingly staffed by faculty who had undertaken postgraduate training in the USA. Most often these graduates had pursued higher degrees in the area of the biological/physical sciences and hence they shaped and created courses in Australian tertiary institutions which were dominated by a scientific/biologistic perspective and which, among other things, devoted considerable curriculum time to understanding the claimed causes of hypo-kinetic diseases and the role which exercise was to play in the amelioration of the problem. Exercise science became the privileged knowledge of the field of PE in the decades of the 1970s and 80s and PE graduates increasingly tended to define their professional mission in terms of the promotion of healthy lifestyles based on the claimed health benefits of involvement in physical activity.

Although the PE profession had long championed the health benefits of its subject matter, most governments, and society in general, other than at times of preparation for war, were not particularly interested in, or committed to, PE in the school curriculum. So the PE profession, particularly those members recently trained in a new science of health, saw the new health consciousness as somewhat of a gift from heaven. At last the community and the government were taking seriously the potential of their subject and physical educators were keen to develop curricula that responded to and captured the new government enthusiasm for physical activity. When these physical educators had a chance to influence or create curriculum for school PE they gave priority to fitness related activities and progressively marginalized other aspects of PE such as the development of the aesthetic, and the development of motor skills. The development of the South Australian Daily Physical Education (DPE) program occurred in that context. It was explicitly conceived as a HOPE program and its first listed benefit of PE was for children to "become fitter and healthier" (Education Department of South Australia, 1982, p. 3).

The new health consciousness intensified attention on care of the body by awarding exercise a major role in the achievement and maintenance of health and happiness, to the point where physical fitness and body shape have increasingly been used by advertisers as cultural symbols of both wellbeing and wealth. One only has to look at the fashion/fitness industry to gain an appreciation of how physical activity (or at least the hint of possible physical activity) has become a major marketing success. Designer track suits that are more at home around the bar-b-que than as post-exercise sweat wear, sneakers which have become status symbols for teenage kids, and aerobics and triathlon fashion gear which emphasize body shape and which come in all the vivid colours of your average packet of fluorescent markers. PE, like it or not, became implicated in the whole commercial marketing endeavour surrounding physical activity and the body.

Although there are dangers in cross-cultural comparisons, the context relating to the new health consciousness in Australia, Britain, Canada and the United States had parallels that enable some cautious comparisons to be made. For example, over 20 years ago the average American citizen was being bombarded by the multiplicity of health hazard and health promotion discourses that convey a sense of "somatic vulnerability" (Crawford, 1987). According to Crawford, their personal "bodily" health is under increased threat from environmental pollution, from "inappropriate" lifestyle habits, and from the failure of the promise of conventional medicine to "guarantee" health. This phenomenon has only intensified over the past two decades.

The new health consciousness was manifest in many contemporary cultural practices (from the purchase of unleaded petrol to the inclusion of fibre in the diet; from the banning of smoking in many workplaces to the mandatory wearing of seat belts) but it had a special significance for PE as a site for the promotion of healthy lifestyles. In the mid-1980s Crawford (1987, p. 101) told us that "Health education is a burgeoning profession, and fitness cheerleaders like Jane Fonda ... have become national celebrities." He also suggested that the themes of body shape, fitness, strength, disease prevention, longevity, youth, beauty and sex appeal had all become entangled. They remain entangled and this is increasingly problematic for PE, although the profession itself seldom recognizes it as such.

In the context of changing expectations associated with the new health consciousness, curriculum writers within the South Australian Department of Education began to produce curriculum materials to assist the "average" teacher take their class for PE on a daily basis. Central to this new initiative was the provision of a daily fitness component. To fund and market this new curriculum, the DPE program, the South Australian Education Department collaborated with the Australian Council for Health, Physical Education and Recreation (ACHPER) and the food company Nabisco.

This arrangement between these three otherwise unconnected organizations was the result of their shared interest in the fostering of a particular version of a healthy lifestyle: one that included daily physical activity and the daily consumption of Nabisco breakfast foods which are claimed to provide important caloric energy and "internal" bodily exercise.

And so during the 1980s, the DPE program won the hearts and minds of thousands of Australian primary school principals and teachers. But even more significant was the fact that as schools attempted to implement the program (which recommended a 15-minute fitness session per day in addition to a 30-minute skills lesson) many found it convenient to eliminate the skills lesson and accordingly PE often became a 15-minute fitness session each day (Tinning, 1987; Kirk *et al.*, 1989). PE had therefore been defined in practice as fitness only. Daily fitness activities as a particular form of HOPE in these schools of the 1990s became the de facto PE curriculum.

I am not attempting to argue why such a conception of PE is inadequate, but rather to consider the state of affairs that created HOPE as the curriculum reality for PE in many primary schools. To do this I want to return to the notion of how the profession defines or sets its problems.

Defining the problems for which the profession offers a solution

There are usually two ways in which problems become defined in a profession. One is that the profession recognizes certain social trends or conditions that are considered ripe for exploitation and accordingly the profession changes its "mission" statement (of aims, objectives) to accommodate responses to these trends. In other words the profession recognizes that its cause can be advanced by attachment to a new social concern. Lawson (1984) cites the changing cultural role prescriptions for women and the heightened interest in fitness and lifestyle as two examples that the PE profession has been able to capitalize on by increasing what it has to offer.

The other way in which problems become defined is where a trend in society or cultural practice is considered to be controversial, troublesome or potentially dangerous (to the profession) in that it may threaten the ideals of the profession. In this context, rather than accept a change in ideals, the profession attempts to change the trend. Thus, for Lawson, "Problem-setting begins with ... a fundamental, ideological disturbance and proceeds as people frame selectively and then name as problems either part, or the entirety, of the aforementioned trends and conditions" (Lawson, 1984, p. 50). Then "once problems have been selectively framed and named, attention may be directed toward their solutions" (ibid). The process of problem-setting proceeds through the complementary process of framing then naming.

Frames provide a perspective for defining a problem as a problem. They are "editing mechanisms that function to transform the unfamiliar into familiar categories and situations" (Lawson, 1984, p. 52). Professionals bring to a particular situation a number of frames or perspectives that they use in order to interpret and locate a particular "problem". Importantly, they "frequently are unable to identify the composition and consequences of their frames because they are tacit" (ibid). In this sense, frames are ideological and the ideological work done by such frames often works to mask the interests that are being served by a particular action.

Framing the problem to which "HOPE" is the solution

If then, as Lawson (1984) tells us, the genesis for problem-setting is either a response to a perceived threat or to the recognition of an opportune moment, what were the perceived threats and opportune moments which set the problem of healthy lifestyles as a challenge for the PE profession? What were the frames or perspectives in which HOPE was conceived as a solution to the problem?

In relation to a perceived threat of irrelevance, 30 years ago MacDonald Wallace (1978, p. 9) argued that "If physical educationists do not take up the challenge, the currently developing – and published – projects in health education curricula will soon leave them out on an isolated limb, regarded as irrelevant by educationists and the public alike." In this case the perceived threat of irrelevance comes from PE failing to promote the purported health benefits of physical activity. Defining health as a problem that can be solved (at least partly) by PE was, in part, a response by the PE profession in Britain to the perceived threat of irrelevance.

The opportunism associated with the development of HOPE in Britain is evident in the following example. Len Almond (1983), one of the chief promoters of HRF (a specific form of HOPE), made the claim that the medical profession in the late 1970s/early 1980s had identified circulatory and heart disease as a major contemporary health problem and an active lifestyle as a necessary preventative measure. He further contended that physical activity is valuable in creating a sense of wellbeing and feeling good. "These points," he suggests "are strong indications that the PE profession could play an important role in raising public consciousness about the value of exercise, being physically active as a part of one's lifestyle, and providing access to ways in which people can look after themselves" (p. 5). Indeed Almond provides a rationale for HRF which centres on "Encouraging and promoting an active lifestyle", and "Making the most of oneself". For Almond and others involved in the HOPE movement in Britain, HRF was the solution to the problem defined by the medical profession.

Of course responding to threat and opportunism is not in and of itself a bad thing, and the developers of HRF and DPE were not acting out of anything but good intentions. And positive things have been accomplished through such HOPE programs. However, and I am sure that HOPE promoters such as Almond in Britain and Wayne Coonan in Australia would be the first to agree, their programs have been less than universally successful and there still remains much work to be done to improve the healthy lifestyles of our children and adolescents.

From heart health HOPE to obesity HOPE (old wine …?)

HOPE in first decade of the twenty-first century has shifted its emphasis from "immunizing" kids against future CHD to "fighting the war against obesity".

The current media obsession with obesity fuels some genuine medical concerns regarding the health issues associated with the morbidly obese. It also fuels calls for school PE (or HPE) to become the front line in the war.

The following two vignettes present a fictitious representation of the lives of two primary school aged Australian students and their HPE experiences in school. Tara is from a middle class family in a "leafy" part of town and Luke is from a working class family in the barren treeless suburb miles from the city centre. Both students attend school in the state of Queensland, which in response to the obesity "crisis", has introduced an initiative called *Smart Moves*. A brief explanation of *Smart Moves* provides something of the context for these two stories.

From the Queensland Government website:

> Smart Moves – Physical Activity Programs in Queensland State Schools – has been developed to increase the curriculum time students are engaged in physical activity at school and to improve the quality of that activity.
>
> All primary schools must allocate 30 minutes per day of physical activity of at least moderate intensity as part of the school curriculum.
>
> (http://education.qld.gov.au/schools/healthy/
> physical-activity-programs.html)

Vignette 1: Tara

Tara is ten and attends Beattie State School in Brisbane. She is usually driven to school although she lives only four blocks away. Tara is, however, quite physically active since she enjoys playing netball on Saturday morning with the school team (they play in a local competition) and on two nights after school they have a training session under the direction of the school PE teacher.

When she arrives at school she usually hangs around with some of her girlfriends and, while practising their netball goal-shooting they often chat about what they saw on TV the previous night. Tara's favourite shows are *The Biggest Loser* and *Australian Idol*.

When the bell goes it's into class and after some preliminary organization it's down to the "work" of the day including maths, language, some social studies, a LOTE (Language other than English) lesson and a library session.

Up until the end of last year Tara received one PE lesson a week from the school specialist PE teacher and a health lesson by their classroom teacher. Collectively these two lessons comprise the HPE curriculum. The PE lesson focus is on games playing and it is not explicitly connected to anything they do in the health lesson. If they do discuss an issue of healthy lifestyles it is usually focused on health knowledge like what are the three food groups. "Theory" about health is separated from the practice of health.

This year however, since the introduction of *Smart Moves* the school has been desperately trying to meet the mandated requirements of *30 min-utes per day of physical activity of at least moderate intensity as part of the school curriculum.* This is not an easy task given the already crowded curriculum and the fact that there is only one PE teacher for the whole school of 340 kids. The principal expects every class teacher to take their class outside for physical activity on the days when the class doesn't have either sport (Friday afternoon for the whole school) or a lesson from the PE specialist.

So, in addition to her regular netball sessions, her weekly PE lesson and Friday afternoon sport, Tara now also has a couple of 30-minute class physical activity sessions with her grade teacher. It is rare that they get three of these sessions in a week simply because they run out of time to fit it in. Although this technically might not meet the *Smart Moves* guidelines of 30 minutes activity per day, the principal reckons that the school meets the "spirit" of the policy.

Tara and her friends are conscious of how they look. They like to wear designer labelled jeans and T-shirts. At home she sees her mum always conscious of how she looks and concerned with her own weight. Her mum is constantly on some sort of diet and regularly attends Curves exercise classes at the local gym to help her look and feel good. The magazines that her mother buys portray images of slender women and fine foods. On the TV all the desirable women are slim and "attractive", and the ads bombard the lounge-room with images of desirable females and the consumption of fast food.

Tara's father is into cycling. He is a keen competitor and spends a considerable amount of time and money on the pursuit of his sport. He is a naturally lean guy who has always been able to eat what he likes and never put on weight. Now that he is training hard he is constantly hungry and eating. He is usually training when the food is being prepared but is very health conscious and concerned with eating the "right" food. Interestingly, Tara sometimes thinks that for such a health "nut" he is often injured because one or other of his body parts seems to break down under the stress of constant training. Tara thinks that she will be like her mum when she matures, she will always be worried about staying slim to look good.

The messages about health (and by association, fitness and looking good) that Tara is exposed to at home and at school are about self-discipline, abstinence, control and will-power. These messages are in tension with those she gets from the TV which highlight the enjoyment, desirability, sensuality, and pleasure that are associated with the consumption of food and alcohol, travel and exotic holidays, luxury cars and other material goods. Nowhere in her home or in her school curriculum is there serious discussion about these contradictions between abstinence and consumption. Living with the tensions involved in these contradictions is part of family life for Tara. She is learning to accept the contradictions as natural and normal.

Vignette 2: Luke

Luke attends a primary school in a different part of town from Tara. He is also ten and is in Grade 6 at Warn Street Primary. He rides his BMX bike to school (a distance of about 1 km) and his school day begins with meeting his mates on the school oval for a game of pick-up soccer.

Like most (but significantly not all) of the boys in his class, Luke loves sport (especially Friday "arvo" sport) but sees it (albeit unconsciously) not in terms of a "healthy" pursuit but rather as a venue in which to assert his developing masculinity. Even before the recent *Smart Moves* initiative the class teacher often took Luke's class outside for "PE" in order to allow them to "let off steam and get rid of some of their energy". PE at Warn Street is seen as cathartic and in an instrumental sense to make students more receptive to their class work.

When they do have health education it is about food groups, or the dangers of drug use. The class teacher and the PE teacher are always telling them that if they get fit they will be healthy, and conversely that being unfit is tantamount to being unhealthy. There is an assumption that PE will "make them healthier" and that the school is contributing to the development of a healthy lifestyle.

After school Luke attends a program of physical activity sponsored by the government *Smart Moves* initiative. The reason Luke participates is that he is mad on sport and since both his mum and dad work and don't get home until 5.30 p.m., he might as well stay at school and play.

At home Luke sees his mother and father take no exercise. His dad used to play footy but gave that up when, at 34, he "got too old". He thinks his mum played netball once but she doesn't talk about it like dad does his footy. Both parents smoke, consume alcohol often to excess, and are generally "unconcerned" about their health unless they get sick. Luke watches a lot of TV and reckons that slim females are the most attractive and that Hungry Jack's is better than McDonald's. The pursuit of a healthy lifestyle is not part of Luke's family agenda.

For Luke health is not an issue, even at the level of the subconscious. The dominant messages he receives about health and fitness from his home environment are markedly different from those that Tara receives. These two vignettes are illustrative of the similarities and differences in contexts in which HOPE pedagogy is located and experienced.

Healthism and HOPE

Those who determined that HOPE was to be a solution to the problem of improving the healthy lifestyle of school children in the 1980s conceived their solution from a perspective which is embedded in healthism. As mentioned in Chapter 6, healthism is the set of assumptions and beliefs which represent the taken-for-granted with respect to health. Contemporary initiatives that place school PE at the front line of the war against obesity have perpetuated these assumptions. Healthism remains an ideology central to contemporary HPE initiatives (see Rich *et al.*, 2004). When people think about health it is typically through (within) the frame that is provided by healthism. As a regulative discourse in PE and health education (Kirk and Colquhoun, 1989), healthism has a number of main assumptions: that health is a self-evident good; that individuals are responsible for their own health; that the body can be considered as analogous to a machine; and that exercise equates with fitness which in turn equates with health. According to Kirk and Colquhoun (1989), "The implicit belief among many physical educators is that exercise through fitness leads to health, that exercise is essential to health, and that being fit and having a slender body is proof of health" (p. 10).

When HOPE is framed within the ideology of healthism there is no recognition of the darker side of the cult of the body that is implicated in the plight of many women and an increasing number of men who, through the contemporary ill-health practices such as excessive dieting, obsessive exercising, bulimia and anorexia nervosa, do daily battle with unattainable and unnatural images of body shape. Commenting on the situation in the 1980s, George and Kirk (1988) claimed that the ideology of healthism pervaded the PE profession, and Colquhoun (1989) argued that it was also the dominant ideology for the teaching of health education in Australian schools. It is still the dominant ideology underpinning contemporary conceptions of HPE and the field of HMS more generally.

Early versions of HOPE (e.g. DPE) and their contemporary manifestations (e.g. *Smart Moves*), for all their good intentions with respect to promoting healthy lifestyles, actually fail to challenge the entanglement of the themes of body shape, fitness, strength, disease prevention, longevity, youth beauty and sex appeal (Crawford, 1987) which has become a taken-for-granted of our contemporary culture and which causes such misery to millions. Part of the problem is the strong moralist language that is used within the discourses of healthism.

The moral discourses of healthism

Crawford (1987) claims that health (and for the purpose of this chapter we can read health as "healthy lifestyle") "is a metaphor, a moral discourse, an opportunity to express and reaffirm shared values, and an extremely important cultural site where the social self is constructed" (p. 103). What he means is that health is not an objective thing but rather a sort of agreement amongst certain members of society with respect to certain shared values. For example, we know of the differences between the way the Western medical profession defines health and the practices and beliefs of "alternative" medicines.

The fact that alternative medicines and practices are termed alternative speaks of the dominance of Western medicine in our culture. It is the baseline against which other practices and beliefs are positioned. It is no accident that the PE profession relates to the notions of health that are supported by our Western medical profession.

Crawford claims that there are two dominant themes that structure our conception of health; namely "control" and "release". I think that they are useful concepts that aid an understanding of the success of HOPE programs as a site for the promotion of healthy lifestyles. These two concepts are not mutually exclusive and exist contemporaneously for most individuals. For health as control, the attainment and maintenance of health requires effort, discipline, choice and determination. It is something to be achieved. Failure to achieve is associated with guilt, lack of will-power, character deficits and so on. It is something that might describe the orientation to health in Tara's home. Health is considered to be a representation of self-control and "evidence" of health carries certain strong moralistic assumptions. Within PE, healthism assumes that exercise relates directly to fitness which in turn leads directly to health. Also body shape is seen to be a metaphor for health and it is thought that it is through the physical that health is manifest. Jack Wilmore (a world renowned exercise physiologist and physical educator) revealed the moral tenor of the body shape metaphor when he argued "How can we [PE professionals] be effective in promoting health and fitness if our bodies are not living testimonies of our commitment? What we are communicates more than what we say" (Wilmore, 1982, p. 43).

An example of control as a form of moral language in HOPE can be seen in the common reaction of the PE profession to the "problem" of obesity (the obese individual is defined as a "loser" in our winning oriented society). The solution rests with the individual. It is classic "victim blaming" (Colquhoun, 1989) – "Just eat less and exercise more, its simple!" Not exercising "sufficiently" and/or "over" eating is thought to be simply a problem of lack of control, will-power or motivation, or just plain laziness on the part of the individual. There is little recognition of the strong social, cultural, emotional, ethnic or economic constraints/factors that also must be understood in any analysis of individual action or non-action. For example, the opportunities to exercise as a form of weight control are not equally available to all individuals. Mothers who work both in and outside the home, shift workers, certain ethnic groups, and economically impoverished families etc. have less "individual" choice with respect to exercising than, for example, a single male primary school teacher who is relatively well paid and who has generous leisure time. Tara's mother for example, who works at home as wife and mother is more able to find time to exercise than Luke's mum who works long hours in the local food processing factory.

For health as release, the emphasis is on enjoyment rather than achievement. It's about a positive attitude and a sense of not worrying about the things over which some control might be possible. "In the 'release' conception, health is not rejected as a value, but it is often repudiated as a goal to be achieved through instrumental actions. It is perceived more as an outcome of the enjoyment of life and the positive state of mind derived from such enjoyment" (Crawford, 1987, p. 108). According to Crawford, it is the working class and the poor who are more likely to consider health in terms of release rather than control. He claims that

> It is not that values of control are unimportant for working-class people ... but for most non-professional and non-managerial wage workers, self-direction and continuous striving are not the usual job require-ments, nor are rewards for such effort plentiful. Supervision and imposed disciplines of time, activity, behaviour, speech and body are the more prevalent type of work experience .... Demands for bodily controls during time off are likely to be regarded as an invasion of time reserved for enjoyment (ibid.).

Certainly Luke's parents do not rate control as a high priority for their lifestyle. When they leave the factory at the end of a day's work it is to the enjoyment of release from control that they turn.

Control and release are not just applicable to the concept of health. PE also contains these elements. Exercise is often perceived by people as involv-ing both control and discipline, and release from stress. Indeed sports are a classic case of both control and release in the PE context. Within PE lessons, with its attendant values of discipline, hard work and "no gain without pain" mentality, it is little wonder that the "messages" of a healthy lifestyle are less often accepted by kids from working class schools than those from middle class settings. Evans and Clarke (1988) describe the middle class view of the child as the "active mesomorph" (like Tara) and PE treats kids as if they were this "ideal". Mostly PE fails to recognize that for many kids (like Luke) the values associated with being an active mesomorph (those of control) are at odds with the values in the home context to which they return at the end of the school day.

Rationality, politics, individualism and the success of HOPE

One of the assumptions that underpins HOPE programs is that an individual actually has freedom to choose one set of lifestyle practices from another. For example, to choose to exercise regularly and to eat nutritious healthy food, rather than to take no exercise and eat predominantly fatty fast foods is not simply a matter of "making the right decision". Life is never that simple. The reasons we behave as we do have puzzled philosophers, historians, scientists and other researchers for thousands of years. More recently it has become the focus of marketing researchers, for obvious reasons.

Whatever the theory of human behaviour that you like to choose we can be sure of two things: first, individual agency is limited by structural factors over which the individual has no control (for example the current economic recession has restricted the choices available to many individuals, particularly those who are unemployed); second, individuals don't make choices based only on what might be called "rational" grounds (how many people know that it is rational to give up cigarette smoking yet continue to smoke in the face of the rational medical evidence?). Another way of thinking about this is to recognize that while their choice might be rational to them, it is based on a different logic and therefore seems irrational. The driver behind many choices is often as much emotional as rational.

In PE's work in health promotion we must recognize that it is unrealistic to expect that individuals will change their behaviour (their lifestyles) simply by acquiring some new knowledge. This rational change model has been shown to be inadequate time after time. To expect that knowing "that" will translate into doing "that" is naive. To expect that Luke will, as a direct consequence of his PE experiences at school, make choices regarding his behaviour that will contribute to a healthy lifestyle is to fail to understand the complex interconnection of factors that influence our personal behaviour.

Now this does not mean that we should not try to influence individual behaviour. Of course one way or another that is what our professional mission is all about. But it does mean that we should be less moralistic in our blaming those who continue with behaviours that we would deem to be counter-productive to a healthy lifestyle. There are always good, and mostly not so obvious, reasons why people behave as they do. In our HOPE programs we must recognize the different contexts in which individuals live and we must tailor our programs accordingly.

I remember a discussion I had with a woman from the local equal opportunity resource centre of the Education Ministry. She was describing how various videos that had been produced by the Ministry on the topic of sexual harassment and domestic violence were only successful for *certain* kids in *certain* areas. Videos that featured interactions of inner city, multicultural kids depicting sexual harassment via profane verbal abuse were not seen to be relevant to most kids in Anglo-Saxon, rural area schools. Context is important. Another example comes to mind: when DPE was introduced in Australian schools in the 1980s it was soon revealed that the tropic environment of Darwin severely circumscribed some of the DPE activities that were successful in the more temperate south (Pettit and Robinson, 1989). The message here is that we need more discussion about the different contexts in which our HOPE programs operate so that we can more specifically adapt them to be responsive to the differences in the lifestyles of families like Tara and Luke, to different ethnic and religious groups, and to different climatic conditions.

We need to recognize that healthism, as the framing ideology of HOPE, acts in a politically conservative way. Problems that are framed and named in a person centred, individualistic way preserve and reproduce existing political institutions and operations (Lawson, 1984). Sparkes (1988) makes the point that "it is not surprising that the ideological bedrock of HRF is that of individualism which does little, if anything, to challenge the conventional social categories and status hierarchies that exist both within schools and the larger society in relation to class, race, and gender" (p. 5).

But recognition of the broader social structures that limit individual agency is unpopular with the dominant power groups within our society. For example, it is in the interests of governments and industry to claim, for example, that a person's health is simply the outcome of their personal choice and to fail to give credence to such social structures as unemployment, dangerous work conditions (e.g. working with asbestos), chronic poverty and so on. Kirk and Colquhoun (1989) point out that all ideologies mask power and make less visible the promotion of one or more groups' interests over other interests. In the case of HOPE, it is the ideology of healthism that masks the interests of those who have most to gain by defining health as ultimately an individual responsibility, and that health can be unproblematically achieved through the "correct" attention to exercise and diet. In the context of the promotion of healthy lifestyles, those with the most to gain from this individualist conception of the problem are the fitness industry – those who own and operate the commercial fitness centres and gyms, the drug companies who produce and market the diet pills and supplements, and the manufacturers of the specific exercise clothing and equipment. Also implicated as interest groups are the medical professions who diagnose and treat conditions associated with the problem; the PE profession whose "expert" services are sought to remediate the problem and to promote healthy lifestyles through HOPE curriculum in schools; and the government and big business who seek greater productivity through less sick leave.

Perhaps all this talk of vested interests sounds rather conspiratorial but, for the most part, the ideological work which is done in the process of problem-setting actually occurs at the level of the implicit, the taken-for-granted, and the subconscious. Of course that's part of the problem, for when things are not obvious they are difficult to challenge. When we think of the lives of Tara and Luke we can get some sense of the way in which schooling in general, and HOPE programs in particular, reproduce a *particular* conception of a healthy lifestyle. The fact that neither school program actively problematizes health by challenging, for example, the media purveyed images of health and fitness, or by relating their daily physical activity sessions to the contexts of their home life, indicates to me that the school is implicated in reproducing notions of a healthy lifestyle which are ill-conceived, and lacking in contextual reality. Programs of physical activity that fail to address context are at best window-dressing, and at worst a reinforcement of the values and assumptions of healthism that ignore the social and political context of health.

Both Tara and Luke experience HOPE in the form of daily physical activity programs that represent a solution to the socially constructed problem of sedentary lifestyles and the obesity "crisis". As pedagogical strategies, HOPE programs do different pedagogical work depending on the context and the background of the participants. Moreover, some of that pedagogical work might be counter productive to the mission of HOPE. As a regulative discourse, healthism works to mask the assumptions implicit in defining healthy lifestyles as a problem and HOPE programs as a possible solution. HOPE programs are, as a function of the politics of problem-setting, essentially conservative and focused on individual solutions to issues which have structural influences. It's not that individuals do not have a responsibility for their own health – of course they do. But to ignore the fact that individual choice is always limited by certain structural conditions is to perpetuate a notion of blaming the victim that conveniently absolves governments, industry, and families from their share of responsibility for the health of the community.

If HOPE programs are to do more than raise the heart rates of children for the duration of the physical activity session they must begin to educate children about the problematic relationships that exist between health, exercise and fitness. For this to happen teachers themselves must recognize the assumptions implicit in the current conceptions of HOPE that operate in various forms in their schools. Moreover, professional organizations such as BPEA, ACHPER, AAPHERD etc. must begin to recognize how their own promotion of HOPE is failing to address the factors involved in the construction and maintenance of healthy lifestyles that exist outside the control of the individual. Advocating for physical activity is a professional responsibility of the field of HMS but in so doing there needs to be recognition of the fact that physical activity is not an unproblematic good. It is not the panacea to "the good life". And neither is the notion of a "healthy lifestyle" an objective, uncontested "fact". It is the creation of certain groups within our society who have particular, and usually implicit, values and opinions that happen to be most appropriate for other members of that particular group. If our HOPE programs are to really offer hope for all school children we must begin to analyze our own professional assumptions and become less moralistic, class biased, gendered and individualistic. Unless we do this we will never understand the causes of the gaps between HOPE and happening.

Note

1 This chapter is based on Tinning, R. (1991). Health oriented physical education (HOPE): The case of physical education and the promotion of healthy lifestyles. *ACHPER National Journal*, 134, 4–11.

Part V
Researching pedagogy

11 Research on pedagogy in HMS

In thinking about research on pedagogy in HMS I was tempted to provide an overview of what had been done and by whom. However, not only has this already been done by many (e.g. Silverman, 1991; Silverman and Ennis, 2003; Siedentop, 2000; O'Sullivan, 2003), including myself (Tinning, 1997), such an overview would not address some aspects that I now think are important in a consideration of research on pedagogy in HMS. Accordingly I have arranged this chapter in three parts. The first presents an autobiographical account of my own research history to share where I have come from. The second part provides my account of the history and traditions of research in sport pedagogy while the third part discusses the research shifts that have come from moving from a faculty of education to a faculty of health science.

My own eclectic research history

I have been asked on many occasions how someone with a critical pedagogy persuasion came to be a doctoral student of Daryl Siedentop. Asian colleagues, in particular, find it rather perplexing since they recognize that there are different epistemological perspectives that underpin much of the work of Siedentop and myself. Accordingly I give a brief account of my own research history so that you might have some understanding of "where I am coming from".

As young PE students we never learned about research. We just learned stuff about the body and physical activity without ever being encouraged to think about how this knowledge came to be "discovered" in the first place. It really wasn't until I did a masters degree in education that I seriously had to engage the research process. This came in the form of a number of very traditional courses in statistics, one of which I remember was called *Theory and Method of Educational Research (Experimental)*. This course positioned the hypothetico-deductive model as *the* way to do research in education. Qualitative methods were not mentioned.

I completed my masters degree (with a thesis that involved factor analysis) and was employed as a lecturer in PE at a new university (Deakin) in a provincial city 80 km from Melbourne. As the new Faculty (then called a School) of Education grew I found myself working with new colleagues who came to Deakin with new PhDs from the USA or Canada. They introduced me to critical theory, case study and action research and the epistemological tenets of these research methods/perspectives began to dominate my thinking with regard to educational research.

While maintaining my full-time lecturing position I enrolled as a part-time PhD student under the supervision of Stephen Kemmis. Kemmis was a critical theory advocate who had done his PhD at the University of Illinois with Professor Robert Stake, an expert on case study as method. Having had a favourable experience of the American PhD structure Kemmis suggested that I should apply for study leave from Deakin and pursue my PhD in the USA as a full-time student. I took his advice and sought to find out about the doctoral programs in PETE at the University of Massachusetts with Larry Locke, Teachers College Columbia with Bill Anderson, and the Ohio State University (OSU) with Daryl Siedentop. As it turned out, it was the OSU program that offered the best structure and credit for my already completed work and so I travelled to Columbus, Ohio with my (then) wife and two daughters to become a full-time doctoral student. It was a heady time and I was fortunate that my fellow students included such special people as Mary O'Sullivan, Ken Alexander, Hans van Der Mars, Donna Dugas, and Melissa (Missy) Parker.

Spared the sequence of statistics courses because of credit given in recognition of similar courses I had completed in my Australian MEd degree, I was free to pursue a sequence in the College of Education in what was called at the time naturalistic inquiry. I did however have to complete a number of courses in behaviour analysis that were mandatory for all PETE students in the OSU program. So there I was spreadeagled across different paradigms that seemed to disdain each other.

I learned a great deal from my time at OSU and still rate Daryl Siedentop as one of the brightest, most widely read, and serious scholars in the field of sport pedagogy. I also consider him to be a good friend. Under Daryl's supervision I managed to complete my doctorate with a thesis titled "A task theory of student teaching: Development and provisional testing". The thesis used Doyle's (1977) concept of task structures that had previously been studied in the PE context by Tousignant (1981) and Alexander (1982). I used a mixed method approach that entailed qualitative data collection and analysis and a form of theory construction that owed much to behaviour analysis. Like most doctoral theses it serves as a good dust collector, having not shaken the academic world as I had hoped. However, the process of completing that research, and the course work that preceded it, was an invaluable learning experience for me.

When I returned to Deakin I moved relatively easily back into the discourse community of the critical educational theory "camp". However, I was rather more suspicious of the grand narrative of critical theory as the only epistemological pathway to a more socially just world. I remember going to a conference of behaviour analysis held in Milwaukee during my time at OSU. Not only did I have the privilege of hearing Professor B.F. Skinner present (he was an old man by that time) but was rather amazed to find that there was a group of serious researchers/scholars who called themselves "behaviourists for social action". Their intentions and their commitments seemed to be no less commendable regarding the mission of making a more equitable world than those critical theorists of the critical project (e.g. Apple, Giroux). However, my Deakin colleagues eschewed behaviourism in all its forms, even though their knowledge of what it stood for was often limited. I learned that the two groups would never talk to each other and never cross the epistemological and discourse divide.

As new faculty members arrived at Deakin the range of theoretical perspectives grew but always remained focused on a critical edge informed by social theory. It was a very special time, and as Joe Kincheloe has remarked, "the amazing Deakin Mafia (Deakin University) ... provided innovative and unprecedented critical scholarship on education for a few short years" (Kincheloe, cited in Smyth, 2001). Informed by various theoretical perspectives (e.g. critical theory, neo-Marxist, poststructuralist, postcolonial, feminist, critical literacy, Bourdieuian, Foucauldian) key Deakin scholars such as Richard Bates, John Smyth, Stephen Kemmis, Robin McTaggart, Fazil Rizvi, Jane Kenway, Bill Green, Chris Bigum, Maree Brennan, Lindsay Fitzclarence and Jill Blackmore pursued their commitments to social justice through education. Individually and collectively they, and others, made Deakin synonymous with critical educational thought.

Attracted by Deakin's growing reputation in the 1980s, numerous internationally renowned education scholars (e.g. Michael Apple, Henry Giroux, Tom Popkewitz, Ivor Goodson, Patti Lather, Wilf Carr, John Codd, Lawrence Iannaccone, Lyn Yates, John Prunty, Valerie Walkerdeen) came to Deakin and wrote monographs for the Deakin Monograph series and generally engaged in the stimulating intellectual discourse about education for social justice. These invited scholars were part of the extended influence and connection of the "Deakin Mafia" and further promoted the work of Deakin in the context of education, social change, and social justice. My own work focused mainly on engaging the discourses and methods of the critical project within the context of PE and PETE and during that time I was greatly influenced by my association with colleagues Lindsay Fitzclarence and David Kirk who, for a number of years, were both at Deakin.

From education to HMS

As I explained in the Introduction, in 2000 I moved from Deakin to the University of Queensland (UQ). The move was significant not only geographically (Geelong and Brisbane are some 1600 km apart) but also in terms of intellectual community. I moved from a faculty of education to a faculty of health science. The UQ Faculty of Health Science comprised "schools" (the equivalent size of a Faculty or College in many other universities) of medicine, dentistry, public health, rehabilitation therapies, pharmacy, nursing, and HMS. HMS sits nicely (but not without tensions of hierarchy) as an "upstream" focused intervention in the field of health. This is manifest clearly in the examples of some of the research that is currently done in the UQ School of Human Movement Studies (see Chapter 8).

Most of my work early on was similar to what I had been doing at Deakin (i.e. teaching and researching in PE/PETE) but over time I became more involved in work beyond the teacher education program. For example, I have worked in the sport coaching postgraduate program, supervised postgraduate students in sports coaching, and been a co-investigator in funded research into pedagogical aspects of sports coaching. In the postgraduate program my contribution was to assist in the development of an online course on *Pedagogies for Coaching*. In this course, which is based on the ideas of reflective practice, students (who are all practising coaches at both junior and elite levels) are required to conduct an action research project involving their own coaching. The research dimension of my involvement with sports coaching has focused on understanding the workplace as a site of learning for coaches. As I mentioned in Chapter 4, sport pedagogy research focusing specifically on sports coaching is very much a developing speciality.

Also, as part of my new responsibilities I also teach on a research skills course (doing the section on epistemology and qualitative methods), and coordinate a course for honours and postgraduate students on interdisciplinary perspectives in HMS. In working with many HMS scientists (not, I hasten to add, on actual research projects) I have come to appreciate and respect their knowledge and skills in new ways. I know I am privileged to work with some genuinely impressive colleagues. However, paradigmatic tensions do arise, for example between quantitative and qualitative research, and in the process of working with these colleagues I have been stimulated to think long and hard about some of the assumptions that underpin our research into physical activity and health, and on the implications of the focus on health in school PE (see for example Tinning, 2008).

Working on the course *Interdisciplinary Perspectives in HMS* with Don Bailey (a specialist on bone growth and physical activity) has been particularly rewarding and enjoyable. Don and I have different epistemological leanings and we have had many engaging debates both in front of the class and privately.

I have come to understand that it is easy to spend time in a small community of scholars (e.g. critical pedagogues) who spend considerable time setting up a caricature of scientists as number-crunching reductionist demons with no political conscience and perhaps an emotional deficit to boot. Of course it is also the case that the reverse tends to happen within groups of exercise scientists who might caricature qualitative researchers as light-weight storytellers. In both cases these caricatures are really straw men that can easily be demolished for the sake of an argument. In many of these situations little time or effort is made to get to know the actual people who are the target of the caricature. Importantly, experience has shown me that much of the fuel that drives paradigm tensions is based as much on personality and ego as it is on epistemological disagreements.

In the increasingly competitive academic environment the value of the research outputs of both paradigms is judged increasingly by supposed objective measures such as impact factors and the citation index. In general terms it is also harder for qualitative researchers to compete with their quantitative colleagues in terms of these measures and also in dollar income derived from competitive grant sources. Accordingly, like it or not, HMS departments are forced to make tough decisions in terms of who they hire and the research agendas they support. In this context, sport pedagogy usually has a difficult time in competition with colleagues from exercise science and physical activity and health who can access serious grant monies targeted on health. I hasten to add that this is less of a personal lament and more of a simple observation of a reality.

Over the years of my career I have learned a great deal from having my ideas (some of them cherished) challenged in many ways and by many people. In what follows I discuss a particular instance of this process and the costs and rewards of having one's ways of seeing the world disturbed.

Challenging beliefs

Some time ago Stephen Thorpe, then one of my doctoral students, and I presented a paper at a conference in Singapore titled "Dilemmas and problematics involved in the process of theorising curriculum development and reform" (Tinning and Thorpe, 1999). The presentation was, in part, a rumination on the process of conducting a funded research project and the impact of having my thinking constantly challenged in new ways by the two research assistants (RAs) who worked on the project. The story provides a window into the complexities of taking a reflexive position with respect to pedagogy research.

The research project that was the focus of the rumination was titled "Competing discourses in school health and physical education" and was conceived over a number of years. It had been previously submitted for funding by Derek Colquhoun, focusing solely on health education. The revised 1995 submission sought to recognize the interconnectedness of health education and PE in the then new Australian Key Learning Area (KLA) named Health and Physical Education. Along with Deborah Lupton (a medical sociologist) I joined the proposal bringing with me my expertise in PE and my theoretical "baggage" of critical theory. I say baggage simply to suggest that there is (was) an ownership of that knowledge – an ownership of knowledge in which I felt comfortable even within the challenging times for critical theorizing (see Anyon, 1994).

The project proposed to investigate the competing discourses at play in the conceptualization of the KLA and its operationalization within school settings. Specifically, and in "grant-speak", it aimed to apply to health and PE a theoretical framework that identifies the dominant sociocultural discourses and power relations of curriculum in health and PE; one which conceptualizes school subjects as sites of contestation, struggle and tension. I was comfortable in using the notions of text and discourse. I was also happy about the notion that there would be a tension between some discourses and that there would be a dominant discourse(s) in the ways in which the KLA was conceptualized and operationalized in schools.

When we began to work on the project at the beginning of 1996 we employed two RAs to help us. Most RAs work mainly at the level of implementation of the principal researchers' ideas and directions. Probably if we had employed RAs who merely worked as directed, then the project would have moved forward in a more technical manner (technical in the sense that the research methods and theoretical framework had been articulated in the original proposal and "all" we would have needed to do was to arrange for the data to be collected, analyzed within the articulated framework and then begin to write about our findings. That would have been the classic linear research model.

It soon became obvious that the two RAs in our project, both of whom were my PhD students, were reading widely in contemporary social theory and that their potential contribution to the project would be wasted if confined to a more functionary role. We discussed with them the idea of them becoming more involved in the conceptual work of the project which was to be the focus of the first year of the project.

And so began the serious roller-coaster ride that was part of re-conceptualizing the project. Ian Hunter's (1994) critique on the principled positions inherent in critical theory accounts of the failure of schooling left a sting in our critical theory cheeks. Rose and Miller (1992), following Foucault, tempted us to think of the political rationalities and governmental technologies that might operate with respect to health and PE, while John Law's (1991) *Organizing Modernity* introduced us to a modest sociology and the need to talk of "ordering processes" rather than an ordered society. All this was heady stuff and a long way conceptually from our original proposal.

Our regular meetings became more like tutorials than research meetings. They were "tutorials" in the sense that Peter Kelly or Stephen Thorpe would typically present an account of the week's reading and I would usually admit to not having done all the required reading. Herein lay a problem. The RA's job (as we conceived it) was to read and extend our theorizing. I was, however, finding that my non-project job (a senior professor in the Faculty of Education) was increasingly limiting the amount of time available for the scholarly activity of reading new theory.

When your hat-rack is removed

When we have an investment in a particular way of seeing the world (a theoretical framework if you like) then it "exists" at levels that are not merely rational. Perhaps we even embody it. Sometimes I wonder if my investments/ commitments to my ways of seeing the world are actually different in *kind* to those of the "flat-earthers". I am so happy to disparage in the comfort of my current knowledge that the earth is a globe.

In the course of the project I read and enjoyed a paper given to me by Peter Kelly. David Blades (1995), in playful way, used the idea of the hat-rack in the hall to discuss the procedures of power in a curriculum discourse. The hat-rack was a metaphor for our frameworks for understanding the world. I understood my hat-rack as critical theory and that, just as Foucault had removed Blades' old hat-rack from his hallway without telling him how to replace it (or even if he should), so Peter Kelly and Stephen Thorpe had removed my hat-rack. I, like Blades before me, entered the "hallway" (of our project) each week and unconsciously attempted to locate my hat-rack to position my thinking – a comfortable "hook" on which to place my ideas. Blades (1995) suggested that

> change is possible, but this is hard work. It begins with critique of those systems of enframing we live within, but it goes further by considering how else it might be. This is an interactive process: we have to be willing to move the frame [hat-rack] out of the house, so to speak, and learn to find new ways to live (p. 129).

In a very important way, "blocks" to new ways of thinking or theorizing about our work are not all, or perhaps even mostly, rational. We can't assume that, just because a new theory might seem to "win the day" at the level of rational debate, it will necessarily be appropriated. One's investment in ideas, ways of seeing and theorizing often exist beyond the conscious realm. I am not talking about Giddens' (1991) notion of practical consciousness here. I think that investment is sometimes registered in the unconscious.

Of course in the academy, as elsewhere, fashion is an important contingency. Theorists and theories become fashionable. For example, some scholars (but certainly not your good self or me!) include a passing reference to Foucault in their work to show that the author is "around", connected with, or otherwise familiar with the work(s) of this fashionable French theorist.

Whatever the explanation for the behaviour or cultural practice (call it what you like) of theorizing, in my view fashion is an unspoken part (agent in the techno-social network [Law, 1994]) that needs to be recognized and factored in to an honest rendering of choice of theory. We need to remember that the history of science is replete with examples of theorists who were considered eccentric (off centre!) because they theorized outside the fashionable and beyond the centre.

My hat-rack was removed and replaced by others. Peter brought the work of Rose and Miller (1992) to the project and Stephen brought the work of Law (1991). Both contributions were destabilizing but they were also stimulating. Personally I was much stimulated by the discussions we had in our project "tutorials". But being stimulated is one thing; being confident to actually engage the new theorizing at an empirical level within the project was another. Before I had read of the hat-rack metaphor I remember thinking that I tended to operate on a sort of theoretical default – when pressed to explain certain social practices I default to the language and discourses of critical theory. Interestingly however, Stephen considered my default was behaviourism. Clearly my OSU experience had been profound.

As I mentioned earlier, as a doctoral student in the early 1980s I learnt that there was (and probably still is) a group of leftist behaviourists dedicated to social justice and their work is unashamedly devoted to this cause (see Moxley, 1982). Yet I was puzzled that there was no reference to any of their work in the work of the critical theorists. Is this because the critical theorists are familiar with, yet reject, the theoretical (and empirical) arguments on the contingencies of reinforcement? Is it considered that behaviourism no longer offers (or never did) any useful explanations for understanding human behaviour? Or is the whole project of behaviourism simply out of fashion with certain groups of scholars? Perhaps it is paradoxical that behaviourists could explain the phenomenon of fashion in theorizing among certain academic populations by an analysis of the contingencies of reinforcement that operate in that population! Perhaps Stephen was right, but I certainly couldn't admit to having a hook on my hat-rack for behaviourism and remain in fashion with the critical theorists now could I?

The truth is that my default hat-rack is probably eclectic in nature. The tension in this position is that I spent most of the time devoted to that project actually feeling insecure and in a state of what Bill Green (1996) called "existential crisis". Indeed if we think of the project as a site of pedagogy for the researchers, then "What is on offer is access to a discourse and, through this discourse, the possibility of engaging the social world differently in such a way as to generate what might well be appropriately called an existential *crisis*" (p. 10; emphasis in original).

I was impressed by what I read of Law's thesis on "ordering modernity" (1994). Perhaps Law's idea of a modest sociology represents something of a paradigm shift in thinking about social theory. On one hand it has the effect of a Kuhnian paradigm shift for me, yet on the other it appeals to my own reservations about some of the less modest, less self-disclosing and partial accounts of social theory that have been appropriated by some educational researchers. Law's own position is reassuring in this regard when he revealingly says "this version of a modest sociology is to expose some of the contingencies and uncertainties – ethnographic, theoretical, personal and political – with which I have wrestled along the way" (p. 17). It is this idea that I later appropriated for my idea of a modest critical pedagogy (see Tinning, 2002).

There is a world of difference between my convenient, good intentioned, but perhaps fashionable, use of Foucault's notion of regimes of truth in discussing dominant discourses in PETE (see for example Tinning, 1991c) and Law's (1994) use of Foucault's notion of discourse which he admits to having "worked in and wrestled with its promise for a decade" (p. 21). What I am saying here is that many of us who work in "applied" settings with "applied" problems (usually set or defined by those of us with an applied focus) need to understand the limits of our understandings of the theories we appropriate and "apply" to our problems. I certainly always feel "out on the limb" and insecure when straying too far into the realm of social theory. Pushing one's theoretical position(s) means moving out of one's comfort zone. Yet this is exactly where we must seek to be if we are to learn. This is exactly where Stephen Thorpe and Peter Kelly took me. In this sense they taught me well and I remain grateful to both of them.

Paradigms, research methods and pedagogy

In order to provide an account of the history and traditions of research in sport pedagogy I will tell the story of a particular conference I attended, since it was a good example of the tensions that exist(ed) within the sport pedagogy research community with regard to paradigms and research method.

Early days in the paradigm wars

As in all wars, the first casualty was innocence.

In 1991 I attended an AIESEP conference in Atlanta, Georgia. Much of the conference focused on research in teaching PE (a dimension of pedagogy research) and although accounts of research studies predominated there were also some polemic-type papers critiquing what was considered to be a technocratic orientation in PE pedagogy. My own paper was on action research and the way that it was used in PE (see Tinning, 1991a). At that time there was a growing literature in sport pedagogy that was providing a critique of the way that PE was taught (Bain, 1990a; Dewar, 1990; Wright, 1990; Kirk, 1986; Hellison, 1988; Tinning, 1984) and of the way it was researched (Schempp, 1988; Kirk, 1989; Smith, 1991; Tinning, 1991c). This work ruffled some feathers not the least because sport pedagogy research was seen to be making some serious progress (e.g. Placek and Locke, 1986; Metzler, 1989; Silverman, 1991) and, presumably, criticism was regarded as unhelpful and perhaps damaging to the cause.

Paul Schempp's (1987) critique was particularly forceful. He first described what he saw as a trend in preference for research methods:

> Recent years have seen an increase in the amount of research activity devoted to teaching in physical education. The result of these efforts has been a substantial growth in the body of knowledge regarding movement

pedagogy. Most of these undertakings have been completed with the natural science mode of inquiry as the research model. Thus the natural science paradigm has emerged as the dominant mode of inquiry and analysis for research on teaching in physical education (p. 111).

Schempp went on in that paper to present the limitations of what he called the "natural science paradigm" and offered support for an alternative paradigm which he called qualitative. Schempp's critique of the natural science paradigm was broadly rebutted by Siedentop (1987). Then there was a rejoinder to Siedentop by Schempp (1988). This was indeed a hotly contested topic. Certianly Schempp and Siedentop were coming from different paradigms.

> Paradigms are basic *belief* systems; they cannot be proven or disproven, but they represent the most fundamental positions we are willing to take. If we could cite reasons why some particular paradigm should be preferred, then, those reasons would form an even more basic set of beliefs. At some level we must stop giving reasons and simply accept whatever we are as our basic belief set – our paradigm (Guba and Lincoln, 1989, p. 80).

> … various paradigms will differ in their assumptions regarding the nature of reality, the nature of truth, and the guidelines for seeking and judging evidence. Finally they will differ in their definition of appropriate strategies for seeking truth (Sparkes 1991, p. 107).

According to Sparkes (1991) although different paradigms produce different truths "this is not to imply that the various conceptualisations of the truth are granted equal status within the research community" (p. 109). For Sparkes, certain individuals are "able to define and legitimate research questions and methodologies. They act as influential *gatekeepers* in their positions as journal editors, editorial board members, reviewers, and conference planners" (ibid.).

I will return to paradigms soon but, for the moment, back to the Atlanta conference. In one presentation Mary O'Sullivan was joined by two of the fathers of pedagogy research, Daryl Siedentop and Larry Locke, in delivering a strong response to what they called the "radical discourse" that was critical of positivistic approaches to research and technocratic approaches to teaching and learning. The presentation carried considerable gravity because of the reputation of the speakers.

After their presentation there was an interesting response from the audience. The Americans in the audience applauded loudly, while most of the European delegates directed their applause at the "critical" scholars who were positioned at the rear of the room. A simplistic reading of this response is that the American academy was, at the time, largely dominated by a positivistic orientation to research while the Europeans were more oriented by the hermeneutic and critical traditions. The European university system has typically placed a greater emphasis on theory than their American counterparts.

The presentation was subsequently published in *Quest* with the title "Towards collegiality: Competing viewpoints among teacher educators" (O'Sullivan *et al.*, 1992). In that paper, they began by indicating that their reaction to the "radical" discourse (as they call critical pedagogy) was mixed:

> We agree with much of what they aspire to for physical education. However, several of their accusations about work within the dominant discourse and some of the assertions about the new discourse have at times made us frustrated, uncomfortable, and even angry (p. 268).

Citing a paper by McKay *et al.* (1990) also published in *Quest* and titled "Beyond the limits of technocratic physical education" as having committed three "sins" of poor scholarship, O'Sullivan and her colleagues (1992) proceeded to challenge the often "overzealous" (their word) language used by some "radicals" in the prosecution of their critical pedagogy "mission"; the perceived high moral ground taken by them; and the lack of evidence to support many of their claims. I think that in terms of language use, claiming the high moral ground, and lack of evidence, the criticisms O'Sullivan and her colleagues made were probably correct. The critical pedagogy literature does contain some rather forceful and less measured language. It does take a high moral ground in its advocacy for "freedom from oppression and unjust social practices". And it does contain claims for which there is no available empirical evidence.

It should be noted that neither Locke nor O'Sullivan were fundamentally opposed to qualitative research. Locke's inspiring qualitative research paper "The ecology of the gym: What the tourist never sees" (1974) is a fine example of interpretivistic research. It was not however, critical. O'Sullivan herself had increasingly worked with qualitative methods and her commitment to issues of equity and social justice were explicit and heartfelt.

Siedentop's position was somewhat more equivocal. As a "radical" behaviourist he was committed to the empirical-analytical paradigm and at that time described his concerns with some of the methodological shortcomings he identified in qualitative research. His reservations at the time were thoughtfully argued in his reply to Locke's (1989) claim that with a good qualitative description of the gym the reader could (almost) smell the gym. The title of Siedentop's paper, "Do the lockers really smell?" (1989), signalled his concerns with Locke's claims.

In the case of the paper by McKay, Gore and Kirk that caused O'Sullivan *et al.* (1991) so much concern, we can better understand why these "sins" of poor scholarship were committed when we understand something of the context in which many of the papers were written.

McKay and colleagues, faced with the very survival of a sociocultural discourse within a science-dominated department of HMS, were passionate in their discursive form. They were pushing the boundaries, making bold claims and generally trying to provoke readers to seriously consider the hegemony of technocratic discourse within PE. To this extent, at least, their work was successful. Their intentions were polemic and not offered as solutions to the perceived problem. Indeed, a good deal of the literature on critical pedagogy has had similar purpose. In terms of rhetorical styles we can identify their paper as *thymos* – a rage against what they saw as injustice. O'Sullivan *et al.* were applying the standards of *logos* – rational scientific discourse in their judgement of this work (see Chapter 6).

Of course this is not to argue that critical pedagogy should be only represented by *thymos* styled rhetoric. As I have argued more recently (Tinning, 2002), a modest critical pedagogy would make use of each of the rhetorical styles, including *thymos*, *mythos* and *logos*.

My reason for explaining this at some length is that the Atlanta presentation and the subsequent *Quest* article by O'Sullivan *et al.* (1992) revealed that the paradigm debate in sport pedagogy was something more than a disinterested, dispassionate, logical debate. It was imbued with emotion and subjectivity. It was imbued with human interests.

It was Habermas (1972) who argued that all human knowledge is connected to human interests in a constitutive sense. This means that human interests make knowledge what it is, and human knowledge is always constitutive of human interests. Table 11.1 illustrates the relationship between the various orientations and the knowledge forms and research paradigms that might be used in pedagogy research.

My own "vested interests"

As I have indicated in other spaces (e.g. Tinning, 1992), I am happy to place myself within the "big tent" of critical pedagogy. As a long-time advocate of critical pedagogy and a socially critical school (Kemmis, 1972), I have argued that issues relating to gender equity, equality of opportunity, catering for diversity, and challenging unjust practices such as motor elitism, should be an integral part of PE (see Tinning, 1985, 1987). I have also been vocal in the need for PE to problematize knowledge construction, legitimation and dissemination, and to critically engage its own ideology, power and culture (see Tinning, 1991c).

In an important sense I have written from a partisan position. This puts me in the company of Liston and Zeichner (1991) who claim that educational research in teacher education should become partisan. By partisan they are not talking about unthinking, unreasoned, adherence to a dogma – they are referring to commitment to a social reconstructivist position with respect to education.

In thinking about the publications of my academic career, I have covered a range of topics from school PE, health education, teacher education, research

Table 11.1 Knowledge, human interests and research

Orientation	World view	Purpose of research	Human interests	Research paradigm
Behaviouristic	Objective reality Science for a better world	Prepare skilled technicians of teaching	Technical Prediction Control	Empirical-analytical Natural science
Personalistic	Multiple realities Subjectivity meaning	To develop the individual teacher as a person	Practical Interpretive understanding	Hermeneutic Interpretive Phenomenological
Critical inquiry	Reality is socially constructed Social inequities, power and oppression	Challenge the school system where necessary	Criticism Liberation Emancipation	Critical theory Action research Case study Feminist Poststructuralist

methodology, critical pedagogy, and the field of HMS. Significantly, most have been analytic and philosophical rather than empirical. With a few notable exceptions, most of my scholarship now consists of interpreting the research/scholarship of HMS within broader analytic frameworks appropriated from other fields. In this way much of my work has been a synthesis, analysis and commentary on trends and developments in the fields of PE, PETE and HMS more broadly. In the language of Basil Bernstein, much of my scholarship is knowledge re-contextualization. I take the knowledge produced by others and translate it into a form that can be understood by teachers, undergraduate and postgraduate students. Each of my books falls into this category. However, I am also a knowledge producer in that through the process of re-contextualization I have attempted to provide new ways of thinking about issues germane to our field.

Since the early 1980s many positive things have happened in terms of a growing interest in a critical agenda within our field. George Sage's (1993) consideration of "Sport and physical education in the new world order" in the pages of *Quest* is an example of how issues relating to social justice have become part of the professional discourse of the broad field of HMS. Importantly, however, such discourses have not been isolated in academic journals. They have also been "taken up" in curriculum reform documents, for example within Australia and New Zealand.

In Figures 11.1–3 I have illustrated what might be conveniently labelled the main research paradigm orientations of the research traditions in sport pedagogy. Beneath each I have included one example that is indicative of the

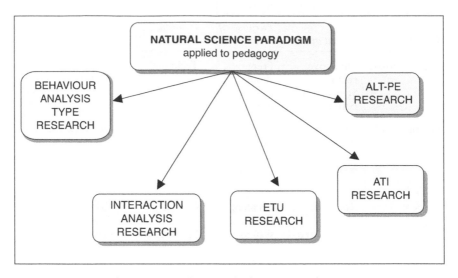

Figure 11.1 Natural science paradigm applied to sport pedagogy.

tradition. You will note that I have only lisited examples of actual empirical research and thus have excluded commentaries, reviews or advocacies.

Behaviour analysis research:

> Eldar, E. (1990). Effect of self-management on preservice teachers' performance during field experience in physical education. *Journal of Teaching in Physical Education*, 9, 307–323.

Interaction analysis research:

> Cheffers, J., and Mancini, V. (1966). Teacher-student interaction. In W. Anderson and G. Barrett (Eds.), *What's Going on in Gym?* Connecticut: Motor Skills Theory into Practice Monograph 1.

ALT-PE research:

> Gagnon, J., Tousignant, M., and Martel, D. (1989). Academinc learning time in physical education classes for mentally handicapped students. *Adapted Physical Activity Quarterly*, 6, 280–289.

ATI (aptitude treatment interaction) research:

> Silverman, S. (1986). Relationship of engagement and practice trials to student achievement. *Journal of Teaching in Physical Education*, 5, 13–21.

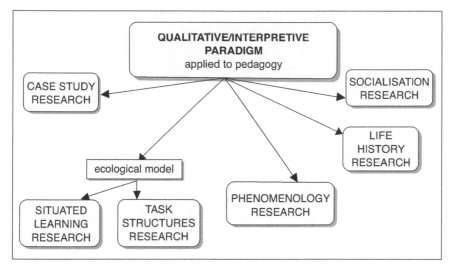

Figure 11.2 Qualitiative/interpretive paradigm applied to sport pedagogy.

ETU (experimental teaching unit) research:

> Yerg, B. (1981). The impact of selected presage and process behaviours on the refinement of a motor skill. *Journal of Teaching in Physical Education*, 1(1), 38–46.

Case study research:

> Tinning, R., and Hawkins, K. (1988). Montaville revisited: A daily physical education program four years on. *ACHPER National Journal*, 121, 24–29.

Task structures research:

> Tousignant, M., and Siedentop, D. (1983). A qualitative analysis of task structures in required secondary physical education classes. *Journal of Teaching in Physical Education*, Fall, 47–57.

Situated learning research:

> Rovegno, I. (1994). Teaching within a curricular zone of safety: School culture and the situated nature of student teachers' pedagogical content knowledge. *Research Quarterly for Exercise and Sport*, 65(3), 269–279.

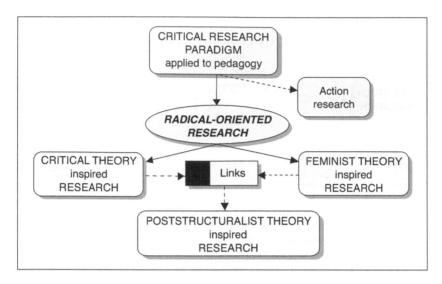

Figure 11.3 Critical research paradigm applied to sport pedagogy.

Phenomenology research:

> Nilges, L. (2004). Ice can look like glass: A phenomenological investiga-
> tion of movement meaning. *Research Quarterly for Exercise and Sport*,
> 75(3), 298–314.

Socialisation research:

> Schempp, P., and Graber, K. (1992). Teacher socialisation from a dialec-
> tical perspective: Pretraining through induction. *Journal of Teaching in
> Physical Education*, 11, 329–348.

Life history research:

> Dowling-Naess, F. (1996). Life events and curriculum change: The life
> history of a Norwegian educator. *European Physical Education Review*,
> 2(1), 41–53.

Action research:

> Tinning, R. Macdonald, D. Tregenza, K and Boustead, J. (1996). Action
> research and the professional development of teachers in the health and
> physical education field: The Australian NPDP experience. *Educational
> Action Research*, 4(2), 391–406.

Critical theory inspired research:

> Bain, L. (1990). A critical analysis of the hidden curriculum in physical education. In D. Kirk and R. Tinning (Eds.), *Physical Education, Curriculum and Culture: Critical Issues in the Contemporary Crisis* (pp. 23–42). Basingstoke: Falmer Press.

Feminist theory inspried research:

> Clarke, G. (2004). Threatening space: (physical) education and homophobic body-work. In J. Evans, B. Davies and J. Wright (Eds.), *Body Knowledge and Control: Studies in the Sociology of Physical Education and Health* (pp. 191–203). London: Routledge.

Poststructuralist inspired research:

> Oliver, K., and Lalik, R. (2004). Critical inquiry on the body in girls' physical education classes: A critical post-structuralist perspective. *Journal of Teaching in Physical Education*, 23(2), 162–195.

Clearly the range of research types is wide and inevitably advocates of one (or more) types tend to champion their prefered type. In making sense of the paradigms used in research on pedagogy in HMS it is necessary to understand that the choice of paradigm will be influenced by the conception of pedagogy used in the first place. For example, if pedagogy is considered as merely a technical matter of arranging the spatial, temporal and human factors such that the explicit lesson objectives are achieved in the most efficient manner then reductionist, objectivist-type research would be most suited. If, however, you use a Lusted (1986) conception of pedagogy such as underpins this book, then the research paradigm needs to be able to "handle" subjectivity, meaning, dispositions, values, ambiguity, and identities. The natural science research paradigm is not intended to, nor can it, handle such matters.

Sport pedagogy: A more mature research field?

It seems to me that sport pedagogy has come a long way since the days of the paradigm wars. For example, in Kirk *et al.*'s (2006) *Handbook of Physical Education* there are chapters on a wide range of methodological perspectives from behaviour analysis (Ward, 2006) to poststructuralism (Wright, 2006). This might indicate a level of maturity and acceptance of different truth tales in our field. I am, however, a little more skeptical in my interpretation of this apparent tolerance of methodological difference.

Take the chapters of Ward and Wright cited above for example. Ward's chapter, titled "The philosophy, science and application of behaviour analysis in physical education" is an excellent account of the philosophical and methodological assumptions underpinning behaviour analysis. But I wonder how seriously it would be read by those who reject behaviourism out of hand as some sort of politically incorrect throwback! In Wright's case, her chapter, titled "Physical education research from postmodern, poststructural and postcolonial perspectives" is rich in analytic power yet I wonder if it would also be glossed over, or ignored by those who define themselves as empirical-analytic researchers.

To put it bluntly, there is still a large degree of ignorance and superficiality about our newfound eclecticism.

There was a time when I, like Crum (1997), held that American research in sport pedagogy was under-theorized compared with work done in Europe in particular, but also the UK and Australasia. Now I am not so sure and am more than a little concerned that the non-course work, dissertation-only approach used in the UK and Australia in particular is actually limiting graduate students' exposure to and understanding of multiple research methodologies. Accordingly, some new PhD graduates enter the field of HMS with an inadequate conceptual base for their careers. I make this criticism not just of sport pedagogy scholars. It seems also to apply to our colleagues in the sciences of HMS. For example, I am always puzzled by the fact that so many of our sport psychology graduates know absolutely nothing about behaviour analysis as a research methodology. They spend all their time learning about psychometrics and inferential statistics and ignore single case design completely.

Notwithstanding this observation, it is increasingly the case that professionals in the field of HMS, like professionals everywhere, are being required to provide evidence for their practice. While this may indeed be a good thing, there is a danger that, since reductionist forms of quantitative data are relatively easy to collect and to display, these forms of evidence will come to dominate. In Macdonald's (2004) opinion "Despite the criticism of evidence-based practice, we have a political and educational climate in which the HPE profession must be vigilant. ... Tradition, routine and unfounded assumptions will not suffice" (p. 24). Let us consider this issue for a moment.

Evidence based pedagogy?

If you want to choose a pedagogy based on research evidence that works what's the chance? Well, firstly we must go back to the question of what is the intent of the pedagogy. If all you want to do is to determine which pedagogical strategy to use to teach a volleyball dig then you might find some specific research that focused on that skill. More than likely, in the absence of a particular study that used the same type of class (same age, same skill level, same sex, same age etc.) you would have to "go generic". By that I mean consider the results of research into the teaching of motor skills in general and then make some generalizations to your particular context. Now this is not really like evidence based medicine. You might remember that in Chapter 9 I explained that even in the area of physical activity and health, the exercise physiology research cannot give you the exact (read "best") dose of exercise to "give" a particular school age child for particular health benefits. The science is not that certain. Well it's the same with motor skills. Typically a teacher or coach works with a group or a whole class and the best we have are some generalizations that might work for most of the group/class.

If, however, you want to teach a positive attitude to physical activity (a disposition for a lifetime of participation) then what pedagogy research would you draw on? The answer is that there is none. None that is specific that is. What we have is plenty of research to show that many kids are turned off PE and sport because of the experiences they have in PE and sports classes (see for example Carlson, 1995). And we can generalize that certain active mesomorphs are easier to engage and we are more likely to achieve our objectives with them than with some others in the class.

Over 20 years ago Placek and Locke (1986) argued that despite the developments in and proliferation of research on teaching physical education over the 20 years from the mid-1960s, "Most physical educators working in school settings ... continue to teach much as they always have, quite untouched by research findings. It is that fact that lends the cautious tone to any contemplation of pedagogical knowledge in physical education" (p. 24). Hal Lawson (1990) then claimed that although there had been a great deal of *information* gathered on PE pedagogy over two decades or more of research on teaching PE, there was far less useful *knowledge*. I wonder what their judgement would be today after another 20 years of research in pedagogy?

David Kirk (1989) argued that the way in which the research was conceived and conducted had something to do with the fact that research into PE teaching has made little impact on curriculum practice. He framed this as part of the perceived theory–practice gap that is much bemoaned by researchers from universities. According to Kirk (1989), part of the problem was that the research has been dominated by an orthodoxy which privileges natural science research methods and this resulted in "theory [being] often treated with indifference, even held in contempt, by many educational practitioners" (p. 124).

Doune Macdonald (2007) notes that it would be short-sighted to unproblematically accept that scientific type evidence will provide the "gold standard" for evidence based practice since "much cannot be understood through a technical, positivistic logic" (p. 6). Macdonald recognizes that although the "gold standard" might sometimes be fool's gold, it is unwise to dismiss quantitative evidence out of hand, citing Alan Luke's (2003) observation that "quantitative educational research is not antithetical to social justice, nor is qualitative research necessarily empowering, transformative, and progressive" (p. 6).

Unfortunately, we must understand that policy makers and bureaucrats are only interested in the sort of evidence that is represented by the voice of *logos*. It is no use approaching policy makers with a wonderful case study or autoethnography and expect that this will influence policy.

A question of research training

Research in sport pedagogy and in the pedagogy of HMS itself faces a number of significant issues. The first relates to the training of future pedagogy researchers and the second to the increasingly competitive academic environment.

In terms of training, what research methods should our graduate students in pedagogy receive? Should they be competent in quantitative methods? Qualitative methods? Poststructural methods? Should they have a working knowledge of pheneomenology, critical theory, postcolonialsm, behaviour analysis, and life history? Should they know some Foucault, Bourdieu, Bernstein? How about Piaget, Vygostky, Lave and Wenger?

Acknowledging that research training takes many forms and is generally a part of graduate education, Silverman and Keating (2008) conducted a descriptive analysis of introductory graduate research methods classes in departments of kinesiology and PE in the USA. They found that most classes had a range of objectives including the ability to understand research, to apply research to professional situations, to critique the research literature, and how to plan for research. From my experience, introductory courses can at best give only a superficial level of understanding and competence in these objectives and further, more specialized courses would be needed.

In terms of curriculum emphasis Silverman and Keating (2008) found that quantitative design and analysis topics were emphasized more strongly than qualitative design and analysis topics and alternative research methodologies have not been quickly added to the research methods curriculum. Again, the breadth and variety of research methods and issues would militate against a comprehensive coverage in an introductory level course.

Obviously, how you define pedagogy will influence the sort of research training that might be necessary for graduate students. If pedagogy is thought of as the science of teaching then presumably research traditions of the sciences would be necessary. But since science is a broad church and the range of research methods and designs is extensive, which sciences? The natural sciences? Hypothetico-deductive science? The behavioural sciences? These distinctions are not trivial. For example, the earth sciences (e.g. geology, archaeology) typically do not use experimental method with control and experimental groups (it's hard to intervene in the formation of an igneous rock formation!) and the psychological sciences use extensive psychometric measures and use statistics to analyze their results. Behaviour analysts doing their science would use single-case design with observation and recording of human behaviour rather than psychometric measures (pencil and paper tests) as data, and graphical, rather than statistical analysis techniques. Underpinning these differences are epistemological distinctions between measures used in the natural sciences and those used in the psychological sciences (see Johnson and Pennypacker, 1980). Should students learn about such distinctions early on in their training? I think they should.

If, however, you think of pedagogy more broadly as the process of coming to know (Lusted, 1986), then perhaps other research methods are necessary. For example, perhaps cultural studies, feminist research and poststructuralist analysis would be useful. In such research there is no attempt to measure human behaviour (e.g. teacher and pupil behaviours) but rather the emphasis is on trying to illicit the meaning of behaviour to the participants themselves and to understand how that meaning is possible (i.e. under what conditions certain meanings be entertained?).

There is no doubt that different conceptual approaches to pedagogy will require different paradigmatic research methods. Of course how undergraduate HM students learn about research, whether for sport pedagogy research, historical research, or research in the biophysical sub-disciplines, will be a significant factor in stimulating interest in graduate (postgraduate) study. There is little more off-putting to facilitating an interest in research than a poorly conceived and taught research methods course. In the next and final chapter I turn attention to the ways in which the stories or tales of our work (both research and practice) are communicated to students and the professional community of HMS.

12 Telling tales about pedagogy and the pedagogy of telling tales

Consistent with my argument that the study of pedagogy is the study of the process of coming to know (about something), we can think of the various stories or tales about pedagogy as themselves doing pedagogical work by the very nature of their particular narrative genre. This idea picks up on the famous Marshall McLuhan (1964) saying "The medium is the message". These tales are related in journals, books, conference presentations and the like and they all have a pedagogical intent. Interestingly, however, I have not read of any analysis of these tales as pedagogy from the perspective of their genre doing pedagogical work.

In his book *Telling Tales in Sport and Physical Activity: A Qualitative Journey*, Andrew Sparkes (2001) describes a range of stories from scientific tales, realist tales, confessional tales, autoethnography, poetic representations, ethno-drama and fictional representations. These representations provide a useful framework for thinking about how the stories about pedagogy are told. Each of these narrative genres has its own tacit rules of storytelling. Theoretically, the genres are narrative strategies that have different purposes, different intent. Importantly, as Nelson *et al.* (1987, p. 3) point out,

> Scholarship uses argument, and argument uses rhetoric. The "rhetoric" is not mere ornament or manipulation or trickery. It is rhetoric in the ancient sense of persuasive discourse. In matters mathematical proof to literary criticism, scholars write rhetorically. Only occasionally do they reflect on that fact (cited in Sparkes, 2001, p. 12)

Sparkes' tales represent rhetorical styles that I have earlier (see Chapter 6 in particular) described in terms of Plato's discourses of *logos*, *thymos* and *mythos*. In what follows I will discuss some of these genres with respect to their work as particular forms of pedagogy.

Scientific tales

Most people probably don't think of a scientific article as a form of rhetoric. Science, it is thought, is above rhetoric, it is concerned with facts and proof rather than story and form. However, the scientific tale is constrained by strict rules regarding how to communicate what the research did and found. Consider the APA's *Publication Manual of the American Psychological Association* that outlines with pedantic detail how the writer must prepare a manuscript for publication. Such is the formality with which scientific tales are told that readers are perhaps seduced into believing its story largely because of the authoritative voice in which it is told. Indeed this is part of the implicit pedagogical work of the scientific genre.

Within the field of HMS scientific tales dominate. This is in part because of the dominance of the biophysical sciences in most departments of HMS. As I have said earlier, *logos* is the lingua franca of the field and is now the rhetorical style across most sub-disciplines.

It is important to recognize that *logos* does not simply mean science. Plato's *logos* is the analytic voice of critique associated with the truth games of science and philosophy (Carlson, 1998). Rational analytic thought and reasoning certainly underpins science but, equally important, this epistemology also informs philosophy and then, in consequence, many other academic discourses in addition to science. By this logic, even sports history operates largely through the voice of *logos*. In this context, Carlson's (1998) words about the rise of *logos* find their own truth in HMS:

> Plato's mission, and one might say, the mission of much Western philosophy, science, and education in the modern era, was to separate and divide these voices, privilege a "pure", supposedly detached, voice of *logos*, and subordinate other ways of speaking as not only less truthful, but as ways of speaking that can lead us away from the truth (p. 543).

Most of the literature on pedagogy research in PE has been conducted in the "image" of science and reported as a scientific tale. The pages of the *Journal of Teaching in Physical Education* are dominated by such tales. Scientific tales are mainly based on quantitative type data and in the tale-telling process such data can often be reduced and displayed in summary form which renders them accessible to a readership with restricted space and time available. The scientific tale is, however, but one form of representation, and as Eisner (2001) points out, "scientific frameworks do not exhaust the ways in which we experience the world or render our experience of it public" (p. 140).

Qualitative data, which forms an increasingly important dimension of communicating experiences of human movement, are however, often more long-winded, messy, and less easily reduced to fit tight publication lengths or conference presentation time slots. Sparkes' book *Telling Tales* provides a thoughtful account of the various types of tales that are based on qualitative, *emic* (insider) perspectives of participants in movement culture.

The realist tales

A realist tale is characterized by extensive, closely edited quotations intended to convey to the reader that the views expressed are those of the participants rather than the researcher (van Manen, 1990). Such data (the quotations) are used in shedding light on the particular research question or topic under investigation. The authority of the realist tale is, to some extent at least, derived from the fact that it is the participants' voices that are used in the process of finding out.

Confessional tales

According to Sparkes (2002) the confessional tale takes the reader behind the scenes of the research process. In the realist tale the voice of the researcher is usually only heard briefly, if at all, within the methods section whereas in the confessional tale the reseacher's subjectivity is very much centre stage. "Confessional tales ... explicitly problematize and de-mystify the field work or participant observation by revealing what actually happened in the research process from start to finish" (p. 58). The pedagogy of the confessional tale intends to take the reader on a journey into the messiness of the project and the subjectivity of the researcher. To some people however, such confessionals are self-indulgent and the pedagogical work done in the tale-telling has the effect of devaluing the power of the research.

The fictional tale

A very good example of this form of tale telling exists in the work of Swan (1995). Swan included a series of ethnographic fictional stories under the collective title of "Between the rings and under the gym mat: A narrative" as part of his doctoral thesis. The fictions were included because Swan felt that after writing his case study, titled "Studentship and oppositional behaviour within physical education teacher education", in the classical case study (realist) genre, he was left feeling (knowing) that it did not (could not) represent all the nuances and "truths" of the phenomenon he had studied for years. Constructing the ethnographic fictions allowed him the freedom to tap into "other knowledges" and represent them in an engaging form.

When Swan gave his colleagues a copy of his fictional tales they all agreed that they "'captured" the student culture of studentship as they understood it. It also left them puzzling over which part of the story and which characters represented themselves as individuals. Of course Swan had been careful to construct his stories and his characters not only from his "factual" realist research data, but also from his own interpretations based on his many years' experience in the institution. Accordingly his stories were more like "factional" than fictional representations and the characters were constructed as hybrids with pseudonyms.

Ethno-drama tales

Leanne Brown (1998), a student of Peter Swan, completed her PhD thesis on "Image, Identity and Investment in Physical Education" using tales from ethno-drama to portray how certain forms of identity and investment are reproduced within a PETE program.

The thesis, together with the scripts *I Can Be This! Plays from the Identity Playground*, the CD-ROM containing the video clip of the ethno-drama (play) *Boys' Training* and *I Can Be This: A Phototext* collectively take the reader "into" the inner sanctum of the identity playground in a vivid and challenging way. The pedagogical intent of the genre was to bring the reader closer to the sub-culture of the students. When I read the thesis and the ethno-drama they had a profound effect on me. As a teacher educator with considerable investment in PETE I found the portrayal of the reproduction of a certain form of hyper-masculinity to be very troubling. It was not a pretty picture that Brown painted of the social practices of these prospective PE teachers. But the depressing portrayal is not a criticism of the thesis. Rather, it was a strength of the three creative components, especially the ethno-drama, that elicited such a strong emotional response in me.

Of course a PhD is not judged on the extent to which it creates an emotional response in its reader. Rather it must satisfy certain more "rational" *logos* expectations such as:

- Does the thesis comprise a coherent investigation of the chosen topic?
- Does the thesis deal with a topic of sufficient range and depth to meet the requirements of the degree?
- Does the thesis make an original contribution to knowledge in its field and contain material suitable for publication?
- Does the thesis meet internationally recognized standards for the conduct and presentation of research in the field?
- Does the thesis demonstrate both a thorough knowledge of the literature and the candidate's ability to exercise critical and analytical judgement of that literature?
- Does the thesis display mastery of appropriate methodology and theoretical material?

In my view, as an examiner of the thesis, Leanne Brown's thesis satisfied all these expectations. However, as Sparkes (1991) has pointed out, there are many dilemmas and judgement calls that must be made in considering which rhetorical style to use.

Autoethnographic tales

Natalie Barker-Ruchti, a PhD student of mine at UQ, chose to tell the tale of her doctoral project as an (auto)ethnographic one (Barker-Ruchti, 2007).

Natalie was heavily invested in gymnastics as a one-time elite gymnast and she wanted to write herself and her subjectivity into her thesis. In some sense Natalie's thesis speaks with the voices of *logos* and *thymos*. She uses the voice of *logos* in that her Foucauldian analysis of bio-power in women's gymnastics relies on sophisticated rational and analytical work. She uses the voice of *thymos* in the sense that it contains a rage against the injustices of certain pedagogical practices used to prepare elite gymnasts for competition.

The point about all these rhetorical styles is that they are pedagogical. They are designed to communicate about research. And as with most pedagogical encounters, the actual pedagogical work done is unpredictable and this is why the examination of a PhD thesis is usually characterized by considerable risk and uncertainty. To select an examiner who has no experience of, or who is not receptive to the genre, is a very risky path.

Thankfully, in sport pedagogy and in HMS generally there is now a growing number of scholars who are open to various forms of representation and accordingly we are seeing a wider range of genres for telling tales of our research endeavours.

Conference presentations as pedagogy

A few years ago I attended a conference at which there were a number of presentations related to the "obesity crisis". The keynote speaker, a famous American researcher on physical activity and health, gave an up-to-date overview of the extant literature on the relationship between inactivity and morbidity and mortality. It was presented in PowerPoint form and included numerous graphs showing "telling trends". There were references to learned journals (e.g. the *New England Journal of Medicine*) scattered throughout and this all gave the presentation a sense of authority. This was expert knowledge presented by an expert. The credentials of the expert speaker were reverently listed when the session chairman provided the introduction. The whole format of the presentation was explicitly pedagogic. It was designed to communicate, to teach the audience about the "facts" related to something important. However, the presenter did not just stick to the "facts". He seamlessly slipped from the science into a moral discourse regarding what we *should* do about it (Gard and Wright, 2001). It became a moral discourse on how we should live our lives with a not-so-implicit message that those who made the wrong choices were irresponsible or just plain slothful. In essence there was the clarion call for individual responsibility for one's own health and a sort of an implicit Nike inspired "Just Do It" subtext. The audience, or most of them, lapped it up and believed in the message. After all, most of the audience were HMS/HPE professionals who stand to gain from having their services as exercise scientists, personal trainers, PE teachers etc. in increasing demand from such evidence and advocacy.

In a keynote address it is often expected that the speaker will be a bit provocative, maybe give some personal slant to the issue and even offer some opinion. The problem I had with this particular presentation was that the speaker made no attempt to separate or dissociate the "evidence" from the moral pronouncements. This had the effect of giving the moral advice the legitimacy of science. The science, however, on which the "should do" advice was based is far from unequivocal. For example, as Johns (2005) and Gard and Wright (2001) show, although there is good evidence that physical activity may be good for health, the exact dose of activity that might be good for each individual is illusive. This "dose-response" dilemma is seldom mentioned in universal moral calls regarding what we all should do.

At the same conference there was a session in which two speakers who had just published a paper in which they put the "obesity crisis" in a cultural context of risk society, presented an oppositional voice to the dominant obesity crisis hype. They explained that in re-contextualizing the biomedical discourse, many of the caveats, limitations and precautions of the original research were omitted with the result that the "evidence" for the relationship between physical activity and health was presented as more certain than the science actually claimed. In their presentation they also pointed out that the process of slipping from science to moral discourse was common in the context of the obesity crisis discourse and that the keynote speaker that morning had done just that.

In their presentation they used some overhead transparencies of a number of textual passages to show how such slippage occurs. The genre of their presentation was the antithesis of the slick PowerPoint slides and graphs of the other presenters in the session and also the keynote in the morning. The audience, accustomed to dot-points, PowerPoints and graphs were unimpressed. I sensed that they closed down and didn't attempt to follow the line of the argument. It was a case of the medium getting in the road of the message. It was also a case of some not wanting to hear anything that might shake their security in certainty. Speaking to a colleague after the presentation I was shocked to hear him claim that "those two are dangerous and should not be let near undergraduates", presumably lest they corrupt their understanding of the truth of the "obesity crisis". As far as I was concerned this comment was evidence that my colleague had not really listened to the argument presented. He had closed-off perhaps because it was an argument he did not want to hear and/or because he found the genre of the presentation so unconvincing that he simply didn't concentrate.

So what am I saying with this example? I am arguing that the conference presentation is a pedagogical act and that the pedagogical work done in any particular presentation might be very different from what the presenters expect. In the example presented above, it seemed to me that their intent was not realized and, rather, had the effect of consolidating prejudice and further marginalizing the oppositional position they were offering.

Poster presentations as pedagogy

You might have seen them at airports checking in with a long tube as part of their cabin baggage. They are off to a conference and in the tube is their presentation. The presentation is a poster that is attached to a display board and displayed at a certain time in the conference program. On the day of the presentation the scholar will typically stand beside their poster and respond to any questions the readers might have. Readers (other conference delegates) wander around the presentations reading ones that interest them.

In one sense the poster is a very useful form of communication and in some disciplines this is the most common form of presentation for doctoral and junior researchers. Preparation of a poster is good training in pedagogy since to do it well it should engage the reader immediately, be succinct in its message, and be visually appealing.

As the number of delegates at conferences has increased, and because not every delegate can be offered an oral presentation slot, poster presentations have become increasingly popular. In such presentations the format is closely mandated (specific size requirements) and size restrictions favour the sort of data that can be condensed (maybe into graphs, tables etc.). Nuanced understandings that might need relatively long passages of text (for example in some qualitative studies) typically do not fit well in the poster genre. Since the body of the presenter is virtually eliminated (they stand to the side and answer questions), there is little if any embodiment in the presentation. The pedagogy of the poster is disembodied. This does not, however, limit the potential for interaction between a reader and the presenter.

The oral presentation: 10–15 minutes of glory?

Travelling for 26 hours from Australia to Europe or the eastern USA for a 10–15-minute conference presentation might seem inefficient and even ridiculous in a world increasingly connected by the Internet and suffering from increased CO_2 levels and global warming. However, for most academics in Australia this is a regular feature of our work.

Notwithstanding pleasurable aspects of conference attendance such as those portrayed so humorously by David Lodge in his novel *Nice Work* (1989), it is a fair question to ask whether, as a form of pedagogy, the 10–15-minute conference presentation actually does the pedagogical work intended by the presenter. As we saw in the example above, conference presentations sometimes don't communicate what is intended.

Consider the actual pedagogy of the 10–15-minute presentation. In HMS conferences increasingly the presenter will use PowerPoint as the medium. Often this means that a number of dot-points, graphs or images are presented and "talked to". They offer a stimulus and framework on which the presenter may elaborate. This is usually claimed as a more engaging presentation style than simply reading a paper. However, this judgement lacks nuance.

Reading a written paper can be dead boring. Or it can be engaging. It all depends on the presenter and the degree to which they need to keep their eyes on the paper or are sufficiently practised to shift between the written paper and the audience. In the field of sport pedagogy both Daryl Siedentop and Larry Locke provide fine examples of the fact that a "read" paper can be stimulating and engaging. Both men were (they have now retired) consummate performers and both would script their presentations and practise them. They didn't rely on a few dot-points to prompt their elaboration. I certainly have learned much from watching their presentations and have long advised my own students to both script and practise their presentations.

In a short 10–15-minute presentation it is easy to run out of time. "Talking to" some PowerPoint slides often results in the speaker spending too long on some points and having to rush/gloss over others. Scripting what is to be said, even if using PowerPoint slides is, to my mind, sensible. Staying on time is also respectful of the time allocated to other presenters. To travel to the other side of the world and have your precious 10–15 minutes in the spotlight reduced to 8 minutes because the previous speaker was allowed to run over time is not an uplifting experience.

Interestingly, to my knowledge, there is no research published that has investigated exactly what individual delegates in the audience take from a presentation, no account of what might be the pedagogical work of the lecture. Of course there are the ubiquitous conference evaluation forms that can rate popular and less popular presentations, but that is not what I am interested in.

A tale about university pedagogy

Pedagogy has moved increasingly into the spotlight in the contemporary university context. However, even though modern teaching technologies have made increasing purchase in our universities, the lecture lives on as a central pedagogical device. It is supposed to be an efficient way of imparting knowledge to large groups. There is research to support such claims, but there is also considerable opposition to the lecture (see for example Bligh, 1971).

In the past decade I have witnessed and experienced a shift in expectations surrounding pedagogy and higher education. Students, especially in large classes, expect lectures to be in PowerPoint form. Moreover, they also expect that the PowerPoint slides will be posted on the Internet (in *Blackboard* or other such web-based platforms) before the lecture so they can download, print them and bring them to class (or not come to class at all!).

It's hard to resist this trend. Failure to entertain and engage will lead to student unrest and talking will pervade the lecture. Failure to satisfy student needs can lead to poor teaching evaluations and increasingly these "measures" are used to judge teaching quality. I have certainly complied with these expectations and universally use PowerPoint in all my large lectures (and also my conference presentations). I do not, however, post my lectures on the Internet before class – I am usually still "tweaking" them 30 minutes before the lecture! Significantly the time necessary to prepare lectures has increased simply because there is a never ending search for better images to better engage with a generation used to visual images and the overlap of entertainment, advertising and education (Kenway and Bullen, 2001).

By way of contrast, one of the best lectures I remember from my undergraduate days was in a course titled "Introduction to Education". It was 1969, the Vietnam War was raging and at Macquarie University there were frequent student protests on campus. The lecturer, a man in his late 40s (I think) would sit on a table down the front of the 250-seat lecture theatre. The theatre was packed and continued to be so throughout the entire semester. He started his lecture by lighting a cigarette (he smoked throughout the 2-hour lecture) and then began to talk. There were no special aids such as overhead transparencies and certainly no PowerPoint. He occasionally used the blackboard (no whiteboards back then) but otherwise he lectured with barely a reference to his notes. And he was captivating in an intellectual sense rather than an entertaining sense. He sparked my interest like few others before or since.

In making this observation I hasten to add that am not taking a nostalgic or fundamentalist line and arguing for a return to a mythical golden age of education. Nor am I sanctioning smoking in lectures or interested in technology-bashing. Rather, I use this example to show how far things have moved. Certainly that lecturer would now be sanctioned for smoking in class, but I wonder how a modern audience of students would respond to such a lecturing style.

Lest you quickly judge my lament as just another case of what Mark Davis calls "baby boomer-whinge" (Davis, 2000), I want to explain that my concerns over the hegemony of PowerPoint are grounded in something of a *deeper crisis* across our educational institutions in general. The crisis is manifest in the atomization of learning into bits or pieces of knowledge, attitudes and behaviours that are purporting to connect with the world beyond the school or university gate. Graduate attributes are now all the go and increasingly we are required to identify which particular graduate attributes are being developed in each lecture! This of course is a manifestation of what Alan Luke (2002) described as "a now internationally rampant vision of schooling, teaching and learning based solely on systemic efficiency and the measurable technical production of human capital" (p. 1).

In our Western school systems this logic plays out in the explication of so-called essential learnings and of complex assessment criteria and standards that are veiled attempts to teacher-proof the curriculum and to regulate for *certainty* of pedagogical outcomes. Moves towards "Total Quality Assurance" in universities (and schools) now require the detailing of specific criteria and learning outcomes in an attempt to standardize the outcomes of pedagogy. However, in an increasingly complex and uncertain world, the sceptre of certainty is an anachronism of the hopes of modernity (Giddens, 1991).

This raises the issue of how we tell our tales of pedagogy within the modern university. Increasingly we are required to tell our stories in the language and genre that embody the discourses that derive from management rather than education (see Smyth, 2001).

In Australian universities today we now have highly resourced departments whose mission it is to formally improve the quality of teaching and learning. These departments are not part of academic faculties of education, or any other faculty for that matter. They are part of the university administrative system. At first glance this focus on improving teaching and learning might be considered a good thing. After all, who would object to improvements in university teaching? Well the problem is that improvement is judged using criteria determined by the government. They control the purse strings and they dictate what stands for good pedagogy. The government makes the allocation of certain funding contingent on universities showing improvement in pedagogy in the terms that they dictate (e.g. reduced student dropout rates, use of standardized student evaluations etc.). But these are not really improvements in pedagogy at all. They are more of a smoke screen for control over the work of academics. As Kniest (2004) argues, "The [Federal Government] Learning and Teaching Fund is yet another way of the Government trying to achieve its policy agenda by leveraging its objectives against funding" (p. 22) and in the process pedagogy becomes another governmental technology.

These new departments and the bureaucratic requirements they set in place represent a particular *way of thinking* with respect to claimed deficits in current pedagogical practice and what is necessary to improve them. Increasingly they are seen as solutions to problems defined or set (Lawson, 1984) by those who champion conceptions of pedagogy in which reductionist processes are used to "identify" the claimed essential component skills and competencies of teaching.

Significantly, these departments or organizational units now contribute to an increase in the cost of compliance for academic staff who must spend time providing an account of their curriculum and pedagogy, what they teach and how they will teach it, their objectives, the sequence of lectures, tutorials and pracs, assessment procedures and the like, in a standardized format. In my own university this takes the form of an electronic course profile (ECP) which students access from the Internet. No more idiosyncratic course profiles constructed by vague or maverick professors. What is needed is standardization! Like the formal APA rules for writing scientific tales, our pedagogy tales are now increasingly rule governed. They have become a rhetoric of impression management. Ironically in a context of evidence based practice (see Chapter 11), it seems there is little to support the contribution of such compliance procedures to actual student learning.

I'm afraid I remain unconvinced that such standardization measures lead to improvements in pedagogy. Moreover I remain sceptical of the "measures" used to judge quality pedagogy in the university context. In a context in which we are increasingly asked to cater for difference and diversity in our student population it seems somewhat ironic that pedagogy must be increasingly standardized. Given that the quality of any pedagogy will depend upon the pedagogical work done as a result of that encounter, it seems axiomatic that the idiosyncratic be celebrated if it leads to genuinely intellectual and emotional engagement with the subject matter.

In a context in which *logos* dominates the truth game regarding pedagogy and in which such tales can, at best, represent only partial accounts and partial truths, it is time to give more voice to *thymos* and *mythos* to portray more of the emotions and the complexity of how we come to know in HMS. A serious engagement with pedagogy and pedagogical work demands it.

References

Abraham, A., and Collins, D. (1998). Examining and extending research in coach development. *Quest*, 50(1), 59–79.

Alexander, K., Taggart, A., and Thorpe, S. (1996). A spring in their steps? Possibilities for professional renewal through sport education in Australian schools. *Sport, Education & Society*, 1(1), 23–46.

Almond, L. (1983) A rationale for health related fitness in schools. *Bulletin of Physical Education*, 19(2), 5–11.

Alter, M. (2004). *Science of Flexibility* (3rd ed.). Champaign, IL: Human Kinetics.

Amade-Escot, C. (2006). Student learning within the *didactique* tradition. In D. Kirk, M. O'Sullivan and D. Macdonald (Eds.), *The Handbook of Physical Education* (pp. 347–367). London: Sage.

Anyon, J. (1994). The retreat of Marxism and socialist feminism: Postmodern and poststructural theories in education. *Curriculum Inquiry*, 24(2), 115–132.

Apple, M. (1982). *Culture and Economic Reproduction in Education*. Boston: Routledge and Kegan Paul.

Armour, K. (1999). The case for a body-focus in education and physical education. *Sport, Education & Society*, 4(1), 5–17.

Armstrong, N. McManus, A. Welsman, J. and Kirby, B. (1996). Physical activity patterns and aerobic fitness among prepubescents. *European Physical Education Review*, 2(1), 19–29.

Arnold, P. (1988). *Education, Movement and the Curriculum*. London: Falmer Press.

Aronowitz, S., and Giroux, H. (1985). *Education under Siege*. South Hadley, MA: Bergin and Garvey.

Avery, D. (1978). "A Comparison of Interaction Patterns of Effective and Less Effective Coaches". Unpublished Masters dissertation, Ithaca College, Ithaca.

Bailey, S., and Vamplew, W. (1999). *100 Years of Physical Education 1899–1999*. Warwick: Warwick Printing Company Limited.

Bain, L. (1988). Beginning the journey: Agenda for 2001. *Quest*, 40, 96–106.

Bain, L. (1989). Interpretive and critical research in sport and physical education. *Research Quarterly for Exercise and Sport*, 60(1), 21–24.

Bain, L. (1990a). A critical analysis of the hidden curriculum in physical education. In D. Kirk and R. Tinning (Eds.), *Physical Education, Curriculum and Culture: Critical Issues in the Contemporary Crisis* (pp. 23–42). Basingstoke: Falmer Press.

Bain, L. (1990b). "Research in sport pedagogy: Past, present and future:. Jose-Marie Cagigal Memorial Lecture, AIESEP World Congress, Loughborough, July.

Bale, J., and Vertinsky, P. (2004). Introduction. In P. Vertinsky and J. Bale (Eds.), *Sites of Sport: Space, Place, Experience* (pp. 1–8). London: Routledge.

Bale, J., Christensen, M., and Pfister, G. (Eds.). (2004). *Writing Lives in Sport: Biographies, Life Histories and Methods*. Aarhus: Aarhus University Press.

Barker-Ruchti, N. (2006). "Stride jump – begin!": Swedish gymnastics in Victorian England. *Sporting Traditions*, 22(2), 13–29.

Barker-Ruchti, N. (2007). "Women's Artistic Gymnastics: An (Auto-)ethnographic Journey". Unpublished PhD thesis, University of Queensland, Brisbane, Australia.

Barr, P. (1978). "The Effects of Instruction and Supervision of Interaction Analysis on Coaching Behaviours". Unpublished Masters thesis, Ithaca College, Ithaca.

Bates, R. (1986). *Management of Culture and Knowledge*. Geelong: Deakin University Press.

Bateson, G. (1973). *Steps to an Ecology of Mind*. Frogmore: Paladin.

Baudrillard, J. (2005). The finest consumer object: The body. In M. Fraser and M. Greco (Eds.), *The Body: A Reader* (pp. 277–283). London: Routledge.

Bauman, Z. (2001). *The Individualized Society*. Cambridge, UK: Polity.

Beck, U. (1992). *Risk Society: Towards a New Modernity*. London: Sage.

Behets, D. (1996). Comparison of visual information processing between preservice students and experienced physical education teachers. *Journal of Teaching in Physical Education*, 16, 79–87.

Bennett, L and Stone, N. (1980) Introduction to *Huff'n Puff: A Life Be In It Resource for Vigorous Games and Activities*. Leongatha District Education Committee: Victoria.

Bernstein, B. (1975). *Class, Codes and Control: Towards a Theory of Educational Transmission*. London: Routledge and Kegan Paul.

Bernstein, B. (1996). *Pedagogy, Symbolic Control and Identity: Theory, Research, Critique*. London: Taylor & Francis.

Bernstein, B. (2000). *Pedagogy, Symbolic Control, and Identity: Theory, Research, Critique*. Lanham, MD: Rowman and Littlefield Publishers.

Bibik, J. (1996). Differential treatment of whole classes by a university dance teacher. *Sport, Education & Society*, 1(2), 215–225.

Biesta, G. (1998). Say you want a revolution … Suggestions for the impossible future of critical pedagogy. *Educational Theory*, 48(4), 499–510.

Bilborough, A., and Jones, P. (1966). *Physical Education in the Primary School*. London: University of London Press.

Billett, S. (1999). Guided learning at work. In D. Boud and J. Garrick (Eds.), *Understanding Learning at Work* (pp. 151–164). London: Routledge.

Billett, S. (2001). *Learning in the Workplace: Strategies for Effective Practice*. New South Wales: Allen & Unwin.

Billett, S. (2006). Relational interdependence between social and individual agency in work and working life. *Mind, Culture and Activity*, 13(1), 53–69.

Biscan, D., and Hoffman, S. (1976). Movement analysis as a generic ability of physical education teachers and students. *Research Quarterly*, 47, 161–163.

Blackburn, S., and Portney, L. (1981). Electromyographic activity of back musculature during Williams' flexion exercises. *Physical Therapy, Journal of the American Physical Therapy Association* (June).

Blades, D. (1995). Procedures of power in a curriculum-discourse: Conversations from home. *Journal of Curriculum Theorising*, 11(4), 125–155.

Blair, S., and Brodney, S. (1999). Effects of physical inactivity and obesity on morbidity and mortality: Current evidence and research issues. *Medicine and Science in Sports and Exercise*, 31(11), 646–662.

Bligh, D. (1971). *What's the Use of Lectures?* Middlesex, England: Penguin Books.

Bloom, B. (1956). *A Taxonomy of Educational Objectives, Handbook 1: Cognitive Domain*. New York: McKay.

Blume, L. (2003). Embodied by dance: Adolescent de/construction of body, sex and gender in physical education. *Sex Education*, 3(2), 95–103.

Bourdieu, P. (1990). *The Logic of Practice*. Stanford: Stanford University Press.

Bourdieu, P., and Passeron, J-C. (1977). *Reproduction in Education, Society and Culture*. London: Sage.

Bowles, S., and Gintis, H. (1976). *Schooling in Capitalist America*. New York: Basic Books.

Branta, C., Haunbenstricker, J., and Seefeldt, V. (1984). Age changes in motor skill during childhood and adolescence. *Exercise and Sports Science Reviews*, 12, 467–520.

Brennan, R. (1991). *Alexander Technique: Natural Poise for Health*. Rockport, Massachusetts: Element.

Bresler, L. (2004). Dancing and the curriculum: Exploring the body and movement in elementary schools. In L. Bresler (Ed.), *Knowing Bodies, Moving Minds: Towards Embodied Teaching and Learning* (pp. 127–153). Dordrecht: Kluwer Academic Publishers.

Brettschneider, W-D. (1991). "The many faces of sport as a challenge for sport pedagogy and physical education". Jose-Marie Cagigal Memorial Lecture, AIESEP/NAPEHE World Congress, Atlanta, Georgia.

Brewer, B., Van Raalte, J., & Linder, D. (1993). Athletic Identity: Hercules' Muscles or Achilles' Heel? *International Journal of Sport Psychology*, 24, 237–254.

Broekhoff, J. (1972). Physical education and the reification of the human body. *Gymnasion*, ix, 4–11.

Brooker, R., Kirk, D., Braiuka, S., and Bransgrove, A. (2000). Implementing a game sense approach to teaching junior high school basketball in a naturalistic setting. *European Journal of Physical Education*, 6, 7–26.

Broudy, H. (1963). Historic examplars of teaching method. In N. Gage (Ed.), *Handbook of Research on Teaching* (pp. 1–44). Chicago: Rand McNally.

Brown, D. (1999). Complicity and reproduction in teaching physical education. *Sport, Education & Society*, 4(2), 143–160.

Brown, D. (2002). "Living links and gender resources in teaching PE: The social construction of masculinity in teaching physical education". Paper presented at the Association for Physical Education in Higher Education (AIESEP), LaCoruna, Spain.

Brown, D., and Evans, J. (2004). Reproducing gender? Intergenerational links and the male PE teacher as a cultural conduit in teaching physical education. *Journal of Teaching in Physical Education*, 23(1), 48–71.

Brown, L. (1998). "Boy's training": The inner sanctum. In C. Hickey, L. Fitzclarence and R. Matthews (Eds.), *Where the Boys Are: Masculinities, Sport and Education* (pp. 83–97). Geelong: Deakin Centre for Education and Change.

Brownwell, S. (1995). *Training the Body for China: Sports in the Moral Order of the People's Republic*. Chicago: The University of Chicago Press.

Buckingham, D. (Ed.). (1998). *Teaching Popular Culture: Beyond Radical Pedagogy*. London: University College London Press.

Bunker, D., and Thorpe, R. (1982). A model for the teaching of games in secondary schools. *Bulletin of Physical Education*, 18(1), 5–8.

Bunton, R., and Burrows, R. (1995). Consumption and health in the "epidemiological" clinic of late modern medicine. In R. Bunton, S. Nettleton, and R. Burrows (Eds.), *The Sociology of Health Promotion: Critical Analyses of Consumption, Lifestyle and Risk* (pp. 206–223). London: Routledge.

Bunton, R., Nettleton, S., and Burrows, R. (Eds.). (1995). *The Sociology of Health Promotion: Critical Analyses of Consumption, Lifestyle and Risk*. London: Routledge.

Caddick, A. (1886). Feminism and the body. *Arena*, 74, 60–90.

Calnan, M. (2004). "Lifestyle" and its social meaning. In G. Albrecht (Ed.), *Advances in Medical Sociology: Volume 4* (pp. 69–88). Greenwich, Conn: JAI Press.

Cannon, R. (2001). Pedagogy: a point of view. *Teaching in Higher Education*, 6(3), 415–419.

Carlson, D. (1998). Finding a voice, and losing our way? *Educational Theory*, 48(4), 541–554.

Carlson, T. (1995). We hate gym: Student alienation from physical education. *Journal of Teaching in Physical Education*, 14(4), 467–477.

Carr, W. and Kemmis, S. (1986). *Becoming Critical: Education, Knowledge and Action Research*. London, Falmer Press.

Cassidy, T. (2000). "Investigating the Pedagogical Process in Physical Education Teacher Education". Unpublished PhD thesis, Deakin University.

Cassidy, T., Jones, R., and Potrac, P. (2004). *Understanding Sports Coaching*. London: Routledge.+

Chambers, W. (1984). *Putting Nature in Order*. Geelong: Deakin University.

Chan, H. (2008). "Production and Reproduction of Healthism in Hong Kong Schools". Unpublished PhD thesis, University of Queensland, Brisbane.

Cheffers, J. (1977). Observing teaching systematically. *Quest*, 28, 17–28.

Cheffers, J., and Mancini, V. (1966). Teacher-student interaction. In W. Anderson and G. Barrett (Eds.), *What's Going on in Gym?* Connecticut: Motor Skills Theory into Practice Monograph 1.

Chopra, D. (1993). *Ageless Body, Timeless Mind*. Sydney: Random House.

Chow, J., Davids, K., Button, C., Shuttleworth, R., Renshaw, I., and Araujo, D. (2006). Nonlinear pedagogy: A constraints-led framework for understanding emergence of game play and movement skills. *Psychology and Life Sciences*, 10(1), 71–103.

Clarke, J. (1995). On becoming skillful: Patterns and constraints. *Research Quarterly for Exercise and Sport*, 66, 173–183.

Collins, C. (Ed.). (1993). *Competencies: The Competencies Debate in Australian Education and Training*. Canberra: Australian College of Education, Canberra.

Colquhoun, D. (1989) "Healthism and Health Based Physical Education: A Critique". Unpublished PhD thesis, University of Queensland, Australia.

Connell, R.W. (1995). *Masculinities*. St Leonards, NSW, Australia: Allen & Unwin.

Connolly, M. (1995). Phenomenongy, physical education, and special populations. *Human Studies*, 18, 25–40.

Cook, S. (1983) A health education approach to physical education. *Bulletin of Physical Education*, 19(2), 11–21.

Coonan, W., Worsley, A and Maynard, E. (1984). *Body Owner's Manual*. Life Be In It Publications.

Cooper, J., Heron, T., & Heward, W. (2007). *Applied Behavior Analysis* (2nd ed.). New York: Prentice Hall.

Cratty, B. (1973). *Movement Behaviour and Motor Learning* (3rd ed.). Philadelphia: Lea & Febiger.

Crawford, R. (1980) Healthism and the medicalisation of everyday life. *International Journal of Health Services*, 10(3), 365–389.

Crawford, R. (1987) Cultural influences on prevention and the emergence of a new health consciousness. In N. Weinstein (Ed.), *Taking Care: Understanding and Encouraging Self-Protective Behaviours* (pp. 45–61). Cambridge: Cambridge University Press.

Crowdes, M. (2000). Embodying sociological imagination: Pedagogical support for linking bodies to minds. *Teaching Sociology*, 28, 28–40.

Crum, B. (1986). Concerning the quality of the development of knowledge in sport pedagogy. *Journal of Teaching in Physical Education*, 5, 211–220.

Crum, B. (1997). In search of paradigmatic identities: General comparison of North America and German contributions to sport pedagogy. *International Journal of Physical Education*, xxxiv, 130–141.

Crum, B. (2001). A review of meta-theoretical discourses in sport pedagogy (1999–2000). *International Journal of Physical* Education, xxxviii, 144–153.

Cushion, C.J., Armour, K.M., and Jones, R.L. (2003). Coach education and continuing professional development: Experience and learning to coach. *Quest*, 55, 215–230.

Davids, K., Yi Chow, J., and Shuttleworth, R. (2005). A constraints-based framework for non-linear pedagogy in physical education. *Journal of Physical Education New Zealand*, 38(1), 17–29.

Davis, B. (2004). *Inventions of Teaching: A Genealogy*. New York: Lawrence Erlbaum.

Davis, K. (1979). An approach to the analysis of a coach's performance. *Sports Coach*, 3(1), 6–12.

Davis, K., and Fitzclarence, L. (1979). A critical analysis of on-field training of a leading AFL team. *Sports Coach*, 3(2), 12–20.

Davis, M. (1999). *Gangland: Cultural Elites and the New Generationalism*. Sydney: Allen & Unwin.

Day, P. (2001). *Health Wars*. Tonbridge, Kent: Credence Publications.

Dean, M. (1999). *Governmentality: Power and Rule in Modern Society*. London: Sage Publications.

De Knop, P., Engstrom, L.-M., Skirsad, B., and Weiss, M. (Eds.). (1996). *Worldwide Trends in Youth Sport*. Champaign, IL: Human Kinetics.

Delorme, D., Kreshel, P., and Reid, L. (2003). Lighting up: Young adults' autobiographical accounts of their first smoking experiences. *Youth and Society*, 34(June), 468–496.

Den Duyn, N. (1996). Why it makes sense to play games. *Sports Coach*, 19(3), 6–9.

Denison, J., and Markula, P. (Eds.). (2003). *Moving Writing: Crafting Movement in Sport Research*. New York: Peter Lang.

Department of Education, V. (1996). *Fundamental Motor Skills: A Manual for Classroom Teachers*. Melbourne: Education Department of Victoria.

Devís-Devís, J., and Sparkes, A. (1999). Burning the book: A biographical study of a pedagogically inspired identity crisis in physical education. *European Physical Education Review*, 5(2), 135–152.

Dewar, A. (1990). Oppression and privilege in physical education: Struggles in the negotiation of gender in a university programme. In D. Kirk and R. Tinning (Eds.), *Physical Education, Curriculum and Culture: Critical Issues in the Contemporary Crisis* (pp. 67–100). Basingstoke: Falmer Press.

Dewar, A. (1991). Feminist pedagogy in physical education: Promises, possibilities, and pitfalls. *JOPERD*, 62(6), 68–77.

Dodds, P. (1993). Removing the ugly "isms" in your gym: Thoughts for teachers on equity. In J. Evans (Ed.), *Equality, Education and Physical Education* (pp. 28–39). London: Falmer Press.

Dowling, F. (2008) Getting in touch with our feelings: The emotional geographies of gender relations in PETE. *Sport, Education and Society*, 13(2), 247–66.

Dowling-Naess, F. (1996). Life events and curriculum change: The life history of a Norwegian educator. *European Physical Education Review*, 2(1), 41–53.

Doyle, W. (1979). Classroom tasks and students' abilities. In P. Peterson and H. Walberg (Eds.), *Research on Teaching: Concepts, Findings and Implications* (pp. 183–209). Berkeley, CA: McCutcheon.

Doyle, W. (1990). Themes in teacher education research. In W.R. Houston (Ed.), *Handbook of Research on Teacher Education* (pp. 3–24). New York: Macmillan.

Doyle, W. (1992). Curriculum and pedagogy. In P. Jackson (Ed.), *Handbook of Research on Curriculum* (pp. 486–516). New York: Macmillan.

Doyle, W., and Ponder, G. (1977). The practicality ethic in teacher education. *Interchange*, 8(3), 1–12.

Dunkin, M. and Biddle, B. (1974). *The Study of Teaching.* New York: Holt, Rinehart and Winston.

Education Department of South Australia. (1982). *Daily Physical Education, Levels 1–7.* Adelaide: Australian Council for Health, Physical Education & Recreation.

Education Department of Victoria. (1970). *Suggested Course of Study for Primary Schools: Physical Education.* Melbourne: Government Printer.

Education Department of Queensland. (2007). *Smart Moves: Physical Activity Programs in Queensland State Schools*, Brisbane: Education Department.

Edut, O. (Ed.). (2000). *Body Outlaws: Young Women Write About Body Image and Identity.* Toronto: Seal Press.

Eisner, E. (2001). Concerns and aspirations for qualitative research in the new millennium. *Qualitative Research*, 1(2), 135–145.

Eldar, E. (1990). Effect of self-management on preservice teachers performance during field experience in physical education. *Journal of Teaching in Physical Education*, 9, 307–323.

Ellsworth, E. (1989). Why doesn't this feel empowering? Working through the repressive myths of critical pedagogy. *Harvard Educational Review*, 59(3), 297–324.

Ellsworth, E. (1997). Teaching positions: Difference, pedagogy, and the power of address. New York: Teachers College Press.

Ellsworth, E. (2005). *Places of Learning.* London: Routledge.

Encarta® *World English Dictionary* (1999). Microsoft Corporation. All rights reserved. Developed for Microsoft by Bloomsbury Publishing Plc.

Ennis, C., Ross, J., and Chen, A. (1992). The role of value orientations in curricular decision making: A rationale for teachers' goals and expectations. *Research Quarterly for Exercise and Sport*, 63, 38–47.

Erdmann, R. (1996). Empirical sport pedagogy. In P. Schempp (Ed.), *Scientific Development of Sport Pedagogy* (pp. 174–203). New York: Waxmann Münster.

Evans, J and Clarke, G. (1988), Changing the face of physical education. In J. Evans (Ed.), *Teachers, Teaching and Control in Physical Education*. Lewes, UK: Falmer Press.

Evans, J. and Davies, B. (1993). Equality, equity and physical education. In J. Evans and B. Davies (Eds.), *Equality, Equity and Physical Education* (pp. 1–27). London: Falmer Press.

Evans, J., Davies, B., and Penny, D. (1999). The social construction of teaching and learning: The politics of pedagogy. In C. Hardy and M. Mawer (Eds.), *Learning and Teaching in Physical Education* (pp. 9–21). London: Falmer Press.

Evans, J., Davies, B., and Wright, J. (Eds.). (2003). *Body Knowledge and Control. Studies in the Sociology of Education and Physical Culture*. London: Routledge.

Fernandez-Balboa, J.-M. (1995). Reclaiming physical education in higher education through critical pedagogy. *Quest*, 47: 91–114.

Fernandez-Balboa, J.M. (1999) "Poisonous pedagogy in physical education". *AIESEP World Congress Proceedings* (Long Island, NY: Adelphi University), pp. 83–87.

Fernandez-Balboa, J-M (Ed.). (1997). *Critical Postmodernism in Human Movement, Physical Education and Sport*. Albany: SUNY.

Fernandez-Balboa, J.-M. (2003). Physical education in the digital (postmodern) era. In A. Laker (Ed.), *The Future of Physical Education* (pp. 137–152). London: Routledge.

Fitzclarence, L. (1991). "Remembering the reconceptualist project". Paper presented at the Curriculum Theorising Conference, Bergamo, USA.

Fitzclarence, L. (1997). "Marketing education: A critical overview". Keynote address to the New Zealand National Teachers Union Conference, Auckland.

Fitzclarence, L. (1993). Social violence and physical activity. In D. Kirk (Ed.), *The Body, Schooling and Culture*. Geelong: Deakin University.

Fitzclarence, L., Green, B., and Kenway, J. (Eds.). (1998). *Changing Education: New Times, New Kids*. Geelong: Deakin University.

Fitzclarence, L., Hickey, C., and Matthews, R. (1997). Getting changed for football: Challenging communities of practice. *Curriculum Perspectives*, 17(1), 69–73.

Fitzclarence, L. and Tinning, R. (1990). Challenging hegemonic physical education: Contexualising physical education as an examinable subject. In D. Kirk and R. Tinning (Eds.), *Physical Education, Curriculum and Culture: Critical Issues in the Contemporary Crisis* (pp. 169–193). London, Falmer Press.

Foer, F. (2004). *How Soccer Explains the World: An Unlikely Theory of Globalization*. New York: HaperCollins.

Foucault, M. (1986). *The Care of the Self, The History of Sexuality* (R. Hurley, Trans. Vol. 3). New York: Vintage Books.

Fraser, M., and Greco, M. (Eds.). (2005). *The Body: A Reader*. London: Routledge.

Freire, P. (1972). *Pedagogy of the Oppressed*. Harmondsworth: Penguin Books.

Friedman, S. (1985). Authority in the feminist classroom: A contradiction in terms? In M. Cully and M. Portuges (Eds.), *Gendered Subjects: The Dynamics of Feminist Teaching* (pp.203–208). New York: Routledge.

Fusco, C. (2004). The space that (in)difference makes: (Re)producing subjectivities in/through abjection – a locker room theoretical study. In P. Vertinsky and

J. Bale (Eds.), *Sites of Sport: Space, Place, Experience* (pp. 157–176). London: Routledge.

Fussell, S. (1991). *Muscle: Confessions of an Unlikely Bodybuilder.* London: Cardinal.

Gage, N., (Ed.). (1963). *Handbook of Research on Teaching.* Chicago: Rand McNally.

Gage, N.L. (1977). *The Scientific Basis of the Art of Teaching.* New York: Teachers College Press.

Gagnon, J., Tousignant, M., and Martel, D. (1989). Academic learning time in physical education classes for mentally handicapped students. *Adapted Physical Activity Quarterly,* 6, 280–289.

Gambetta, V. (1998). How much strength is enough? *Sports Coach,* 21(1), 7–9.

Gard, M. (2004). Movement, art and culture: problem-solving and critical inquiry in dance. In J. Wright, D. Macdonald and L. Burrows (Eds.), *Critical Inquiry and Problem-Solving in Physical Education* (pp. 93–105). London: Routledge.

Gard, M., and Meyenn, R. (2000). Boys, bodies, pleasure and pain: Interrogating contact sports in schools. *Sport, Education & Society,* 5(1), 19–34.

Gard, M. and Wright, J. (2001). Managing uncertainty: Obesity discourses and physical education in a risk society. *Studies in Philosophy and Education,* 20(6), 535–549.

Gard, M., and Wright, J. (2005). *The Obesity Epidemic: Science, Morality and Ideology.* London: Routledge.

George, L., and Kirk, D. (1987) "Barriers to change in physical education". Paper presented to the Conference on Ethnography and Inequality, St Hilda's College, Oxford, September.

Gibson, J. (1986). *The Ecological Approach to Visual Perception.* Hillsdale, NJ: Lawrence Erlbaum.

Giddens, A. (1990). *The Consequences of Modernity.* Stanford: Stanford University Press.

Giddens, A. (1991). *Modernity and Self-Identity. Self and Society in the Late Modern Age.* Cambridge, UK: Polity Press.

Giddens, A. (1994). *Beyond Left and Right: The Future of Radical Politics.* Cambridge, UK: Polity Press.

Gilbert, W., and Trudel, P. (2001). Learning to coach through experience: Reflection in model youth sport coaches. *Journal of Teaching in Physical Education,* 21, 16–34.

Giroux, H. (1989). *Schooling for Democracy: Critical Pedagogy in the Modern Age.* London: Routledge.

Giroux, H. (1992). *Border Crossings. Cultural Workers and the Politics of Education.* London: Routledge.

Glasby, T. (2000). "Teacher Constructions of Health: A Case Study of School Health Education in Queensland", Unpublished PhD thesis, University of Queensland.

Glassner, B. (1995). In the name of health. In R. Bunton, S. Nettleton and R. Burrows (Eds.), *The Sociology of Health* (pp. 159–176). London: Routledge.

Gleyse, J. (1998). Instrumental rationalization of human movement: An archeological approach. In G. Rail (Ed.), *Sport and Postmodern Times* (pp. 239–261). Albany: State University of New York Press.

Goldfarb, B. (2002). *Visual Pedagogy: Media Cultures In and Beyond the Classroom.* Durham: Duke University Press.

Gomez, N. (1992) Somarhythms: Developing somatic awareness with balls, *Journal of Physical Education, Recreation and Dance,* April, 74–76.

Gore, J. (1990). Pedagogy as text in physical education teacher education: Beyond the preferred reading. In D. Kirk. and R. Tinning (Eds.), *Physical Education, Curriculum and Culture: Critical Issues in the Contemporary Crisis* (pp. 101–138). Basingstoke: Falmer Press.

Gore, J. (1993). *The Struggle for Pedagogies: Critical and Feminist Discourses as Regimes of Truth*. New York: Routledge.

Graber, K. (2001). Research in teaching physical education. In V. Richardson (Ed.), *Handbook of Research on Teaching* (4th ed.) (pp. 491–520). Washington, DC: American Educational Research Association.

Gray, R. (1985a). From drills to skills: Changes in physical education in Australian schools 1945–1970. *ACHPER National Journal*, 107, 50–54.

Gray, R. (1985b). From drills to skills: Movement education. *ACHPER National Journal*, 109, 70–73.

Gray, R. (1985c). From drills to skills: Scientific discoveries. *ACHPER National Journal*, 108, 26–31.

Green, B. (1992). "Living (in) media culture". Paper presented at the "Facing the Future" National Media Education Conference, Perth.

Green, B. (1996). Teaching for difference: Learning theory and post-critical pedagogy. In D. Buckingham (Ed.), *Teaching Popular Culture: Beyond Radical Pedagogy* (pp. 177–197), London: Taylor & Francis.

Green, M. (1986). Philosophy and teaching. In M. Wittrock. (Ed.), *Handbook of Research on Teaching* (3rd ed.) (pp. 479–505). New York: Macmillan.

Griffin, L., Mitchell, M., & Olsin, J. (1997). Teaching Sport Concepts and Skills: A Tactical Games Approach. Champaign, IL: Human Kinetics.

Grossberg, L. (Ed.). (1997). *Bringing it All Back Home: Essays in Cultural Studies*. Durham: Duke University Press.

Grossley, N. (1995). Body techniques, agency and intercorporeality: On Goffman's *Relations in Public. Sociology*, 29(1), 133–150.

Gruneau, R., and Whitson, D. (1993). *Hockey Night in Canada: Sport, Identities, and Cultural Politics*. Toronto: Garamond Press.

Grupe, O., and Krüger, M. (1996). Sport pedagogy: Anthropological perspectives and traditions. In P. Schempp (Ed.), *Scientific Development of Sport Pedagogy* (pp. 155–174). New York: Waxmann Münster.

Guba, E., & Lincoln, Y. (1989). Fourth Generation Evaluation. London: Sage Publications.

Gur-Ze'ev (1998). Toward a nonrepressive critical pedagogy. *Educational Theory*, 48(4), 463–486.

Haag, H. (1989). Research in "sport pedagogy": One field of theoretical study in the science of sport. *International Review of Education*, 35(1), 5–16.

Haag, H. (1996). Sport pedagogy theory and research in the Federal Republic of Germany. In P. Schempp (Ed.), *Scientific Development of Sport Pedagogy* (pp. 143–155). New York: Waxmann Münster.

Haag, H. (2005). Concerning the concept of sport pedagogy by help of the macro-mezo-micro paradigm. In F. Carreiro da Costa *et al.* (Eds.), *The Art and Science of Teaching in Physical Education and Sport* (pp. 41–49). Lisbon: Faculdade de Motricidade Humana, Universidade Technica de Lisboa.

Haag, H. (Ed.). (1978). *Sport Pedagogy: Content and Methodology*. Balitmore: University Park Press.

Habermas, J. (1972). *Knowledge and Human Interest*. London: Heinemann.

Hamilton, D., and McWilliam, E. (2001). Ex-centric voices that frame research on teaching. In V. Richardson (Ed.), *Handbook of Research on Teaching* (4th ed.) (pp. 17–43). Washington, DC: American Educational Research Association:.

Hannula, D., and Thornton, N. (Eds.). (2001). *The Swim Coaching Bible*. Champaign, IL: Human Kinetics.

Hansen, J., and Kayser Nielsen, N. (2000). Body, health and physical education, 1870–1930. In J. Hansen and N. Kayser Nielsen (Eds.), *Sports, Body and Health* (pp. 21–47). Odense: Odense University Press.

Hardman, A. (2001). Physical activity and health: Current issues and research needs. *International Journal of Epidemiology*, 30, 1193–1197.

Hardman, A. and Stensel, D. (2003) *Physical Activity and Health: The Evidence Explained*. London: Routledge.

Hargreaves, J. (1986). *Sport, Power and Culture*. Cambridge: Polity Press.

Harwood, V. (2008). Theorising biopedagogies. In J. Wright and V. Harwood (Eds.), *Biopolitics and the "Obesity Epidemic": Governing Bodies*. London: Routledge.

Hastie, P., and Siedentop, D. (1999). An ecological perspective on physical education. *European Physical Education Review*, 5(1), 9–27.

Hay, P., and lisahunter. (2006). "Please Mr Hay, what are my poss(abilities)?": Legitimation of ability through physical education practices. *Sport, Education & Society*, 11(3), 293–310.

Hellison, D. (1988). Our constructed reality: Some contributions of an alternative perspective to physical education pedagogy. *Quest*, 40: 84–90.

Henry, J. (1998). Bull riding into manhood. In C. Hickey, L. Fitzclarence and R. Matthews (Eds.), *Where the Boys Are: Masculinity, Sport and Education* (pp. 97–109). Geelong: Deakin Centre for Education and Change.

Heron, J. (1981). *Paradigm Papers*. London: British Postgraduate Medical Federation.

Hickey, C. (1995). "Beyond critical idealism: Using critical discourses as an intellectual resource to guide teaching in physical education". Paper presented at the Australian Association for Research in Education (AARE).

Hickey, C. (2008). Physical education, sport and hyper-masculinity in schools. *Sport, Education & Society*, 13(2), 147–163.

Hickey, C., and Fitzclarence, L. (1999). Educating boys in sport and physical education: Using narrative methods to develop pedagogies of responsibility. *Sport, Education & Society*, 4(1), 51–62.

Hoffman, S. (1971). Traditional methodology: Prospects for change. *Quest*, 15, 55–57.

Hoffman, S. (1983). Clinical diagnosis as a pedagogical skill. In T. Templin and J. Olson (Eds.), *Teaching in Physical Education* (pp. 35–46). Champaign, IL: Human Kinetics.

Holland, B. (1986). "Development and Validation of an Elementary Motor Performance Test for Students Classified as Non-Handicapped, Learning Disabled, or Educable Mentally Impaired". Unpublished PhD thesis, Michigan State University.

Howell, J., and Ingham, A. (2001). From social problem to personal issue: The language of lifestyle. *Cultural Studies*, 15(2), 326–351.

Hunter, I. (1994). *Rethinking the School: Subjectivity, Bureaucracy, Criticism*. Sydney: Allen & Unwin.

Hunter, L. (2004). Bourdieu and the social space of the PE class: Reproduction of Doxa through practice. *Sport, Education & Society*, 9(2), 175–192.

Hytten, K. (1999). The promise of cultural studies of education. *Educational Theory*, 49(4), 527–543.

Imwold, C., and Hoffman, S. (1983). Visual recognition of a gymnastics skill by experienced and inexperienced instructors. *Research Quarterly for Exercise and Sport*, 54, 149–155.

Janssens, J. *et al.* (Eds.). (2004). *Education Through Sport: An Overview of Good Practices in Europe*. Nieuwegein, The Netherlands: Michel van Troost.

Johns, D. (2005). Recontexualising and delivering the biomedical model as a physical education curriculum. *Sport, Education & Society*, 10(1), 69–85.

Johns, D., and Johns, J. (2000). Surveillance, subjectivism and technologies of power: An analysis of the discursive practices of high performance sport. *International Review for the Sociology of Sport*, 35, 219–234.

Johns, D., and Tinning, R. (2006). Risk reduction: Recontextualizing health as a physical education curriculum. *Quest*, 58, 395–410.

Johnston, J., and Pennypacker, H. (1980). *Strategies and Tactics of Human Behavioural Research*. Hiilsdale, New Jersey: Lawrence Erlbaum Associates.

Kanpol, B. (2002). A sweaty pedagogy of bodily resistance: Critical implications. In S. Shapiro and S. Shapiro (Eds.), *Body Movements: Pedagogy, Politics and Social Change* (pp. 117–133). Cresshill, NJ: Hampton Press.

Kelly, L., Reuschein, P., and Hauebstricker, J. (1989). Qualitative analysis of bouncing, kicking and striking motor skills: Implications for assessing and teaching. *Journal of the International Council for Health, Physical Education and Recreation*, 26(2), 28–32.

Kelly, P., Hickey, C., and Tinning, R. (2000). Processes of expert knowledge production about PE pedagogy: Problematising the activities of expertise. *Quest*, 52(3), 284–296.

Kemmis, S. (1982). "The socially critical school". Paper presented at the Australian Association for Research in Education (AARA), Brisbane.

Kenway, J. (1992). Making "hope practical" rather than "despair convincing": Some thoughts on the value of post-structuralism as a theory of and for feminist change in schools. Unpublished manuscript, Deakin University.

Kenway, J., and Bullen, E. (2001). *Consuming Children: Education-Entertainment-Advertising*. Buckingham: Open University Press.

Kenway, J., and Modra, H (1989). Feminist pedagogy and emancipatory possibilities. *Critical Pedagogy Networker*, 2(2–3), 1–17.

Kidman, L., and Carlson, T. (1998). An action research process to change coaching behaviours. *Avante*, 4(3), 100–117.

Kidman, L., and Hanrahan, S. (1997). *The Coaching Process: A Practical Guide to Improving Your Effectiveness*. Palmerston North: Dunmore Press.

Kinchin, G. (2006). Sport education: a view of the research. In D. Kirk, D. Macdonald and M. O'Sullivan (Eds.), *The Handbook of Physical Education* (pp. 596–610). London: Sage.

Kirk, D. (1986). A critical pedagogy for teacher education: Toward an inquiry-oriented approach. *Journal of Teaching in Physical Education*, 5(4), 230–246.

Kirk, D. (1989). The orthodoxy in RT-PE and the research/practice gap: A critique and an alternative view. *Journal of Teaching in Physical Education*, 8, 123–130.

Kirk, D. (1991). "Languaging physical education teaching". Presentation to the AIESEP/NAPEHE Convention, Atlanta, Georgia.

Kirk, D. (1992a). Physical education, discourse, and ideology: Bringing the hidden curriculum into view. *Quest*, 44: 35–56.

Kirk, D. (1993a). "Physical education, the body and modernity: Is a postmodern curriculum possible?". Paper presented at the Annual Conference of the National Association of Physical Education in Higher Education, Fort Lauderdale.

Kirk, D. (1993b). *The Body, Schooling and Culture*. Geelong: Deakin University.

Kirk, D., and Colquhoun, D. (1988). Healthism and daily physical education. Unpublished manuscript, University of Queensland.

Kirk, D., and Macdonald, D. (1998). Situated learning in physical education. *Journal of Teaching in Physical Education*, 17(3), 376–387.

Kirk, D., Macdonald, D., and O'Sullivan, M. (2006). *The Handbook of Physical Education*. London: Sage.

Kirk, D., Nauright, J., Hanrahan, S., Macdonald, D., and Jobling, I. (1996). *The Sociocultuural Foundations of Human Movement Studies*. Melbourne: Macmillan Education.

Kirk, D., and Spiller, B. (1993). Schooling for docility-utility: Drill, gymnastics and the problem of the body in victorian elementary schools. In D. Meredyth and Deborah Tyler (Eds.), *Child and Citizen: Genealogies of Schooling and Subjectivity* (pp. 103–127). Brisbane: Institute of Cultural Policy Studies, Griffith University.

Kirk, D., and Tinning, R. (1992b). "Physical education pedagogical work as praxis". Paper presented at the American Educational Research Association, San Francisco.

Klein, N. (2000). *No Logo*. London: Flamingo.

Kniest, P. (2004). Proof of performance. *Advocate: Journal of the National Tertiary Education Union*, 11(1), 22–23.

Kohli, W. (1998). Critical education and embodied subjects: Making the poststructural turn. *Educational Theory*, 48(4), 511–519.

Kretchmer, S. (2007). What to do with meaning? A research conundrum for the 21st century. *Quest*, 59(4), 373–383.

Landsdorf, E. (1979). "A Systematic Observation of Football Coaching Behaviour in a Major University Environment." Unpublished PhD dissertation, Arizona State University.

Laker, A. (Ed.). (2003). *The Future of Physical Education: Building a New Pedagogy*. London: Routledge.

Lather, P. (1991). *Getting Smart: Feminist Research and Pedagogy within the Postmodern*. London: Routledge.

Lather, P. (1998). Critical pedagogy and its complicities: A praxis of stuck places. *Educational Theory*, 48(4), 487–497.

Launder, A. (2001). *Play Practice: The Games Approach to Teaching and Coaching Sports*. Champaign, IL: Human Kinetics.

Lave, J. (1997). The culture of acquisition and the practice of understanding. In D. Kirshner and J. Whitson (Eds.), *Situated Cognition: Social, Semiotic and Psychological Perspectives* (pp. 17–37). New York: Lawrence Erlbaum.

Lave, J., and Wenger, E. (1991). *Situated Learning: Legitimate Peripheral Participation*. Cambridge: Cambridge University Press.

Law, J. (1994). *Organizing Modernity*. Oxford: Blackwell.

Lawson, H. (1984). Problem-setting for physical education, *Quest*, 36, 48–60.

Lawson, H.A. (1990). Sport pedagogy research: From information-gathering to useful knowledge. *Journal of Teaching in Physical Education*, 10(1), 1–20.

Leahy, D. (2008). Disgusting pedagogies. In J. Wright and V. Harwood (Eds.),

Biopolitics and the "Obesity Epidemic": Governing Bodies (pp. 172–182). London: Routledge.

Lee, A., and Green, B. (1997). Pedagogy and disciplinarity in the "new university". *The UTS Review*, 3(1), 1–25.

Lee, A., and Solmon, M. (2005). Pedagogy research through the years in RQES. *Research Quarterly for Exercise and Sport*, 76(2), s108–s121.

Lee, M. (Ed.). (1993). *Coaching Children in Sport: Principles and Practice*. London: E & FN Spon.

Light, R. (2007). Re-examining hegemonic masculinity in high school rugby: The body, compliance and resistance. *Quest*, 59(3), 323–338.

Light, R., and Kirk, D. (2000). High school rugby, the body and the reproduction of hegemonic masculinity. *Sport, Education & Society*, 5(2), 163–177.

Light, R., and Wallian, N. (2008). A constructivist-informed approach to teaching swimming. *Quest*, 60(3), 387–405.

Linden, P. (1994). Somatic literacy: Bringing somatic education into physical education. *Journal of Physical Education, Recreation & Dance*, September, 16–21.

Lindqvist, S. (2003). *Bench Press* (S. Death, Trans.). London: Grant Books.

Liston, D., and Zeichner, K. (1991). *Teacher Education and the Social Conditions of Schooling*. New York: Routledge.

Locke, L. (1977). Research on teaching in physical education: New hope for a dismal science. *Quest*, 28, 2–16.

Locke, L. (1979). "Teaching and learning processes in physical activity: The central problem of sport pedagogy". Keynote address to the ICHPER Congress, Kiel, Germany.

Locke, L. (1982). "Research on teacher education for physical education in the USA, Part 2: Questions and conclusions". Paper presented at the International Symposium on Research in School Physical Education, University of Jyvaskyla, Finland.

Locke, L. (1989). Qualitative research as a form of scientific inquiry in sport and physical education. *Research Quarterly for Exercise and Sport*, 60(1), 1–20.

Locke, L., Mand, C., and Siedentop, D. (1981). The preparation of physical education teachers: A subject-matter-centred model. In H. Lawson (Ed.), *Undergraduate Physical Education Programs: Issues and Approaches* (pp. 33–54). Washington, DC: American Alliance for Health, Physical Education, Recreation and Dance.

Locke, L.F. (1974). "The ecology of the gymnasium: What the tourists never see". Paper presented at the SAPECW Workshop, Gatlinburg, Tennessee.

Lodge, D. (1989). *Nice Work*. New York: Viking Penguin.

London County Council (1962). *Educational Gymnastics: A Guide for Teachers*. London: W.F. Houghton.

Lounsbery, M., and Coker, C. (2008). Developing skill-analysis competency in physical education teachers. *Quest*, 60, 255–267.

Luke, A. (2002). Curriculum, ethics, metanarrative: Teaching and learning beyond the nation. *Curriculum Perspectives*, 22(1), 49–55.

Luke, C. (Ed.). (1996). *Feminisms and Pedagogies of Everyday Life*. Albany, NY: SUNY.

Luke, C., and Gore, J. (Eds.). (1992). *Feminisms and Critical Pedagogy*. New York: Routledge.

Lundgren, U. (1983). *Curriculum Theory, Between Hope And Happening: Text and Context in Curriculum*. Geelong: Deakin University.

Lupton, D. (1994). *Medicine as Culture*. London: Sage.

Lupton, D. (1996). *Food, the Body and the Self*. London: Sage.

Lupton, D. (1997). Consumersim, reflexivity and the medical encounter. *Social Science and Medicine*, 45(3), 373–381.

Lusted, D. (1986). Why pedagogy? *Screen*, 27(5), 2–14.

Lynch, A. (1996). *Thought Contagion: How Belief Spreads Through Society*. New York: Basic Books.

McCallister, S., Blinde, E., and Weiss, W. (2000). Teaching values and implementing philosophies: Dilemmas of the youth sport coach. *The Physical Educator*, 57(1), 35–46.

McCloy, C. (1940). *Philosophical Bases for Physical Education*. New York: Century-Crofts.

McCuaig, L. (2008). "Teaching the Art of Healthy Living: A Geneological Study of H-PE and the Moral Governance of Apprentice Citizens". Unpublished PhD thesis, University of Queensland.

McCullick, B., Belcher, D., Hardin, B., and Hardin, M. (2003). Butches, bullies and buffoons: Images of physical education teachers in the movies. *Sport, Education & Society*, 8(1), 3–16.

Macdonald, D. (2003). Curriculum change and the postmodern world: Is the school curriculum-reform project an anachronism? *Journal of Curriculum Studies*, 35(2), 139–149.

Macdonald, D. (2004). Commentary: Evidence-based practice in health and physical education. *Waikato Journal of Education*, 10, 21–27.

Macdonald, D. (2007). "Evidence-based practice in physical education: Ample evidence, patchy practice". Paper presented at the "History and Future Directions of Research on Teaching and Teacher Education in PE" Conference, Pittsburgh, Pennsylvania.

Macdonald, D., and Brooker, R. (2000). Articulating a critical pedagogy in physical education teacher education. *Journal of Sport Pedagogy*, 5(1), 51–63.

Macdonald, D., Cote, J., and Kirk, D. (2007). Physical activity pedagogy for junior sport. In S. Hooper, D. Macdonald and M. Phillips (Eds.), *Junior Sport Matters: Briefing Papers of Australian Junior Sport* (pp. 29–41). Canberra: Australian Sports Commission.

Macdonald, D., and Kirk, D. (1999). Pedagogy, the body and Christian identity. *Sport, Education & Society*, 4(2), 131–142.

Macdonald, D., Kirk, D., and Braiuka, S. (1999). The social construction of the physical activity field at the school/university interface. *European Journal of Physical Education*, 5(1), 31–51.

MacDonald-Wallace, J. (1978). Is health your concern? *British Journal of Physical Education*, 9(1), 8–9.

Mackay, H. (1997). *Generations: Baby Boomers, Their Parents and Their Children*. Sydney: Pan Macmillan.

McKay, J., Gore, J., and Kirk, D. (1990). Beyond the limits of technocratic physical education. *Quest*, 42(1), 52–75.

McLaren, P. (1998). Revolutionary pedagogy in post-revolutionary times: Rethinking the political economy of critical education. *Educational Theory*, 48(4), 431–462.

McLuhan, M. (1964). *Understanding Media: The Extensions of Man*. New York: Mentor.

McNay, L. (1992). *Foucault and Feminism: Power, Gender and the Self*. Cambridge: Polity Press.

MacPhail, A., Gorley, T., and Kirk, D. (2003). Young people's socialisation into sport: A case study of an athletics club. *Sport Education & Society*, 8(2), 251–267.

McWilliam, E. (1996). Touchy subjects: A risky inquiry into pedagogical pleasure. *British Educational Research Journal*, 22(3), 305–317.

McWilliam, E. (1999). *Pedagogical Pleasures*. New York: Peter Lang.

McWilliam, E., and Taylor, P. (1996). *Pedagogy, Technology and the Body*. New York: Peter Lang.

Magill, R. (2003). *Motor Learning and Control: Concepts and Applications* (7th ed.). Boston: McGraw-Hill.

Maher, F. (1985). Toward a richer theory of feminist pedagogy: A comparison of "liberal" and "gender" models of teaching and learning. *Journal of Education*, 169(3), 91–100.

Maisel, E. (1970). *The Alexander Technique: The Resurrection of the Body*. New York: University Books.

Major, J. (1994). 'Sport in Schools', Address to the Conservative Party Conference, UK, 14 October, 1994.

Mallett, C. (2004). Reflective practices in teaching and coaching: Using reflective journals to enhance performance. In J. Wright, L. Burrows and D. Macdonald (Eds.), *Critical Inquiry and Problem-Solving in Physical Education* (pp. 147–159). London: Routledge.

Martens, R. (2004). *Successful Coaching* (3rd ed.). Champaign, IL: Human Kinetics.

Marton, F., and Booth, S. (1997). *Learning and Awareness*. Mahwah, NJ: Erlbaum Publishers.

Mawer, M. (1984) Physical education and health education. In G. Campbell (Ed.), *Health Education and Youth: A Review of Research and Development* (pp. 338–343). UK: Falmer Press.

Melville, D., and Maddalozzo, J. (1988). The effects of a physical educator's appearance of body fatness on communicating exercise concepts to high school students. *Journal of Teaching in Physical Education*, 7(4), 343–352.

Mercer, N. (1992). Culture, context and the construction of knowledge in the classroom. In P. Light and G. Butterworth (Eds.), *Context and Cognition* (pp. 28–46). Hillsdale: Erlbaum Publishers.

Metcalfe, A. (1993). Living in a clinic: The power of public health promotions. *Anthropological Journal of Australia*, 4(1), 31–44.

Miller, A. (1987). *For Your Own Good: Hidden Cruelty in Child-Rearing and the Roots of Violence* (H. and H. Hannum, Trans.). London: Virago.

Ministry of Education. (1952). *Moving and Growing: Physical Education in the Primary School Part 1*. London: HMSO.

Moran, K. (2001). Aquatics education and the advent of the primary school learners' pool in post World War II New Zealand. *New Zealand Journal of Educational Studies*, 36(1), 57–69.

Moran, K. (2002). Final year student teachers' perceptions of their training and readiness to teach aquatics education in New Zealand primary schools. *Journal of Physical Education New Zealand*, 35(1), 55–75.

Moran, K. (2008). Taking the plunge: Diving risk practices and perceptions of New Zealand youth. *Health Promotion Journal of Australia*, 19(1), 68–71.

Morrison, C., and Reeve, E. (1988). Effect of instruction and undergraduate major on qualitative skill analysis. *Journal of Human Movement Studies*, 15, 291–297.

Mosston, M. (1966). *Teaching Physical Education: From Command to Discovery.* Columbus, OH: Charles Merrill Publishing Co.

Mosston, M., and Ashworth, S. (1994). *Teaching Physical Education.* Columbus, OH: Merrill.

Moxley, R. (1982). Graphics for three term contingencies. *The Behaviour Analyst,* 51(1), 45–53.

Myerson, J. (2005). *Not a Games Person.* London: Yellow Jersey Press.

Nauright, J. (1996). Sustaining masculine hegemony: Rugby and the nostalgia of masculinity. In J. Nauright and T. Chandler (Eds.), *Making Men: Rugby and Masculine Identity* (pp. 227–244). London: Cass.

Nel, B. (1973). The phenomenological approach to pedagogy. *Journal of Phenomenological Psychology,* 3(2), 201–15.

Nestle, M. (2003). *Food Politics: How the Food Industry Influences Nutrition and Health.* Los Angeles: University of California Press.

Nettleton, B. (1976). Physical competence as an educational objective. *New Zealand Journal of Health, Physical Education & Recreation,* 9(2), 39–47.

Nettleton, B. (1985). *The Image of the Physical Education Teacher.* Eastwood: ACHPER Publications.

Nettleton, S., and Bunton, R. (1995). Sociological critiques of health promotion. In R. Bunton, S. Nettleton and R. Burrows (Eds.), *The Sociology of Health Promotion: Critical Analysis of Consumption, Lifestyle and Risk* (pp. 39–56). London: Routledge.

Newell, K. (1986). Constraints on the development of coordination. In M. Wade and H.T.A. Whiting (Eds.), *Motor Development in Children: Aspects of Coordination and Control* (pp. 341–360). Boston: Martinus Nijhoff.

Nilges, L. (2004). Ice can look like glass: A phenomenological investigation of movement meaning. *Research Quarterly for Exercise and Sport,* 75(3), 298–314.

Nisbett, R. (2003). *The Geography of Thought: How Asians and Westerners Think Differently – And Why.* New York: Free Press.

Norman, J. (1995). Zen and the art of body maintenance. *Good Weekend: The Age Magazine,* 2 September, pp. 22–27.

O'Farrell, C., Meadmore, D., McWilliam, E., and Symes, C. (Eds.). (2000). *Taught Bodies.* New York: Peter Lang.

Oliver, K. (2001). Images of the body from popular culture: Engaging adolescent girls in critical inquiry. *Sport, Education & Society,* 6(2), 143–164.

Oliver, K., and Lalik, R. (2004). Critical inquiry on the body in girls' physical education classes: A critical post-structuralist perspective. *Journal of Teaching in Physical Education,* 23(2), 162–195.

Olsin, J., and Mitchell, S. (2006). Game-centered approaches to teaching physical education. In D. Kirk, M. O'Sullivan and D. Macdonald (Eds.), *The Handbook of Physical Education* (pp. 627–651). London: Sage.

Orbach, S. (1978). *Fat is a Feminist Issue.* New York: Berkeley Books.

O'Sullivan, M., Siedentop, D., and Locke, L. (1992). Toward collegiality: Competing viewpoints among teacher educators. *Quest,* 44(2), 266–280.

Ovens, A. (2002). "Discourse communities and the social construction of reflection in teacher education". Paper presented at the HERDSA, Perth.

Oxendine, J. (1968). *Psychology of Motor Learning.* New York: Appleton-Century-Crofts.

Oxford English Dictionary (1989), 2nd Edition, Oxford: Clarendon Press.

Paffenbarger, R.S., Hyde, R.T., Wing, A.L., and Hseih, C. (1986) Physical activity, all cause mortality, and longevity of college alumni. *New England Journal of Medicine*, 314, 605–613.

Paffenbarger, R.S., Wing, A.L., Hyde, R.T., and Jung, D. (1983) Chronic disease in former college students; physical activity and incidence of hypertension of college alumni. *American Journal of Epidemiology*, 117, 245–257.

Park, R. (2004). For pleasure? Or profit? Or personal health?: College gymnasia as contested terrain. In P. Vertinsky and J. Bale (Eds.), *Sites of Sport: Space, Place, Experience* (pp. 177–205). London: Routledge.

Penny, D. (2003). Sport education and situated learning: Problematizing the potential. *European Physical Education Review*, 9(3), 301–308.

Penny, D., and Waring, M. (2000). The absent agenda: Pedagogy and physical education. *Journal of Sport Pedagogy*, 6(1), 4–38.

Peters, J., & Peters, H. (1995). *The Flexibility Manual*. Berwyn, PA: Sports Kinetics.

Peters, R. (1981). *Moral Development and Moral Education.*, London: Allen & Unwin.

Petersen, A., & Lupton, D. (1996). *The New Public Health: Health and self in the age of risk*. Sydney: Allen & Unwin.

Petersen, A., & Bunton, R. (Eds.). (1997). *Foucault, Health and Medicine*. London: Routledge.

Peterson, P., and Walberg, H. (Eds.). (1979). *Research on Teaching: Concepts, Findings and Implications*. Berkeley, CA: McGutchan Publishing.

Pettit, A, and Robinson, J. (1989) "That hustle thing": The theory and practice of daily physical education in Darwin, *ACHPER National Journal*, June, 28–30.

Piéron, M. (1983). Teacher and pupil behaviour and the interaction process in PE classes. In R. Telema (Ed.), *Research in School Physical Education*. Jyvaskyla, Finland: The Foundation for Promotion of Physical Culture and Health.

Piéron, M., Cheffers, J., and Barrette, G. (1990). *An Introduction to the Terminology of Sport Pedagogy*. Leige, Belgium: CIEPSS-AIESEP.

Pike, F. (Ed.). (1991). *Better Coaching: Advanced Coach's Manual*, Canberra: Australian Sports Commission.

Placek, J., and Locke, L. (1986). Research on teaching physical education: New knowledge and cautious optimism. *Journal of Teacher Education*, 37(4), 24–28.

Pollack-Seid, R. (1989). *Never Too Thin: Why Women Are at War with Their Bodies*. New York: Prentice Hall Press.

Popenoe, R. (2004). *Feeding Desire: Fatness, Beauty, and Sexuality among a Saharan People*. London: Routledge.

Popkewitz, T., and Brennan, M. (Eds.) (1998). *Foucault's Challenge:Discourse, Knowledge, and Power in Education*. New York: Teachers College Press.

Postman, N. (1989). *Conscientious Objections: Stirring Up Trouble about Language, Technology and Education*. London: Heinemann.

Powell, K.E., and Blair, S.N. (1994) The public health burden of sedentary living habits: Theoretical but realistic estimates. *Medicine and Science in Sports and Exercise*, 26, 851–856.

Pritchard, T., Hawkins, A., Wiegand, R., and Metzler, J. (2008). Effects of two instructional approaches on skill development, knowledge, and game performance. *Measurement in Physical Education and Exercise Science*, 12, 219–236.

Pronger, B. (1995). Rendering the body: The implicit lessons of gross anatomy. *Quest*, 47, 427–446.

Pronger, B. (2002). *Body Fascism: Salvation in the Technology of Physical Fitness.* Toronto: University of Toronto Press.

Queensland School Curriculum Council (1999). *Health and Physical Education Years 1 to 10 Syllabus*, Brisbane: Education Queensland.

Rasmussen, M. (2007). Prescriptions for sex and gender in school architecture. *Redress*, 16(1), 17–22.

Rate, R. (1980). *A descriptive analysis of academic learning time and coaching behaviour in interscholastic athletic practices.* Unpublished PhD, Ohio State University, Columbus.

Rich, E., Holroyd, R., & Evans, J. (2004). 'Hungry to be noticed': young women, anorexia and schooling. In J. Evans, B. Davies & J. Wright (Eds.), *Body Knowledge and Control: Studies in the Sociology of Education and Physical Culture.* (pp. 173–191). London: Routledge.

Richardson, V. (Ed.). (2001). *Handbook of Research on Teaching* (4th ed.). Washington, DC: American Educational Research Association.

Rink, J. (1994). Task presentation in pedagogy. *Journal of Teaching in Physical Education*, 46: 270–280.

Rink, J. (2007). What knowledge is of most worth?: Perspectives on kinesiology and pedagogy. *Quest*, 59(1), 100–110.

Riordan, J., and Krüger, A. (Eds.). (2003). *European Cultures in Sport: Examining the Nations and Regions.* Bristol: Intellect Books.

Roberts, E.A. (1905). *A Handbook of Free-Standing Gymnastics.* London: Sherratt & Hughes.

Rochester, D., Mancini, V., and Morris, H. (1977). "The effects of supervision and instruction in the use of interaction analysis on the teaching behaviour and effectiveness of pre-service teachers". Paper presented at the AAHPER National Convention.

Rogers, C. (1967). *On Becoming a Person: A Therapist's View of Psychotherapy.* London: Constable.

Rogoff, B. (1990). *Apprenticeship in Thinking: Cognitive Development in Social Context.* New York: Oxford University Press.

Rose, M., and Miller, P. (1992). Political power beyond the State: Problematics of government. *British Journal of Sociology*, 43(2), 173–205.

Rose, N. (1993). Government, authority and expertise in advanced liberalism. *Economy and Society*, 22(3), 283–299.

Rose, N. (1996). *Inventing Our Selves: Psychology, Power, and Personhood.* Cambridge: Cambridge University Press.

Rose, N. (1999). *Powers of Freedom: Reframing Political Thought.* Cambridge: Cambridge University Press.

Rossi, A. (2001). "Linking games for understanding with dynamical systems of skill acquisition: Old milk in new bottles or have we really got a new research agenda in physical education and sport?". Paper presented at the "Teaching Games For Understanding in Physical Education and Sport" International Conference, Waterville Valley, New Hampshire.

Rossi, A., and Ryan, M. (2006). Literacy issues and PE. In R. Tinning, L. McCuaig and lisahunter (Eds.), *Teaching Health and Physical Education in Australian Schools* (pp. 70–78). Sydney: Pearson.

Rotsko, A. (1979). "A Comparison of Coaching Behaviours of Successful and Less Successful Coaches". Unpublished Masters thesis, Ithaca College, Ithaca.

Rousseau, J.-J. (1911). *Emile; or Treatise on Education* (W. H. Payne, Trans.). New York: Appleton.

Rovegno, I. (1994). Teaching within a curricular zone of safety: School culture and the situated nature of student teachers' pedagogical content knowledge. *Research Quarterly for Exercise and Sport*, 65(3), 269–279.

Rovegno, I., and Dolly, J. (2006). Constructivist perspectives on learning. In D. Kirk, M. O'Sullivan and D. Macdonald (Eds.), *The Handbook of Physical Education* (pp. 242–261). London: Sage.

Rovegno, I. and Kirk. D. (1995). Articulations and silences in socially-critical work on physical education: Toward a broader agenda. *Quest*, 47(4), 447–474.

Rynne, S.B., Mallett, C., and Tinning, R. (2006). High performance sport coaching: Institutes of sport as sites for learning. *International Journal of Sport Science and Coaching*, 1(3), 223–233.

Rynne, S., Mallett, C., and Tinning, R. (in press). Workplace learning of high performance sports coaches. *Sport, Education & Society*.

Sacks, P. (1996). *Generation X Goes to College: An Eye-Opening Account of Teaching in Postmodern America*. Chicago: Open Court.

Sage, G.H. (1993). Sport and physical education and the new world order: Dare we be agents of social change. *Quest*, 45(2), 151–164.

Sallis, J., and McKenzie, T. (1991). Physical education's role in public health. *Research Quarterly for Exercise and Sport*, 62(2), 124–137.

Sallis, J., and Owen, N. (1999). *Physical Activity and Behavioural Medicine*. London: Sage Publications.

Saltmann, K. (2002). Embodied promise: The pedagogy of market faith in bodybuilding. In S. and S. Shapiro (Eds.), *Body Movements: Pedagogy, Politics and Social Change* (pp. 317–336). Cresskill, NJ: Hampton Press.

Schempp, P. (1987). Research on teaching in physical education: Beyond the limits of natural science. *Journal of Teaching in Physical Education*, 6(2), 111–121.

Schempp, P. (1988). Exorcist II: A reply to Siedentop. *Journal of Teaching in Physical Education*, (7), 79–81.

Schempp, P. (1993). "The nature of knowledge in sport pedagogy". Jose-Marie Cagigal Memorial Lecture at the AIESEP World Congress, Buffalo, New York.

Schempp, P., and Graber, K. (1992). Teacher socialisation from a dialectical perspective: Pretraining through induction. *Journal of Teaching in Physical Education*, 11, 329–348.

Schemmp, P., Webster, C., McCullick, B., Busch, C., and Sannen Mason, I. (2007). How the best get better: An analysis of the self-monitoring strategies used by expert golf instructors. *Sport, Education & Society*, 12(2), 175–192.

Schempp, P., You, J., & Clark, B. (1998). The antecedents of expertise in golf instruction. In A. Farrally & B. Cochran (Eds.), *Science of Golf III: Proceedings of the World Scientific Congress of Golf*. Champaign, IL: Human Kinetics.

Schwarz, G., and Cavener, L. (1994). Outcome-based education and curriculum change: Advocacy, practice and critique. *Journal of Curriculum and Supervision*, 9(4), 326–338.

Scraton, S. (1990). *Gender and Physical Education*, Geelong: Deakin University.

Shulman, L.S. (1986). Those who understand: Knowledge growth in teaching. *Educational Researcher*, 15(February), 4–14.

Siedentop, D. (1983a). *Developing Teaching Skills in Physical Education*. Palo Alto, CA: Mayfield.

Siedentop, D. (1983b). Research on teaching in physical education. In T. Templin. and J. Olson. (Eds.) *Teaching in Physical Education*. Champaign, IL: Human Kinetics.

Siedentop, D. (1987). Dialogue or exorcism? A rejoinder to Schempp. *Journal of Teaching in Physical Education*, 6(4), 373–376.

Siedentop, D. (1989). Do the lockers really smell? *Research Quarterly for Exercise and Sport*, 60(1), 36–41.

Siedentop, D. (1990). *Introduction to Physical Education, Fitness, and Sport*. London: Mayfield.

Siedentop, D. (1994). Curriculum innovation: Towards the 21st century. *ICPHER Journal*, xxx(2), 11–14.

Siedentop, D. (1995). "Physical activity cultures for children and youth: Redefining physical education". Paper presented at the Thirteenth Annual Oberteuffer Lecture, the Ohio State University.

Siedentop, D. (1998). New times in (and for) physical education. In R. Feingold, R. Rees, G. Barrette, S. Fiorentino, S. Virgilio and E. Kowalski (Eds.), *AIESEP Proceedings, "Education for Life" World Congress* (pp. 210–212). New York: Adelphi University.

Siedentop, D. (2002). Content knowledge for physical education. *Journal of Teaching in Physical Education*, 21, 4, 368–377.

Siedentop, D., Birdwell, D., and Metzler, M. (1979). "A process approach to measuring teacher effectiveness in physical education". Paper presented at the AAHPER, New Orleans.

Siedentop, D., and Tannehill, D. (2000). *Developing Teaching Skills in Physical Education*. Palo Alto, CA: Mayfield.

Siegel, B. (1990). *Love, Medicine and Miracles*. New York: Quill.

Silverman, D. (2007). Mingling with our friends: The kinesiology student and pedagogy knowledge. *Quest*, 59(1), 92–99.

Silverman, D., and Ennis, C. (Eds.) (1996). *Student Learning in Physical Education: Applying Research to Enhance Instruction*. Champaign, IL: Human Kinetics.

Silverman, S. (1986). Relationship of engagement and practice trials to student achievement. *Journal of teaching in physical education*, 5, 13–21.

Silverman, S. (1991). Research on teaching in physical education. Research quarterly for exercise and sport, 62(4), 352–364.

Silverman, S., and Keating, X.D. (2002). A descriptive analysis of research methods classes in departments of kinesiology and physical education in the United States. *Research Quarterly in Exercise and Sport*, 73(1), 1–9.

Simon, R. (1997). Forms of insurgency in the production of popular memories: The Columbus Quincentury and the pedagogy of counter-commemoration. In L. Grossberg (Ed.), *Bringing it all Back Home: Essays in Cultural Studies* (pp. 125–142). Durham: Duke University Press.

Simpson, J., and Weiner, E. (1989). *The Oxford English Dictionary* (2nd ed.). Oxford: Clarendon Press.

Singer, P. (1993). *How Are We to Live? Ethics in an Age of Self-Interest*. Melbourne: The Text Publishing Company.

Singer, R. (1968). *Motor Learning and Human Performance*. New York: Macmillan.

Smith, R., Curtin, P., and Newman, L. (1996). "Kids in the 'kitchen': The social implications for schooling in the age of advanced computer technology". Paper presented at the Australian Association for Research in Education, Annual Conference, Hobart, December.

Smith, S. (1991). Where is the child in physical education research? *Quest*, 43: 55–65.

Smith, S. (1998). *Risk and Our Pedagogical Relation to Children*. Albany, NY: SUNY.

Smyth, J. (2001). *Critical Politics of Teachers' Work: An Australian Perspective*. New York: Peter Lang.

Smyth, J., and Dow, A. (1998). What's wrong with outcomes? Spotter planes, action plans and steerage of the educational workplace. *British Journal of Sociology of Education*, 19(3), 291–303.

Smyth, S. (1987). *A Rationale for Teachers' Critical Pedagogy: A Handbook*. Geelong: Deakin University.

Sparkes, A. (1989). Health related fitness and pervasive ideology of individualism. *Perspectives*, 42, 10–14.

Sparkes, A. (1991). Towards understanding, dialogue and polyvocality in the research community: Extending the boundaries of the paradigm debate. *Journal of Teaching in Physical Education*, 10(2), 103–133.

Sparkes, A. (1996). The fatal flaw: A narrative of the fragile body/self. *Qualitative Inquiry*, 2(4), 463–494.

Sparkes, A. (2001). *Telling Tales in Sport and Physical Activity: A Qualitative Journey*. Champaign, IL: Human Kinetics.

Sparkes, A. (2004). From performance to impairment: A patchwork of embodied memories. In J. Evan, B. Davies and J. Wright (Eds.), *Body Knowledge and Control. Studies in the Sociology of Education and Physical Culture* (pp. 157–173). London: Routledge.

Spiecker, B. (1984). The pedagogical relationship. *Oxford Review of Education*, 10(2), 203–9.

Stearns, P. (1997). *Fat History: Bodies and Beauty in the Modern West*. New York: New York University Press.

Stones, E. (2000). Iconoclastes: poor pedagogy. *Journal of Teaching for Education*, 26(1), 93–95.

Stroot, S., and Oslin, J. (1993). Use of instructional statements by preservice teachers for overhand throwing performance of children. *Journal of Teaching in Physical Education*, 13, 24–45.

Swan, P. (1995). Studentship and oppositional behaviour within physical education teacher education: A case study and Between the rings and under the gym mat: A narrative. Unpublished Doctor of Education, Deakin University.

Swan, P. (1999). Three ages of changing. In A. Sparkes and M. Silvennoinen (Eds.), *Talking Bodies: Men's Narratives of the Body and Sport* (pp. 37–48). Jyvaskyla: SoPhi.

Tanner, J. (1964). *The Physique of the Olympic Athlete*. London: Allen & Unwin.

Templin, T., and Olson, J. (Eds.). (1983). *Teaching in Physical Education*. Champaign, IL: Human Kinetics.

Terret, T. (2004). Educative pools: Water, school and space in twentieth-century France. In P. Vertinsky and J. Bale (Eds.), *Sites of Sport: Space, Place, Experience* (pp. 37–56). London: Routledge.

Tharpe, R., and Gallimore, R. (1976). What a coach can teach a teacher. *Psychology Today*, 9(8), 75–78.

Theberge, N. (1991). Reflections on the body in the sociology of sport. *Quest*, 43, 123–134.

Theodorakou, K., and Zervas, Y. (2003). The effects of the creative teaching method and the traditional teaching method on elementary school children's self-esteem. *Sport, Education & Society*, 8(1), 91–104.

Thorpe, R., Bunker, D., and Almond, L. (Eds.). (1986). *Rethinking Games Teaching*. Loughborough, UK: Department of Physical Education and Sports Science, Loughborough University.

Tinning, R. (1982). Improving coaches' instructional effectiveness. *Sports Coach*, 5(4), 37–41.

Tinning, R. (1985). Physical education and the cult of slenderness: A critique. *ACHPER National Journal*, 107(Autumn), 10–14.

Tinning, R. (1987). *Improving Teaching in Physical Education*, Geelong: Deakin University Press.

Tinning, R. (1991a). "If you could see it through my eyes: Notes on reading action research". Paper presented to the AIESEP/NAHAPE World Convention, Atlanta, Georgia, January.

Tinning, R. (1991b). Health oriented physical education (HOPE): The case of physical education and the promotion of healthy lifestyles. *ACHPER National Journal*, 134, 4–11.

Tinning, R. (1991c). Teacher education pedagogy: Dominant discourses and the process of problem solving. *Journal of Teaching in Physical Education*, 11: 1–20.

Tinning, R. (1992). Reading action research: Notes on knowledge and human interests. *Quest*, 44(1), 1–15.

Tinning, R. (1994). If physical education is the answer, what is the question?: Ruminations on the relevance of physical education in the 1990s. *New Zealand Physical Education Journal*, 22(4), 15–24.

Tinning, R. (1997). *Pedagogies for Physical Education: Pauline's Story*. Geelong: Deakin University.

Tinning, R. (1998). "Coaching kids in 'new times': Thoughts on sport pedagogy, coaching and physical education". Keynote address to the Australian National Sports Coaching Conference, Melbourne.

Tinning, R. (2000). Unsettling matters for physical education in higher education: Taking seriously the possible implications of "new times". *Quest*, 52(1), 32–49.

Tinning, R. (2001). Physical education and back health: Negotiating instrumental aims and holistic body-work practices. *European Physical Education Review*, 7(2), 191–207.

Tinning, R. (2002). Towards a "modest" pedagogy: Reflections on the problematics of critical pedagogy. *Quest*, 54(3), 224–241.

Tinning, R. (2008). Who pushed Humpty Dumpty? Dilemmas in physical education circa 2007. In L. Housner, M. Metzler, P. Schempp and T. Templin (Eds.), *Historic Traditions and Future Directions in Research on Teaching*. West Virginia: West Virginia University School of Physical Education International Center for Performance Excellence.

Tinning, R., and Glasby, P. (2002). Pedagogical work and the "cult of the body": Considering the role of HPE in the context of the "new public health". *Sport, Education & Society*, 7(2), 109–119.

Tinning, R., and Kirk, D. (1991). *Daily Physical Education: Collected Papers on Health Based Physical Education in Australia*, Geelong: Deakin University Press.

Tinning, R., Macdonald, D., Tregenza, K., and Boustead, J. (1996). Action research and the professional development of teachers in the health and physical education field: The Australian NPDP experience. *Educational Action Research*, 4:2, 391–406.

Tinning, R., and Thorpe, S. (1999). "Dilemmas and problematics involved in the process of theorising curriculum development and reform". Paper presented at the AARE/SERA Conference, Singapore, November.

Tousignant, M. (2000). Synthesis of the section devoted to research on teacher education. In F-C. da Costa *et al.* (Eds.), *Research on Teaching and Research on Teacher Education: Proceedings of the International Seminar* (pp. 261–264). Lisboa: Edições FMH.

Tousignant, M. (2005). Observational research on teaching in physical education. In F-C. da Costa *et al.* (Eds.), *The Art and Science of Teaching in Physical Education and Sport* (pp. 249–279). Faculdade de Motricidade Humana, Universidade Technica de Lisboa.

Tousignant, M., and Siedentop, D. (1983). A qualitative analysis of task structures in required secondary physical education classes. *Journal of Teaching in Physical Education* (Fall), 47–57.

Travers, M., (Ed.). (1973). *Second Handbook of Research on Teaching*. Chicago: Rand McNally.

Trend, D. (1992). *Cultural Pedagogy: Art/Education/Politics*. New York: Bergin and Garvey.

Trudel, P., and Gilbert, W. (2006). Coaching and coach education. In D. Kirk, M. O'Sullivan and D. Macdonald (Eds.), *The Handbook of Physical Education* (pp. 516–540). London: Sage.

Turner, B. (1996). *The Body and Society: Explorations in Social Theory*. London: Sage.

Ulrich, D. (1985). *Test of Gross Motor Development*. Austin, Texas: PRO-ED inc.

USDHHS. (1980). *Health: United States 1980*. US Government Printing Office: Washington, DC.

Vamplew, W. (Ed.). (1997). *The Oxford Companion to Australian Sport* (2nd ed.). Melbourne: Oxford University Press.

Van Den Berg, J. (1964). The significance of human movement. *Philosophy and Phenomenological Research*, 13, 159–183.

van der Mars, H. (1987). Effects of audio-cueing on teacher verbal praise of student managerial and transitional task performance. *Journal of Teaching in Physical Education*, 6, 157–165.

van Manen, M. (1979). The phenomenology of pedagogic observation. *Canadian Journal of Education*, 4(1), 5–16.

van Manen, M. (1982). Phenomenological pedagogy. *Curriculum Inquiry*, 12(3), 283–99.

van Manen, M. (1990). *Researching Lived Experience: Human Science for an Action Sensitive Pedagogy*. Albany, NY: SUNY Press.

Vertinsky, P. (2004). Locating a "sense of place": Space, place and gender in the gymnasium. In P. Vertinsky and J. Bale (Eds.), *Sites of Sport: Space, Place, Experience* (pp. 8–25). London: Routledge.

Vertinsky, P., and Bale, J. (Eds.). (2004). *Sites of Sport: Space, Place, Experience*. London: Routledge.

Vertinsky, P., McManus, A., & Sit, C. (2007). 'Dancing class': schooling the dance in colonial and post-colonial Hong Kong. *Sport, Education & Society*, 12(1), 73–92.

Wade, A. (1978). *The F.A. Guide to Teaching Football*. London: Heinemann.

Walkley, J., Holland, B., Treloar, R., and Probyn-Smith, H. (1993). Fundamental motor skills proficiency in children. *ACHPER Healthy Lifestyle Journal*, 40(3), 11–15.

Wattchow, B., Burke, G., and Cutter-Mackenzie, A. (2008). "Environment, place and social ecology in educational practice". Paper presented at the Australian Association for Research in Education, Brisbane.

Wellard, I. (2006). Able bodies and sport participation: Social constructions of physical ability for gendered and sexually identified bodies. *Sport, Education & Society*, 11(2), 105–121.

Werner, P., Thorpe, R., and Bunker, D. (1996). Teaching games for understanding: Evolution of a model. *JOHPERD*, 67(1), 28–33.

Whitehead, M. (2001). The concept of physical literacy. *European Journal of Physical Education*, 6, 127–138.

Whiting, H.T.A. (Ed.). (1973). *Personality and Performance in Physical Education and Sport*. London: Kimpton.

Whitson, D., and McIntosh, D. (1990). The scientization of physical education: Discourses of performance. *Quest*, 42(1), 40–65.

Willee, B. (1978). Directive and non-directive methods. *FIEP Bulletin*, 48(4), 20.

Willis, P. (1977). *Learning to Labour*. Farnborough: Saxon House.

Wilmore, J. (1982). Objectives for the nation: Physical fitness and exercise, *Journal of Physical Education, Recreation and Dance*, 53:3, 41–43.

Wilmore, J., and Costill, D. (2004). *Physiology of Sport and Exercise* (3rd ed.). Champaign, IL: Human Kinetics.

Wittrock, M. (Ed.). (1986). *Handbook of Research on Teaching* (3rd ed.). New York: Macmillan.

Worthington, E. (1974). *Teaching Soccer Skill*. London: Lepus Books.

Wright, J. (1990). Remember those skirts: The constitution of gender in physical education. In S. Scraton (Ed.), *Gender and Physical Education* (pp. 63–77). Geelong: Deakin University Press.

Wright, J. (2000). Bodies, meanings and movement: A comparison of the language of a physical education lesson and a Feldenkrais movement class. *Sport, Education & Society*, 5(1), 35–51.

Wright, J., and Burrows, L. (2006). Re-conceiving ability in physical education: A social analysis. *Sport, Education & Society*, 11(3), 275–293.

Wright, J., and King, R. (1990). "I say what I mean," said Alice: An analysis of gendered discourse in physical education. *Journal of Teaching in Physical Education*, 10: 210–225.

Yerg, B. (1981). The impact of selected presage and process behaviours on the refinement of a motor skill. *Journal of Teaching in Physical Education*, 1(1), 38–46.

Young, M.D.F. (1971). *Knowledge and Control: New Directions for the Sociology of Education*. London: Collier-Macmillan.

Zakus, D., and Cruise Malloy, D. (1996). A critical evaluation of current pedagogical approaches in huma movement studies: A suggested alternative. *Quest*, 48(4), 501–518.

Index

References to illustrations and tables are in *italic*.